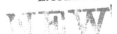

MONETARY TARGETS

MONETARY TARGETS

Edited by
Brian Griffiths
and
Geoffrey E. Wood

Centre for Banking and International
Finance at the City University

First published 1981 by
THE MACMILLAN PRESS LTD
London and Basingstoke
Companies and representatives
throughout the world

ISBN 0–333–28746–0

Printed in Hong Kong

Contents

Notes on the Contributors

The editors

BRIAN GRIFFITHS is Professor of Banking and International Finance and Director of the Centre for Banking and International Finance at The City University, London. Since 1977 he has been a Member of the Panel of Academic Consultants to the Bank of England. He graduated from the London School of Economics, and taught there for a number of years before joining the City University.

GEOFFREY E. WOOD is Senior Lecturer in Banking and International Finance at the City University, London. A graduate of Aberdeen and Essex Universities, he has taught at Warwick University, been a member of the Economic Section of the Bank of England, and Visiting Scholar at the Federal Reserve Bank of St Louis. He has published articles in, among other places, the *Journal of International Economics*, the *European Economic Review*, and the *American Economic Review*.

The authors of papers

BRUCE BRITTAIN is an economist at the Bank for International Settlements in Basle, Switzerland. Formerly employed at Citibank, New York, he has published in the areas of international finance and monetary economics.

MICHAEL FOOT graduated from Cambridge University in 1969 and joined the Bank of England. In 1975 he took a postgraduate course at Yale University. He is currently working in the Economics Division of the Bank.

GEORGE FREEMAN received his master's degree in economics from the University of Toronto in 1946. He joined the staff of the Bank of Canada in 1949, was appointed Chief of the Bank's Research Department in 1965 and Deputy Governor in 1974.

P. E. MIDDLETON was Head of the Financial Economic Unit, HM Treasury, at the time his paper was delivered. He is currently Deputy Secretary responsible for fiscal and monetary policy.

C. J. MOWL has been Economic Adviser in the Policy Analysis Division, HM Treasury, since 1977.

J. C. ODLING-SMEE has been Head of the Policy Analysis Division in the Treasury since 1977.

C. J. RILEY is Senior Economic Adviser in the Monetary Policy Division, HM Treasury.

LAWRENCE K. ROOS graduated from Yale University and entered the US Army. From 1946–50 he was a member of the Missouri House of Representatives. Through the 1950s and into the 60s, he was president of the Mound City Trust Company in St Louis and chairman of the First Security Bank of Kirkwood, Mo. In 1975, he was elected executive vice-president and a director of the First National Bank in St Louis and served in that capacity until becoming president of the Federal Reserve Bank in March 1976.

J. R. SARGENT has been Economic Adviser to the Midland Bank Group since the beginning of 1974. He joined the bank from Warwick University, where he was the first Professor of Economics, founding the Department of Economics in 1965. He started his academic career as a Fellow of Worcester College, Oxford, in 1951 and has also worked as an Economic Consultant with the Treasury.

KURT SCHILTKNECHT studied economics at the University of Zurich, where he received his PhD in 1969. From 1967–9 and 1970–2 he was researcher at the Institute for Economic Research at the Swiss Institute of Technology in Zurich. In 1969–70 and 1973–4 he was visiting researcher at the Econometric Research Unit of the OECD in Paris and Economics Research Unit, University of Pennsylvania. In 1974 he joined the Swiss National Bank. Currently he is head of the Economics Department at the Bank and lectures at the University of Basle and the University of Zurich. He has had a number of books published, including *Monetary Policy under Flexible Exchange Rates: The Swiss Case* (1979).

The discussants

ROY BATCHELOR is Director of Research at the Centre for Banking and International Finance, and editor of the Centre's *Annual Monetary Review*. A graduate of Glasgow University, he has worked in government and in the National Institute of Economic and Social Research. He is co-author of a recent book, *Industrialisation and the Basis for Trade*, and has published many articles on trade and exchange rate policy, monetary control, and the problems of inflation and unemployment.

FRANK BLACKABY works at the National Institute of Economic and Social Research. He is a graduate of Cambridge University, and was for a while an economist in the Treasury; he has been at the National Institute since 1958, as deputy editor and then editor of the National Institute Economic Review, and presently Deputy Director of the Institute. He has edited a number of books, including *British Economic Policy 1960–1974*, *An Incomes Policy for Britain*, and *De-Industrialisation*.

ALAN BUDD is Director of the Centre for Economic Forecasting at the London Business School. He graduated from the LSE and has a PhD from Cambridge University. He has taught at Southampton University and has been Visiting Professor at Carnegie-Mellon University, Pittsburgh. He was in HM Treasury from 1970–4 and is the author of *The Politics of·Economic Planning*.

W. MAX CORDEN is Professor of Economics at the Australian National University. From 1967 to 1976 he was the Nuffield Reader of International Economics and a Fellow of Nuffield College at Oxford University. He is the author of *The Theory of Protection* (1971), *Trade Policy and Economic Welfare* (1974) and *Inflation, Exchange Rates and the World Economy* (1977).

JOHN GASTER is Head of Corporate Planning at Williams & Glyn's Bank Ltd, which he joined as an economist in 1975. A graduate of Cambridge University and the London School of Economics, he worked at the Bank of England for twelve years, latterly in the Economic Section, where he was involved in financial forecasting and flow of funds analysis, on which he has published a number of articles.

CHARLES GOODHART is Chief Adviser at the Bank of England. He is a graduate of Cambridge and Harvard Universities. After teaching at

Cambridge, he became an Economic Adviser in the Department of Economic Affairs for a short spell, and then moved back to academic work as a lecturer in monetary economics at LSE from 1966–8. Since 1969 he has acted as an adviser in the Bank of England, with particular reference to domestic monetary management.

He is the author of *Money, Information and Uncertainty*, and other books and articles mostly on monetary economics and monetary history.

MICHAEL J. HAMBURGER is currently Visiting Professor of Economics at New York University on leave as Adviser from the Federal Reserve Bank of New York. He holds a BS degree from Syracuse University and a PhD from Carnegie-Mellon University and has taught at the University of Pennsylvania, the New School for Social Research and Rutgers University. He has also served as an Economic Adviser to the Bank of England. He is co-author of two books and has published articles in, among other places, the *American Economic Review*, *Econometrica*, the *Journal of Monetary Economics*, the *Journal of Political Economy*, the *Journal of Finance* and the *Manchester School*.

DAVID LAIDLER is Professor of Economics at the University of Western Ontario. He is a graduate of the London School of Economics, the University of Syracuse and the University of Chicago. From 1969 to 1975 he was Professor of Economics at the University of Manchester, and before that held teaching appointments at the London School of Economics, the University of California, Berkeley, and the University of Essex. He has published numerous articles in the areas of monetary economics and the economics of inflation.

RICHARD G. LIPSEY is the Sir Edward Peacock Professor of Economics at Queen's University, Kingston, Ontario, Canada. He holds degrees from UBC, Toronto and London University (at the LSE) and has taught at LSE, Essex, University of California at Berkeley, UBC, and Yale University. He has published articles on theoretical and applied aspects of micro and macro economics and is the author of several textbooks including *An Introduction to Positive Economics*.

PATRICK MINFORD is Professor of Applied Economics at Liverpool University. Before that, in 1975–6, he was editor of the NIESR *Review*. He has also visited Manchester University as a Hallsworth Research Fellow and has been an economic adviser in the external section of HM

Treasury. His publications include *Substitution Effects, Speculation and Exchange Rate Stability* (1978) and articles on trade and macro-economics.

JAMES TREVITHICK is a University Lecturer in the Faculty of Economics at Cambridge and a Fellow of King's College. After graduating from the LSE he taught at Trinity College, Dublin and at the University of Glasgow. The author of two books on the problem of inflation, he has written several articles on, *inter alia*, the theory of inflation and on Keynesian economics.

Introduction

Brian Griffiths
Geoffrey E. Wood

The decade of the 1970s has seen a major change in the role accorded to monetary policy in the developed countries of the western world. From the final breakdown of the gold standard in the 1930s, and continuing after the Second World War and throughout the 1950s and 1960s, most central banks implemented some form of credit policy. They targetted interest rates and imposed controls over the growth of certain categories of credit, such as bank loans, consumer credit and foreign lending. Broadly speaking these were years of economic stability—most countries experienced a low rate of inflation and a low level of unemployment. By contrast the '70s have been a period of instability and uncertainty. All western countries have been affected by a high and varying rate of inflation, which has undermined business confidence, and by larger output fluctuations than characterised previous decades.[1] In trying to bring this inflation under control, and to achieve greater stability in output growth one country after another has given up controlling interest rates and credit conditions and has adopted quantitative targets for the rate of growth of the money supply as the basis of its monetary policy. The conference on which this volume of papers is based was organised as an attempt to evaluate the experience of various countries in implementing this new form of monetary policy.

Two features of this development are of particular interest. First, the switch of emphasis from credit policy (interest rates and credit controls) to monetary policy (money supply growth), follows the acceptance of, if not a thoroughgoing monetarist approach to aggregate economic policy in trying to explain and control inflation, at least a general recognition that monetary expansion plays a necessary role in inflation. It is in explaining inflation that the traditional Keynesian approach is at its

1

weakest. And it was precisely because inflation became the dominant economic problem of the decade that monetarism has been accepted so widely. Second, explicit quantitative targets for the rate of growth of the money supply were adopted as guidelines for monetary policy soon after the breakdown of the Bretton Woods system of fixed exchange rates. It is interesting that Germany adopted monetary targets in 1974, the US, Switzerland and Canada in 1975 and the UK, France and Italy in 1976, following the abandoning of fixed rates in 1973. This seems to us to be no accident. The evidence of history suggests that it is difficult for any government to pursue a purely discretionary monetary policy, independent that is of either fixed exchange rates or monetary rules. Under the gold exchange standard (up to 1914) the gold bullion standard (1925–31) and the gold-dollar-sterling exchange standard (1946–71) individual countries did not need quantitative monetary targets. By maintaining a fixed exchange rate countries were assured of some degree of stability in their domestic price levels. After the gold-dollar crises of 1968 and the conversion of the Bretton Woods system into a *de facto* dollar standard the US should most certainly have adopted a monetary target, rather than continuing to focus on interest rates.[2] It did not switch to a monetary target, and, almost by oversight, excess dollars were pumped into the world economy. The result was a global acceleration in the rate of inflation, leading finally to the breakdown of the international monetary system of pegged exchange rates.

In view of the experience of countries since the time of the gold standard of the late nineteenth century it must be questioned whether it is possible to operate a monetary policy without some method of providing the economy with additional information regarding money supply growth. The papers in this volume are concerned with discussing and comparing the available methods.

I. INSTRUMENTS, INDICATORS AND TARGETS

The dictionary of monetary policy was formalised by Thomas Saving,[3] who argued that what the monetary authorities are concerned with can be divided into four categories. First, there are *instruments*—variables directly controllable by the monetary authorities. Second, are *indicators*—these provide preliminary information to the authorities (and, in general also to the private sector) about the stance of policy. Third, are *proximate objectives*—variables which give an early and unambiguous indication of the way in which *ultimate objectives*, the fourth category, will actually move.

Targets are, according to Saving, another name for proximate objectives. Most participants in this conference conformed to that usage, regarding the monetary authorities as using some variable or set of variables—their instruments—to affect some monetary aggregate or range of aggregates—their target—with the ultimate objective of influencing money National Income. This usage, however, was questioned by Professors Corden and Lipsey in their comments on the papers by Bruce Brittain and Kurt Schiltknecht, respectively, (pp. 86–94 and 226–228). Their dispute with the conventional usage is discussed below.

Aside from the issue of terminology, any discussion of the appropriate choice of a monetary target has to resolve three basic questions of principle. First, should the target be a quantity (some monetary aggregate, such as the money stock or liquidity or bank credit) or a price (some interest rate or exchange rate)?

Second, should policy be 'activist', responding to feedback from the current and prospective state of the economy, or should the authorities follow rules without feedback—for example having the money supply grow at some constant rate irrespective of the state of the economy? And third, should the rules by which the authorities act be published? In this introductory essay we set out a framework for the discussion of these three questions and set the papers to follow in that context.

The answers that are given to the three questions raised above do not in general depend on the goals it is thought appropriate for policy-makers to try to achieve.[4] Most groups seek the goal of 'full employment without inflation'. Nor is the basic dispute about the exact way in which the monetary authorities should respond to disturbances, given their understanding of the economy, what objectives they are trying to attain, and what their trade-offs among these objectives are. What basically determines the answers to these three questions is a particular feature in the model of the economy used in providing the answers. This particular feature is the way in which agents in the economy are thought to form their expectations.

We first consider the choice between policy rules with and without feedback—that is, we ask whether national monetary authorities should adjust their policy instruments according to the state of the economy or whether it is better for them to keep these instruments unchanged whatever the economy is doing. Focusing on this question highlights the role of expectations. We then turn to the choice between an interest rate and a monetary aggregate as a target for policy.

II. POLICY RULES WITH AND WITHOUT FEEDBACK

The case for activist policy—i.e. for 'fine tuning'—rests on certain
assumptions about how the economy can be described. It has generally
been believed by the proponents of fine tuning that the economy can be
modelled by a set of equations describing the behaviour of economic
agents, the parameters of which equations are not influenced by the way
the authorities behave. Basic equations of such models are the
consumption function and the investment demand schedule. These
equations embody the decision rules which determine how people
respond, with regard to consumption and investment, to changes in the
economic environment. If these decision rules are affected by the
intervention of the authorities in the economy, then such intervention
will not have predictable consequences unless the way in which the
decision rules change is itself modelled. An example helps make this
clear. Suppose that investment demand is affected by short-term interest
rates. If the authorities suddenly decide to abandon a policy of not
letting such rates stay above 10 per cent for more than a month, then the
response of investment to a rise in interest rates above that rate is
clearly affected by whether or not investors change their behaviour in
response to the authorities' changed decision rule. If they do not
change their response, then any rise in interest rates above 10 per cent
will have no effect on investment demand, while if they do change then
it will.

The restriction that individuals' decision rules are not affected by the
behaviour of the authorities is clearly a strong one. Indeed, it is clear that
such behaviour by individuals would not be optimising. If agents are
using optimal decision rules, then the assumption that the parameters of
the equations describing the economy are invariant with respect to the
decision rules the authorities use will not hold.

Recognising this has led to attempts to model expectations in a way
which embodies the notion that individuals try to anticipate as best they
can the consequences of all events, *including government actions*, which
influence their well-being.

Rational Expectations

'Rational' expectations (the term originated with John Muth)[5] are
expectations formed in a way consistent with the best available relevant
economic model. They are rational in that sense, not in the sense that

they are based on a full and correct understanding of the working of the economy. (Alan Walters[6] has proposed that a more appropriate name for them is therefore 'consistent expectations', but Muth's rather more striking term seems to have captivated the economics profession.)

They may be described as a way of avoiding imputing to firms and individuals the custom of, systematically and without ever learning to do better, making mistakes. As Barro and Fischer[7] wrote:

> A fundamental difficulty with theories of expectations that are not based on predictions of the relevant economic model (rational expectations) is that they require a theory of systematic mistakes. Such theories are inherently more difficult to formulate than those based on rational behaviour, and it seems to be a reasonable strategy to try to do without them.

Rational expectations therefore make the parameters of the model dependent on, and variable with, the rule the authorities use to guide policy.

This has important implications for monetary policy. It is now fairly widely accepted that the equilibrium output of an economy is determined by real variables, and changes in nominal variables affect this only if they are (incorrectly) thought to be real changes. This widely accepted view of how economies work is embodied, for example, in the natural rate hypothesis, which says that there is an equilibrium level of employment in the economy from which changes in the price level (or rate of change of prices) can produce deviations only if they are unanticipated and therefore produce, until expectations catch up, a change in real wages.

If expectations are rational, (and markets clear quickly) the private sector anticipates that a monetary fluctuation will change only the general level of prices, and adjusts its prices accordingly in response to the monetary fluctuation. These price fluctuations are fully anticipated and therefore have no effect on real output. *Rational expectations combined with a natural-rate-type view of the world means that an activist monetary policy will serve only to produce price level fluctuations.*

In this framework (which helped underpin the work of Henry Simons[8] and Milton Friedman[9]) rules with feedback are no better than rules without. Indeed, they can readily be worse if they increase the uncertainty of the information set of economic agents. Does the evidence support the view that expectations are rational?

The Evidence

Expectations are not generally observed; therefore testing of whether or not they are rational must be of the implications of rationality. Tests must seek to find whether people behave as if expectations are formed rationally, or in some other manner. The evidence is as yet somewhat fragmentary, but it seems to be starting to indicate that rational expectations are fairly widespread.

One type of test examines whether the coefficients in an econometric model change, in response to changes in the authorities' decision rules, as rational expectations lead one to expect. An example of this approach is the study by Meunch et al.,[10] which found that they did. A second approach is to examine prices in particular markets, to see if they behave as if agents in these markets form their expectations rationally. Beenstock's[11] work on the foreign exchanges pursued this approach, and yielded the result that expectations there are rational, as does work such as that of Michael Jensen[12] which shows that capital markets are efficient.

But the body of evidence on this very important point is as yet not substantial. The case for monetary authorities adopting a rule without feedback to guide their behaviour is supported by some evidence, but at least as important in providing support is the observation that any other kind of rule requires the assumption that individuals and firms in the economy persist in forming their expectations in a non-optimising way. The case for a rule without feedback still rests primarily on logic.

Announce or Not?

Discussion of whether or not policy rules should be announced follows naturally from the choice of type of policy rule. That discussion hinges on how expectations are formed; if they are formed rationally, then we are led to a non-feedback rule. Rationality also implies in turn that the rule should be announced. Consider the following example. There is an exogenous unanticipated shock to the economy—a harvest failure would satisfy both adjectives. With this reduction in national income there will be a jump in prices since money growth (supposing that to be the target) does not change. If the rule is not announced, people will not know—unless the rule has been pursued sufficiently long for it to be inferred—just how much prices will jump. In contrast, with an announced rule prices would move quickly to their new equilibrium level, eliminating any possibility of supply responses being misled by a change ‍in the price level being confused with a change in relative prices.[13]

Another way of putting this point is to recollect that, as noted above, a policy rule with feedback is worse than one without only because it is highly likely to add to uncertainty, which is undesirable. If a rule without feedback is adopted, then announcing it will have the desirable effect of reducing uncertainty, since only over a long period of time could a non-announced rule be inferred from observations of actual money growth.

Price or Quantity?

Should the monetary authorities target on an interest rate or a monetary aggregate? This question has been answered several times, in different intellectual frameworks.

The best known of the 'classical' answers is Wicksell's; the authorities should peg the money stock because if they choose an interest rate the price level becomes indeterminate. In certain other classes of model, generally called Keynesian, a certain level of real GNP can be achieved by choosing either an interest rate or a money quantity. The choice is immaterial since the price level is given exogenously—as it is in a small open economy under a fixed exchange rate. But even in a fixed-price model, however, complications can enter. As Poole[14] showed, allowing for the fact that economies suffer random, unpredictable, shocks does affect the choice of target, as between interest rate or money stock. Poole demonstrated that if money markets are more subject to unpredictable shocks than are goods markets, the authorities should target on interest rates, while if the reverse is true they should target on the money stock. These are the choices of target which would be most successful in stabilising nominal income. An example shows the line of argument. If the monetary sector of the economy is highly subject to shocks, then a policy of stabilising money growth will lead to large movements in interest rates, with consequent effects for goods markets. But if an interest rate is targetted, then random disturbances in the monetary sector have no consequences for goods markets. Poole's work therefore did not yield the unambiguous policy recommendation that Wicksell's did.

If, however, one is concerned with price level stability (rather than nominal income stability), and if expectations are rational, the advice to policy-makers once more becomes quite definite. Under these circumstances, a money supply rule gives a determinate course for the price level; an interest rate rule does not. The economics of this are straightforward. Under an interest rate rule, the public (quite correctly) expects that the authorities will supply whatever nominal money stock is required to maintain the interest rate. Hence, any exogenous shock to the price level will be matched by a monetary fluctuation to make the new price level an equilibrium one. The price level is in meta-stable equilibrium and there is *no way* to forecast the expected price level. This is not a consequence of choosing the 'wrong' interest rate rule—no interest rate rule yields a stable price level. (This is the counterpart of Wicksell's result in a model of the economy which allows for random shocks.)The conclusion has to be, then, that an interest rate rule is unambiguously wrong.

Three Principles

That brief summary of the modern rational expectations literature leads to three propositions, all three of which rest on two assumptions. The first is that expectations are formed rationally, and the second is that the natural rate hypothesis holds. The three principles are: (i) that a non-feedback rule is at least as good as, and likely to be better than, discretionary fine tuning; (ii) that the rule should be pre-announced; and (iii) that it should be for a quantity, some monetary aggregate, rather than for a price, some interest rate. How do the papers of this conference fit into that context?

III. THE PAPERS

Michael Foot's paper surveys what countries actually do, and looks at official statements of what motivated their actions. It summarises the response of national monetary authorities to the principles set out above. Bruce Brittain follows a related approach: accepting the above principles, he considers whether the authorities of various countries have made the most appropriate choice of aggregate on which to target. The criterion which has to be satisfied is a dual one, since the aggregate which may be most closely related to future nominal income is not necessarily the one which can be controlled most accurately. What has to be minimised is the *combined* error from these two sources. Dr Brittain argues that he shows that most authorities seem to do this quite well, but his conclusions encountered two objections. One was statistical: in his comment (pp. 81–85) Roy Batchelor argued that the results could not bear the weight put on them, and could be regarded as at most suggestive. Max Corden challenged the whole philosophy of targetting in a subtle and provocative comment (pp. 86–94). He argued that the notion of a target as proximate objective concealed the true objective of policy, namely nominal national income. The authorities should, he maintained, target that directly. To the objection that it was just such policy that had produced accelerating inflation and fluctuations of increasing size in economic activity, he replied that this was because the authorities had accommodated shocks from the labour market, and that he viewed them as eschewing this particular response. There appears, however, to remain a serious problem. What would his policy do to the behaviour of the price level?

Suppose national income dropped because of a transitory fluctuation in demand. The authorities would respond by increasing money growth, and might increase demand if it were believed that the bulge in money would be removed before it caused inflation. (This of course requires considerable nimbleness by the authorities.) Suppose now the cause of the drop is a supply shock. Again the authorities increase money growth, but output is supply-constrained so nominal income can only rise if prices do. In other words, the policy would seem to produce great price-level volatility. This issue needs to be explored both more thoroughly and more formally: Corden's proposal was not found appealing at the Conference on the perhaps less fundamental, but certainly cogent, argument that the authorities could not move with the required precision.

Sargent's and the British Treasury's papers both backed off from the rational expectations framework which produces targetting. Sargent dealt with money market and money stock control complications of targetting, and its implications for the government debt market. The Treasury paper rejected the framework altogether, although it did so implicitly. As David Laidler pointed out in his comment (pp. 176–179), their exercise of using an econometric model to simulate the interest rate consequences of money stock targetting was rather odd, in that if one really had such detailed knowledge of the structure of the economy targetting would always be second-best policy. Given the framework they had established, the question they addressed was trivial. And there is a more fundamental objection, which emerges when the intimate connection between rational expectations and targetting is highlighted. Any feedback policy rule will condition the response of the private sector, and hence the established coefficients of the model. These coefficients will change either when a new feedback rule is adopted or when the authorities move to a non-feedback rule. Not only is the question they address uninteresting in their framework; when the rationality of expectations is a possibility, the answer they obtain is meaningless unless the authorities' reaction function is made an integral part of the estimated model—which it was not.

The remaining papers discuss the experience of individual countries with targetting, and each highlights a different issue. Lawrence Roos observed how flimsy was money stock control in the US, demonstrating that the consequences of targetting on money stock *and* on interest rates, and using interest rates to control the money stock, had been that the monetary target was missed about half the time. His speech was a cogent argument for giving up attempts to manipulate interest rates, and for controlling money growth by controlling the growth of the base.

The same may be said of Dr Shiltknecht's paper, in that it demonstrated the consequences for Switzerland of doing so. It also (implicitly) showed how the private sector reacts to a stable monetary environment, responding to the trend of variables, in particular the monetary base, rather than their transitory fluctuations. The paper was a powerful demonstration both of the rationality of the private sector and of how it quickly learned to distinguish between transitory and permanent fluctuations in variables.

George Freeman's paper showed that Canada had had an apparently unsatisfactory experience with targetting; monetary targets had been lowered year by year, but both inflation and unemployment had risen. That appears a powerful challenge to the rationale of targetting; but as Michael Hamburger points out, (pp. 203–210) there is another interpretation. While monetary *targets* were lowered, *actual* money growth within Canada's very wide target ranges *accelerated*—hence the rising inflation. Further, the uncertainty inevitably produced by the combination of a commitment to tightening money and the symbolic implementation of this, lowering targets, with actually raising money growth must surely have made the private sector somewhat uncertain about the authorities' intentions. It of course requires formal demonstration, but there is certainly a good chance that this uncertainty contributed to the rise in unemployment.

IV. SUMMARY AND CONCLUSIONS

The papers presented at this conference dealt with the experience of various countries in monetary targetting. It is absolutely clear that the experience has not been universally satisfactory: but, as is also clear, most countries have not adhered to the principles to which they committed themselves when announcing they were to target some monetary aggregate. The country which has pursued the policy wholeheartedly, Switzerland, has had the most satisfactory outcome. It is our view that the conclusion of this conference must be that monetary targetting works. It may be resisted by governments and central banks—indeed, since it reduces the scope they have for intervention in markets, it is highly likely to be resisted by those institutions—but until that resistance is overcome countries cannot hope to attain price level stability. The idea that monetary authorities can control interest rates is an illusion; only when they give up pursuing that illusion, and follow instead a policy of steady and pre-announced monetary growth, will price level stability be restored.

NOTES

Individual contributors to this volume have adopted different spellings for the words 'targeting' and 'targeted'. For an explanation of his use of two 'ts' see Roy Batchelor's note on page 85.

1. See e.g. Geoffrey E. Wood and Nancy Ammom Jianakoplos, 'Co-ordinated international economic expansion: are convoys or locomotive the answer?', Federal Reserve Bank of St Louis Review (July 1978).
2. For a description of how policy was conducted, see Roos, pp. 183–190 of this volume.
3. Thomas R. Saving, 'Monetary policy – targets and indicators', *Journal of Political Economy*, 75, no 4 supplement (August 1967). See also R. A. Batchelor's contribution to this volume (pp. 81–85).
4. A notable exception comprises that group of economists and philosophers who seek to minimise the role of the state. They recommend rules with that objective in view. A cogent statement of their philosophical position is Robert Nozick's *Anarchy, State and Utopia* (Oxford: Blackwell, 1974).
5. John Muth, 'Rational expectations and the theory of price movements', *Econometrica*, 29 (July 1961), 313–35.
6. Alan Walters, 'Consistent expectations, lags, and the quantity theory', *Economic Journal*, Cambridge, 81 (June 1971).
7. R. J. Barro and Stanley Fischer, 'Recent developments in monetary theory', *Journal of Monetary Economics* (April 1976).
8. H. C. Simons, 'Rules versus authorities in momentary policy', I.P.E., 44 (1937), 1–30.
9. Milton Friedman, 'A Monetary and Fiscal Framework for Economic Stability', *A.E.R.*, 38 (June 1948), 245–64.
10. T. Meunch, A. Rolnick, N. Wallace and W. Weiler, 'Tests for structural

change and prediction intervals for the reduced forms of two models of the U.S., the FRB–MIT and Michigan Quarterly Models, *Annals of Economic and Social Measurement*, 3, No 3 (June 1974), 491–520.

11. M. J. Beenstock, *The Foreign Exchanges: Theory and Policy* (London: Macmillan, 1978).
12. M. Jensen, 'Capital Markets: Theory and Evidence', *The Bell Journal of Economics and Management Science* (Autumn 1972), pp. 357–398.
13. If the analysis were to be pursued further, at this point it would be necessary to distinguish between permanent and transitory fluctuations in output.
14. W. Poole, 'Optimal choice of monetary policy instruments in a simple stochastic macro model', *Q.J.E.* (May 1970), 197–216.
15. For an elaboration of this see L. C. Andersen and Denis Karnosky, 'Some Considerations in the use of Monetary Aggregates for the Implementation of Monetary Policy', Federal Reserve Bank of St Louis Review (September 1977), and Geoffrey Wood's comment on Dr Schiltknecht's paper in the present volume (pp. 229–234).

1 Monetary Targets: Their Nature and Record in the Major Economies

M. D. K. W. Foot*
Bank of England

INTRODUCTION

Undoubtedly the major change this decade in the presentation—if not
the aims—of monetary policy in many advanced economies has been a
move away from the pursuit of an interest rate objective to the formal
announcement of a target rate of growth for some monetary aggregate.
It is no simple task to trace this development and only certain aspects
receive detailed consideration here. Notes, indicated by superior
numbers and drawn together at the end of the chapter, have therefore
been used extensively, to cover certain points only briefly noted in the
main text and also to illustrate arguments by quotations from senior
central bank officials and their economists. References to published
sources are shown in parentheses and also listed at the end of the
chapter.

Before going any further, it is worth defining the phrase 'monetary
target'. In this paper, it is taken to cover any quantitative target or
ceiling for a generally recognised monetary aggregate, whether set for
that aggregate alone or for some ratio of which that aggregate is part;

---

* The author is an Adviser Principal in the Economics Division of the
Bank of England. The preparation of this chapter has been greatly
assisted by comments from colleagues in the Bank and by the provision of
background material by members of the Overseas Department, notably C. J.
Davies. However, the chapter should be regarded as expressing the views of
the author alone.

always provided that the national authorities have the intention of actively framing their policy in such a way that one aim is to achieve the target. On this view, ceilings on some limited set of bank liabilities (such as the 'corset' in the UK) or on some limited set of bank assets (like those on bank advances in the UK during the second half of the 1960s) are not targets because they are not set with respect to 'recognised aggregates'. Also excluded is the Dutch national liquidity ratio (M2 over net national income), though this is very much a borderline case, because it is not clear that the Dutch actively seek to control M2 so as to achieve the projected liquidity ratio in anything other than, perhaps, the very long run. The establishment of a ceiling for Domestic Credit Expansion (DCE), when the authorities actively seek to achieve it, does count as setting a target; but because none of the countries considered in detail in this paper has set such a target, except as part of recourse to borrowing from the IMF, no great attention will be paid to DCE.

Finally, by way of introduction, it is worth noting briefly that the setting of monetary targets has not been confined to advanced economies. Firstly, many less developed countries have accepted ceilings on DCE or something like it as part of the conditions for an IMF loan. Between 1973 and 1975, eighteen member countries of the IMF accepted such ceilings. Secondly, members of the Eastern bloc have tended to view planning of the rate of money creation as part of the much wider economic planning process which characterises these economies, (Haffner, 1977). In the rather special case of Yugoslavia, monetary targets have also been set since at least 1967 for macroeconomic purposes (Dragas, 1977). Indeed, it has been explicitly argued that, given Yugoslavia's relatively unsophisticated financial system, any untoward increase in real money balances will find its way into real spending (Dimitrijevic, 1977). Finally, there may have been a number of (notably Latin American) sufferers of endemic inflation who have tried monetary targets as part of stringent anti-inflation policies. One suspects that targetry may have been attempted in several such cases but only for Brazil is evidence readily available (see for example Banco Lar/Chase, 1978).

I. THE SPREAD OF TARGETRY

The first major economy to have seriously considered the use of monetary targets unconnected with borrowing from the IMF appears to have been the United States. This observation may depend in part upon the greater availability of information on policy formulation in the USA and also in part upon one's choice of which stage in the 'evolutionary' process of taking more note of monetary aggregates constitutes setting a target. However, Wallich (a Governor of the Federal Reserve Board) and Keir argue that between 1970 and 1972 the Federal Open Market Committee (FOMC) 'stressed bank credit and money as primary targets [for the two months ahead] with money market conditions subordinated to a proviso role' (Wallich and Keir, 1978).[1]

From the early 1970s there is also evidence that Spain began setting formal growth targets for a broad monetary aggregate (McClam, 1978, p. 4), while during these same years the UK authorities came to think increasingly in terms of the growth of the monetary aggregates, beginning from late 1973 to set informal targets for the ratio of M3 growth to national income (Bank of England, 1978, p. 33). However, it was Germany, late in 1974, that became the first advanced economy to announce a formal target for a period as long as a year, unconnected with borrowing from the IMF. This example was followed by the USA early in 1975, in the only instance where the initiative for the move came from the legislature rather than from the central bank or the executive (Davis, 1977). Also in 1975, the Swiss and the Canadians announced formal targets and in 1976 the UK and the French followed suit.[2] Of these six countries, only Switzerland has—at least for the time being—subsequently abandoned targetry. These six, and to a lesser extent Italy—which adopted a form of DCE target in 1974 and subsequently a formal target for the monetary base, while obtaining loans from the IMF and the EEC (Cotula and Micossi, 1977)—constitute the focus of this paper.

It is, of course, possible that other countries have maintained monetary targets in this period but have not let the fact be generally known. However, in so far as targets are intended to have a favourable impact on expectations (see the next section) this would be to reduce the value of targetry and, in a number of the advanced countries not mentioned above, there have been explicit renunciations of targets—usually because (as in the cases of Austria, Belgium and Sweden) the country concerned is a comparatively small open economy, for which an exchange rate commitment has been given preference (McClam, 1978, p. 4). More 'doubtful' are the cases where it is known that the authorities make projections of the money stock but where it is uncertain whether policy is subsequently adjusted to try to validate these projections. Thus, since 1976 Australia has announced 'guidelines' for M3 and, since 1978,

Japan has made 'projections' for M2. The longest standing of these doubtful cases, as noted in the Introduction, is the Netherlands.

II. THE NATURE AND PURPOSE OF TARGETS

Without trespassing on the theoretical province of other papers at this conference, it seems reasonable to distinguish three broad lines of argument that have been advanced to support the adoption of monetary targets and to establish, as far as is possible, which have been the more prominent in countries where targets have been adopted.

The first is essentially Keynesian and may be said to represent the 1970s version of the thinking which underlay the interest rate objectives common in the 1960s, which had to be abandoned when inflation rates (past and prospective) became so high and volatile that nominal interest rates became an increasingly poor guide to the thrust of monetary policy (Bockelmann, 1977). Thus, in the UK while Bank Rate/Minimum Lending Rate[3] rose from 5 per cent in June 1972 to 13 per cent in September 1973—implying a sharp tightening of monetary policy— inflationary expectations almost certainly rose much faster and, on this criterion, monetary policy—as measured by real interest rates—eased (Gowland, 1978). This acceleration of inflation added to a problem that had been evident for some time: namely that it was not always clear whether a rise in interest rates reflected a tightening of policy or was the natural market result of an increase in the demand for money.

Now money can only act as a better indicator than nominal interest rates of the thrust of monetary policy on a Keynesian view, if there is a stable demand for money function—i.e. if one can 'predict' from observation of past and current movements in, say, prices, output, wealth and interest rates what the change in the demand for money will be. If such prediction is possible (an empirical question left over to Section IV) then movements in the monetary aggregates can give an early indication of deviations from forecast of, say, the path of output and prices.[4] Further, although on a Keynesian view, the authorities may not necessarily be able (or may not choose) to control the money supply directly, they can influence the demand for money over time by operating on interest rates. If output or prices (and therefore the demand for money) rise 'too fast' the authorities can push rates of interest up, bringing the demand for money back to some preferred path and inducing a reduction in the rate of growth of aggregate demand (and thus of output and/or prices).[5]

It is thus perfectly possible to present an argument along strictly Keynesian lines in favour of adopting monetary targets. Such an argument might conclude that, in the long term, an appropriate monetary target is a necessary but not sufficient condition for curbing inflation.[6, 7] Monetary policy should not, however, be considered by itself.[8, 9]

However, by no means all Keynesians would agree that monetary targets were desirable. In the first place, there are those, notably the so-called Radcliffians in the UK, who would argue that there is no stable demand for money function. If there is not, then although they might agree with the long-run conclusion of the previous paragraph, they would view an operational target for the money stock over, say, a year as providing no information about the movement of prices or output.

A second, not necessarily related, school of Keynesian thought finds it difficult to understand why the authorities should wish to regulate a variable that is essentially an indicator of past and present price, output and interest rate movements, in preference to operating on variables that have some more direct influence on current and future values of the general economic goals that the authorities set (Friedman, 1977).

On a monetarist view, in contrast, the value of a monetary target is generally self-evident. There are a number of theoretical models that a monetarist may have in mind. But in all cases, he would regard the authorities as controlling the money stock (or at the least its domestic element) directly and he would see some clear causal link between movements in the money stock now and changes in prices, if not output, in the future. In contrast, then, to the Keynesian view, he would see changes in the money stock as more than an indicator of the stance of monetary policy and he would disagree strongly with the Keynesian views set out in the two previous paragraphs. To him, an appropriate monetary target appears as both necessary and sufficient to curbing inflation. It is no surprise then that monetarist support for targets is of long standing; twenty years ago, Milton Friedman was calling for a monetary policy that involved ensuring a set, small, rate of growth of money each year (Friedman, 1960).

Cutting across the Keynesian and monetarist cases in favour of monetary targets, there is a third broad line of argument that is theoretically acceptable to nearly all economists. It rests on the argument that announcing targets can have a psychological effect (notably in reducing inflationary expectations) in either or both the financial and 'real' (notably labour) markets.

It is outside the scope of this paper to discuss the respective merits of these various lines of argument. It is also important to note that the theoretical differences outlined above tend to become blurred when discussion about short-term policy takes place between moderate proponents of the various views. Under such circumstances, a monetarist might well, for example, accept that other policy aims—such as avoidance of disorder in financial markets—might have to take precedence temporarily over the preferred monetary path. That said, however, it seems reasonable to argue that, for most of the countries covered here, the widespread adoption of targets did not indicate an espousal of monetarism on the part of those responsible for introducing targets; indeed there was some explicit repudiation of any such conversion.[10] However, it is fair to note monetarist strands of thought in some of the Swiss discussions, the contribution of monetarist views, notably from the Federal Reserve Bank of St Louis, in the USA and— though this is difficult to quantify—a widespread view that it mattered that many in the financial markets were monetarists. The psychological value of targets was also cited as a contributory factor in a number of cases,[11] although the one central bank to offer supporting empirical evidence, the Bank of Japan (1975), has only a monetary projection and not a target.

Whatever the differences of emphasis, those responsible for introducing targets did, however, tend to agree on three things:

(1) That the prospect of achieving pre-determined monetary targets other than for DCE had become reasonably bright only when the move away from fixed exchange rates in the early 1970s had released monetary policy from its role of always supporting the exchange rate commitment.

(2) That, by setting targets, they were seeking to strengthen the stance of long-run anti-inflationary policy.

(3) That they were not contracting to achieve close short-run control of money[12] nor to meet the targets for the periods specified regardless of other factors.[13]

III. THE PARAMETERS

The single most important choice facing the various authorities was perhaps which aggregate to pick as the target variable. In almost every case, statistics on at least one narrow definition of money (M1 differently defined but always some measure of the demand for transactions balances) and a broader measure (M2 or M3, incorporating all or part of savings deposits with banks) were available. In many cases, though not in Switzerland, the choice was almost embarrassingly wide.[14]

The extent of choice would not matter, of course, if the different aggregates were likely to move in a similar fashion. Not surprisingly, given their very different natures, there can be no such presumption.[15]

Of the six countries considered here in detail which freely adopted targets, M1 alone was chosen by just Canada, the USA selected this aggregate as perhaps the most important of three target aggregates, while Switzerland initially adopted targets for both M1 and the monetary base[16] (the latter being dropped after 2 years). The others— the UK, France and Germany—chose a broad aggregate (M2 or M3), albeit in the German case a version (called central bank money) that can easily be mistaken for a narrow aggregate akin to the monetary base.[17]

There is no simple theoretical explanation for this division in the choice of aggregate. Monetarists might generally be expected to favour the adoption of either the monetary base or a broad aggregate, on the grounds that the target must be for a definition of money which can be directly controlled by the authorities; without such control the monetarist cannot be sure that the authorities can make their policy 'stick'. M1 (notes and coin plus sight deposits) is clearly determined by the demands of individuals and companies and so should not appeal to monetarists.[18]

On the Keynesian side, there is no such obvious theoretical preference. 'Controllability', in the sense of being able to influence demand for the aggregate, is naturally relevant and in the Canadian case this led to a clear preference for M1 (White, 1976, p. 48). However, in principle, demand for both narrow and broadly defined money may be significantly affected by interest rate changes.

It is sometimes argued that Keynesians are likely to prefer a broad definition on the grounds that fiscal policy—a key policy instrument in their thinking—has an obvious connection with money broadly defined. However, although this is so in an accounting sense, fiscal policy is also clearly a major potential determinant of output and prices and consequently the demand for transactions balances.[19]

There is also nothing obvious to be gained by seeking, as is sometimes done, to explain the choice of aggregate by reference to the constitutional position of the central banks concerned. It is true that the Swiss (Leutwiler, 1979) and American central banks have both considerable independence and an M1 target. But the Bundesbank has equal independence and a broad monetary target, while the Bank of Canada's independence (with an M1 target) is much like that of the Bank of England (Courchene, 1976, p. 9) and the Banque de France (with broad targets).

The choice of aggregate is far from being the only aspect of the parameters of targetry in which the various authorities have shown considerable diversity of approach. In a practical sense, once the target has been chosen the key issue is the method of selecting the target number. Here, the Germans have an elaborate procedure— Bockelmann (1977) details, for 1977, considerations that were quantified: the growth of productive potential (estimated at 3 per cent), the desirable change in the utilisation of potential (+2 per cent), the 'unavoidable' rate of price increase (+4 per cent) and an increase in the velocity of circulation of 1 per cent. Implicitly, then, using a demand for money function in which every 1 per cent rise in output or prices leads to a 1 per cent increase in the demand for money, the Bundesbank arrived at its 1977 target of 8 per cent (equals $3 + 2 + 4 - 1$ per cent).

Similar calculations are probably made in each of the other five countries but only in the case of the USA are they discussed to any great extent.[20] However, the lack of any dogmatic economic theory on which to rest the adoption of targets (as illustrated in Section II above) together with widespread scepticism about the stability of the relevant demand for money function (see IV below) must inevitably make the authorities concerned reluctant to appear too mechanistic in their selection of the appropriate growth rate of money. On some views, the Americans have, however, often given such an appearance, by so frequently changing their target ranges by $\frac{1}{2} - 1$ per cent when rolling them forward and thus implying that such small changes have some significance.

This same reluctance to assume exact relationships can be seen in the fact that while Germany, Switzerland and France all began by publishing point (i.e. one figure) targets, now—with Switzerland having abandoned targetry altogether for the moment—only the French do not publish their target in the form of a range. This fits well with the general caveats noted earlier about the feasibility of precise control over the target aggregate, as well as with a general view among the authorities concerned that attempts to produce a uniform rate of growth of money over, say, specific quarters cannot be justified on theoretical grounds. Where ranges have been adopted, a margin of 4 per cent has been the norm for Canada and the UK, the Germans' current target has a 3 per cent spread, while the margin allowed by the USA has varied over time and between aggregates, but until recently has rarely been less than 2 per cent or more than 3 per cent.

Disparity has also been shown over the question of how frequently to renew targets. The Americans have rolled their targets forward every three months until recently but now the Humphrey–Hawkins Act requires the Federal Reserve Board to set targets for the current calendar year; the UK now roll-forward every six months, having initially chosen one year, while others have set new targets once a year. In favour of frequent review, it can be argued that circumstances change quickly and thus so does the outlook for output and prices. Also in favour of a rollover well before the end of the existing target period, it can be said that this lessens the risk of overshooting if the relevant aggregate rises fast towards the end of the period;[21] none of the central banks have claimed the ability to bring back deviations within a few months, and, in the case of Germany in 1976 and the UK in 1977/78, the target was exceeded when unexpected rises in the money stock showed through towards the end of the target period. Against that it may be argued that frequent rollovers actually reduce each target period to the length of time between new targets, exacerbating the authorities' problems of maintaining credibility, because the shorter the effective target period the greater the importance of random influences and special factors on the money stock (Davis, 1977).

Finally, we may note one point of agreement. So far, discounting the UK's minor change from M3 to £M3 and the Federal Reserve's recent problems with M1 (see Appendix) because of developments in the banking system, no country has yet switched its target variable.

IV. METHODS OF CONTROL OF THE TARGET VARIABLE

For a country seeking to meet a particular monetary target, other Government policies, notably on fiscal and exchange rate matters, can have the greatest importance. However, in this section, we are concerned only with what may be termed the proximate controls of the target aggregate that would generally be described as within the ambit of 'monetary policy'. Indeed, to avoid being drawn into enumeration of all the individual features of the economies covered in this paper, we shall concentrate on two that are potentially common to all the countries concerned. This is not to deny that the operational problem in any specific case is likely to be much more complex. Thus, for example, in the

USA the Federal Open Market Committee sets targets for several monetary aggregates; but in seeking to meet these targets, it has to have regard to the stance of Government policies, conditions in financial markets and, in closer operational terms, the level of bank reserves, money market interest rates, changes in the monetary base (to a lesser extent) and the growth of bank credit. All the central banks involved have responsibilities, either under statute or self-imposed, to meet aims such as the maintenance of orderly and stable financial markets as well as to achieve given monetary targets.[22]

The first operational control considered here is one available to and used by all the authorities covered in this paper; namely, influence over short-term interest rates. How this influence is achieved in practice (and exactly why it is attempted) varies considerably between countries but the general approach is for the central bank to conduct open market operations or to vary banks' reserve requirements so as to cause or validate changes in some key short-term rate, such as MLR in the UK or the Federal Funds Rate in the USA.

In order to meet an M1 target, influence over some short-term interest rate is a necessary but not sufficient condition for success, for then the authorities will normally be able to vary the gap between the rate of return on M1 (which in most countries has normally been either zero or very low and fairly constant) and on competing short-term assets.[23] Thus in the UK the authorities can expect to reduce the demand for M1 by raising MLR.

To ensure that an M1 target is *successfully* met, however, there are three additional requirements:

(1) The authorities are prepared to pay the necessary price in terms of foregoing other policy objectives.

(2) The authorities face a known and stable demand for money function so that they know for a given forecast of the other determinants of the demand for M1 (prices, output and so on) what action they must take on short-term interest rates to achieve their target. (This is true, however, only if it is assumed that changes in interest rates do not significantly affect incomes in the target period; if this assumption cannot be made the authorities must have a complete model of the economy to determine the interest rate policy necessary to achieve the monetary target.)

(3) The lags in the response of the demand for M1 to changes in interest rates are sufficiently short and the effects of the changes sufficiently strong that the impact on the demand for money of any

deviation in prices or output from their predicted path can be offset by appropriate interest rate changes within the target period.

To achieve a target for a broad aggregate, the authorities must, in similar fashion, be able to influence the relative yield between deposits counted within M3 and competing assets, as well as be able to meet the requirements listed above. However, for any definition of money that includes saving deposits on which competitive rates of interest are paid it may be no easy matter for the central bank concerned to influence the appropriate interest rate relativity.[24] Indeed, at least in the UK, it is possible that the initial impact of a rise in short-term rates engineered by the authorities as a restrictive measure may lead immediately to a rise in banks' deposits rates relative to competing rates and, initially, *increase* the demand for broad money. Only over time will these other rates tend to rise and also will the demand for bank credit be reduced in response to a higher cost of borrowing.

What constitutes the 'necessary price' mentioned above, of course, depends greatly on circumstances at the time and this issue is deferred to Section V. Here, we are primarily concerned with the question of whether or not stable demand for money functions exist in the countries that have adopted monetary targets.

This is an enormous subject in its own right. The periods chosen for study, the explanatory variables selected, the lag structure tried, and the econometric methods used all have a potentially large impact on the results.[25] Also, studies applying similar hypotheses to a number of countries (and thus of particular interest for a paper like this) are relatively rare, and where attempted at all, have to sacrifice sophistication for the sake of comparability. The approach adopted here— which is to discuss the subject in the context of a recent comparative study by the OECD (Boughton, 1979)—is therefore far from perfect.

Perhaps the most interesting feature of this OECD study is that it concludes that there is stable underlying demand for money functions in the countries covered[26] and yet it can be argued that much of the detailed evidence provides ammunition for those who doubt whether the requirements listed above for meeting a target are generally met. However, two conclusions might find wide acceptance. Firstly, 'in each country examined, at least one market rate of interest has a significant negative influence on the demand for money' (Boughton, 1979, p. 36). In other words, what was described earlier as the necessary but not sufficient condition for meeting a monetary target does appear to hold.

Secondly, the study does *not* produce any evidence that one definition of money performs uniformly better than any other.

For M1, the study accepts that there appears to have been instability in the demand for money function 'during the recent period in the United States, Italy and perhaps in France' but it claims that 'only in the case of the United States has the shift been large enough to have a visible effect on the forecasting ability of the equation'. Certainly, the conclusion for the United States endorses what has long been felt by policymakers there.[27] Whether the authorities in the other countries would agree is perhaps more doubtful. But, even where they do, they would probably require little reminding of the vulnerability to the passage of time of the findings of stable demand functions in any country. Reminder enough is provided close to home, for the OECD study on the UK leads to the same conclusion as work by Coghlan (1978) in the Bank of England over roughly the same data period; namely, that a stable demand for M1 can be identified. However, while this is not the place to report recent work at the Bank on the subject, it will be apparent to anyone who has run the quarterly equations reported by Coghlan, that they have significantly underpredicted the growth in M1 in the year since the article was published.

On the lesser, but still important, question of the size and speed of response of the demand for M1 to changes in interest rates the OECD study gives some mixed results.

Clearly, the larger the fall in the demand for M1 for any given rise in the relevant interest rate, the easier it is likely to be for the authorities to surmount the economic and political difficulties involved in varying interest rates sufficiently to keep to the M1 target. Here the results of the study are mildly encouraging: 'a sustained one-point increase in all interest rates is expected to lower the demand for real money balances by 1½ per cent in the United States, about 4 per cent in Canada, Germany and Japan, more than 5 per cent in France and Italy, and over 6 per cent in the UK' (Boughton, 1979, p. 41). However, caution is suggested by the often somewhat lower figures found by other cross-country studies [ibid, p. 41] (and again near home) by the fact that the figure suggested by Coghlan was only one-third that found by the OECD.

The findings on the speed of adjustment, however, confirm the caution noted earlier (and regularly expressed by central bankers) over the feasibility of offsetting quickly any unexpected deviations of M1 from target. Half the effect of a change in interest rates comes through quite quickly (by the second quarter) only in Germany according to the OECD study, and takes as long as five quarters for France and the UK, a finding, for the UK, not dissimilar from that reported by Coghlan.

The study's results on M3 tell a very similar story. Considerable instability is found for this aggregate in the case of the UK (a result foreshadowed by Hacche, 1974, some years before) and quite serious problems also appear in the United States and Italy. However, for Germany and France (i.e. two of the three countries freely choosing a broad money target), the study does find stable functions. In the German case, this fits with work conducted by the Bundesbank (Gebauer, 1977).

In summary, then, it appears that while the Canadians, the Germans and the French *may* have a target aggregate the demand function for which has exhibited considerable stability, no country can readily assume that such a function will be known and stable when it seeks to achieve its monetary target. Equally, no central bank can expect to achieve rapid reversals of any deviations of the aggregate from target by use of interest rate controls alone.

This helps to explain why the authorities in the UK, France and Italy (and Japan and the Netherlands), all of whom have placed primary emphasis on broad aggregates, have also sought to use the second form of policy weapon to be discussed in this section—direct controls on bank lending.[28] In each case, however, it is important to note that these controls (in some form) pre-dated the adoption of monetary targets. Thus, in the UK, ceilings on lending were in force through most of the 1960s and since 1973 the Supplementary Special Deposits scheme (which is a form of indirect control on the totality of bank lending) has been used three times.

Controls on bank lending, if tight enough, almost guarantee the achievement of the relevant target if the authorities are prepared to run the risk of stifling competition in the banking system, encouraging disintermediation from the banking system to some less regulated part of the financial system (thereby eroding the effect of the target) and the rationing of available funds other than by price. The merits generally claimed for the approach are that it may obviate the need for temporary and unnecessary increases in interest rates, may permit a lower general rate of interest than would be the case if interest rates alone were left to restrain bank lending, and may act sooner and more certainly than interest rates alone.

V. THE RESULTS

None of the countries considered here has had any more than four years'

TABLE 1.1 SETTING AND MEETING MONETARY TARGETS[a]

Country and target variable	Number of times target[b]:			Number of times target[c]:		
	(a) Reduced	(b) Unchanged	(c) Increased	(d) Undershot	(e) Met	(f) Overshot
UK						
M3/£M3*	1	2		1	1(10)	1
USA[d]						
M1*	4	9		1	4	6
M2*	7	5	1		7	4
M3*	6	6	1		6	5
CANADA						
M1*	3				4(7)	
GERMANY						
Central Bank Money[†][e]*	1	3				4
SWITZERLAND						
(i) M1[†]	1	2		1		3
(ii) Monetary base[†]		1		2		
ITALY						
(i) Global credit expansion[e][f]			4	1		4
(ii) Monetary base[g]						1
FRANCE						
M2[†]	2					2

* Indicates target set as a range – e.g. 8–12 per cent.

ᶠ Indicates target set as a point projection – e.g. 8 per cent.

ᵉ Indicates a ceiling.

ᵃ Columns (a)–(c) cover targets announced up to mid-March 1979. Columns (d)–(f) cover performance indicated by data available by mid-March 1979 and exclude cases for which data is available for half the target period or less. For the definitions used, see the individual country entries in the Appendix.

ᵇ To illustrate how the first half of this table was compiled, a target or ceiling was said to have been reduced when the point projection (or, in the case of a range, the centre of the projection range) was reduced between one target period and the next.

ᶜ To illustrate how the second half of this table was compiled, a target or ceiling was said to have been 'met' if the out-turn equalled the point projection/ceiling or, in the case of a range, fell within the projected range. Brackets by the side of an entry indicate that this column contains an unfinished target period; the figure in the brackets indicates the number of months of the period for which data are available.

ᵈ Because of the distortions to the monetary aggregates in the USA in recent months (see Appendix), only targets set before the fourth quarter 1978 are included in the first half of the table and only target periods completed by the fourth quarter 1978 are counted in the second half.

ᵉ The latest target set by the Bundesbank is in the form of a range; earlier targets were point estimates.

ᶠ Targets in Italy have often been revised during the period to which they relate. In such cases, only the revised targets have been considered.

experience of formal monetary targets and it would be unrealistic to pass final judgements on the results. Nevertheless, over the group taken as a whole, targets have been operated in sets of circumstances ranging from low growth, high inflation and capital outflows to moderately rapid growth, low inflation and heavy inflows. This range of experience and the problems associated with each set of circumstances are worth provisional comment.

Judged solely by whether or not the targets were met, the results (summarised in Table 1.1) have been generally poor. Only Canada has consistently met its targets. The UK has had one failure in three for M3/£M3; the USA has overshot between one-third and one-half the targets set, depending on which aggregate is considered; Switzerland (for M1) and Italy[29] have overshot more often than not; while Germany and France have not yet met a target (though the latter came very close in 1978). There has been no obvious difference between the performance of countries with narrow and of those with broad aggregate targets.

The authorities concerned would probably wish to be judged on rather different criteria; the difficulty is that there are no unambiguously 'correct' yardsticks by which success can be measured. Table 1.2 shows one very simple measure, the actual rate of growth of the target aggregate for;

(i) an (inevitably) arbitrarily chosen period before the setting of the first target; and
(ii) the rate of growth since.

At best such a comparison might be taken as a partial, indirect measure of the authorities' commitment to reducing the rate of growth of money and, if so, the relative ranking remains much as noted above. Thus the rate of growth has decelerated in those countries (notably the UK and Canada) which it might be generally agreed have shown most concern for meeting their targets while the growth rate of the money stock has been little changed or has actually risen in the countries with the poorest records of meeting targets. Table 1.2 also suggests these differences are not due to any obvious disparities between the two periods in the rate of growth of real activity.

A more general yardstick for 'success' might be a comparison of rates of inflation before and after the adoption of monetary targets, which after all were generally regarded by the authorities concerned as forming a major part of a long-run attempt to curb inflation. For many, targets were introduced at a time when inflation was at an historically high level.

TABLE 1.2   RATES OF GROWTH OF MONEY AND OUTPUT BEFORE AND AFTER THE ADOPTION OF MONETARY TARGETS

| | Average 1970-setting of first target | | Annual average rates of growth % Average since setting of first target | |
| | (1) | (2) | (3) | (4) |
	Money stock[a]	Real GDP	Money stock[a]	Real GDP
UK	$13\frac{1}{4}$	2	11	$1\frac{3}{4}$
USA	$6\frac{1}{4}$	$1\frac{3}{4}$	$6\frac{1}{2}$	$5\frac{1}{4}$
Canada	$13\frac{1}{2}$	$4\frac{1}{2}$	7	4
Germany	$9\frac{1}{2}$	$2\frac{1}{4}$	$9\frac{1}{4}$	4
Switzerland	$7\frac{3}{4}$	N/A	$10\frac{1}{2}$	N/A
Italy	18	$4\frac{1}{2}$	$23\frac{1}{4}$	1
France	$16\frac{1}{4}$	4	$13\frac{1}{2}$	3

[a] The target aggregate in each case: for the USA, M1 only, for Italy M2 (as no such calculation is possible for their target of GCE); for the UK £M3, but as this is not available for the period before July 1971 the growth of M3 is used as a proxy for the period 1970–July 1971.

In Table 1.3 is shown a comparison, for the same periods as chosen for Table 1.2 for each country, of average rates of inflation before and during the target period and also a comparison of the annual rate of inflation when targets were adopted and in 1978. As with the comparison in the previous paragraph, it must be stressed that the arbitrariness of the choice of the pre-target period and the fact that one is not comparing like with like because each country adopted targets at a different point in time greatly restricts the value of any conclusions. Nevertheless, and in the absence of better measures, it may be said that, in general, recent rates of inflation have been significantly lower in the majority of cases than when targets were first adopted, as a result of the set of policies—including monetary targets—followed in each case. However, the figures for Germany and Switzerland also serve as a reminder, if one were needed, that overshooting of one's monetary target need not, in the short run at least, be associated with unfortunate inflationary consequences.

What has been clear in the experience to date is that many of those

TABLE 1.3 RATES OF INFLATION[a] BEFORE AND AFTER THE ADOPTION OF MONETARY TARGETS

	(1) average 1970 – setting up first target	(2) in year preceding setting of first target	(3) average since setting up first target[b]	Annual average rates of growth % (4) annual rate during 1978[c]
UK	13.5	13.7	11.4	8.4
USA	7.5	11.3	7.5	9.0
Canada	6.6	10.4	8.3	8.4
Germany	6.7	5.9	4.3	2.4
Switzerland	8.0	8.0	1.3	0.7
Italy	9.0	16.0	16.8	11.6
France	8.9	9.9	9.4	9.7

[a] Measured by what are generally described as consumer price indices in most of the countries concerned but which are in practice generally akin to the UK's retail price index (which was used for the UK).

[b] Covers the period to end-1978 or as far into 1978 as the figures available at mid-March 1979 permitted.

[c] Where the figures for the whole year are not available, the rate of growth over the latest twelve months is shown.

setting monetary targets have not been prepared to pay the price necessary to meet these targets. The following general difficulties may be noted. Firstly, for Germany and Switzerland increasingly and for the UK in 1977/78, the strength of foreign demand for their currencies led to a particularly difficult policy choice. In all three countries, money is defined to exclude non-resident holdings, but there are several pervasive channels by which external flows are likely to affect such a country's money stock. The least impact is likely to occur if the authorities do not intervene to maintain the exchange rate. Nevertheless, to the extent that an inflow is the result of a private sector surplus on current and capital accounts, the money stock is likely to rise. Where the authorities do intervene, the risks are greater.[30] There is also a potential second-round effect if the intervention is allowed to lead to a rise in banks' liquidity. Finally, there may be a significant indirect effect, as the inflows tend to push down domestic rates of interest, and thus induce an increase in the demand for credit and M1.

For a country operating a monetary target and faced with heavy inflows there are no easy options. If it does not intervene, the exchange rate may rise far further than is consistent with the orderly development of its industry (during 1978, for example, the Swiss franc rose by 13 per cent in effective terms, despite net intervention amounting to nearly 10 billion Swiss francs.[31] Even then, the money stock will tend to rise. If the authorities do intervene the exchange rate will rise less but the money stock more. Whether there is intervention or not, the first of the responses discussed in Section IV—the raising of short-term interest rates—may curb domestic demands for credit but only at the cost of exacerbating the inflows which are the root of the problem. One possible response is to discourage inflows, for example, by exchange controls or tax penalties; but this is never an easy policy to enforce. An alternative is to have a broad target aggregate and rely on quantitative controls on bank lending to prevent inflows from affecting the money stock too much. Whether this policy of potentially severe rationing is feasible (and whether it too would induce additional inflows from abroad) will no doubt depend on the country and the circumstances involved; but any such approach would, for example, have been a major departure from normal Bundesbank policy.

The resolution of this dilemma in Germany and Switzerland to date has been to let the monetary targets be exceeded as a conscious policy decision.[32] In the Swiss case, the need for stabilisation of the exchange rate has led them to prefer, for 1979, an exchange rate—rather than a monetary—target.

A second explanation of failures to meet targets where inflows have not been a problem has been the unwillingness or inability of the authorities concerned to introduce sufficiently tough or rapid restrictive action (by raising interest rates or tightening fiscal policy). The most general criticism on this score was heard in the United States during much of 1977/78 but there has of course also been recurrent argument on these lines in the UK, specifically with respect to the size of the PSBR,[33] the flexibility of interest rates and, on occasion, exchange rate policy.

Several mitigating factors may be pleaded by the authorities concerned. Short-term changes in the money stock often contain large random or special, once for all, influences and may, for example, depend heavily upon the seasonal adjustment factor. It may therefore take time for a change in trend to be verified as such. Secondly, as noted earlier in the case of Germany in 1976 and the UK in 1977/78, the deviations may occur so late in the target period as to make it most unlikely that correction can be ensured in time. Thirdly—and perhaps most fundamentally—the meanderings of an unstable demand for money function may lead to unexpected out-turns for money, even when the growth of prices, output and the movements in interest rates have been those that *ex ante* appeared appropriate to achieve the target. Finally, there may sometimes have been reluctance, on Keynesian grounds, to restrict monetary growth when the prospects for real growth appeared poor.[34]

A related difficulty, in the USA at least, has occurred as a result of adopting targets in the depressed economic conditions of 1975/76 and subsequently coming under pressure, on the one hand, to bring these targets down as part of the long-run anti-inflationary stance and, on the other, to raise them to finance the recovery in real output of 1977/78. At the outset, the hope may well have been that inflation would have fallen sharply by the time real output picked up but in the USA this did not in fact happen.

By way of partial evaluation of these various mitigating circumstances, it is perhaps worth examining indirect measures of how hard the various authorities have tried. One obvious measure, of course, is the average of short-term interest rates since targets were adopted compared with the pre-target period; generally speaking, the higher short-term interest rates the more one might say the authorities had tried. However, as with earlier comparisons in this section this is vulnerable to the time-periods chosen and perhaps, more importantly, it also tells one nothing about expected real rates of interest which are almost certainly more relevant. Real rates can be constructed by, for example, deducting the past rate of price increase from the nominal interest rate (and this is done in Table 1.4) but no-one would pretend that this was exactly an ideal measure of expected real rates.

A second measure is whether nominal interest rates have been more volatile in the short run since targets were adopted, volatility *perhaps* being a measure of the authorities' preparedness to take quick action to keep the target aggregate on the 'preferred' path. One could not, however, deduce from finding that short-run volatility had increased that active attempts to meet targets were destabilising for financial markets, for it is quite possible that sharp short-run variations in interest rates within a fairly narrow range could reduce the need for large longer run fluctuations in rates over the business cycle.

An attempt to make these measurements is shown in Table 1.4. The results emphasise the need for caution in interpreting these at best very uncertain measures. Nevertheless, it is perhaps of interest that in the USA, Italy and France—the countries with relatively poor target

TABLE 1.4   THE AVERAGE LEVEL AND SHORT-RUN VOLATILITY OF SHORT-TERM INTEREST RATES BEFORE AND AFTER THE ADOPTION OF TARGETS

| | % Average level of representative short-term interest rate:[a] | | Volatility[b] of short-term interest rate: | |
Country	(a) Pre-target	(b) In target period	(a) Pre-target	(b) In target period
UK	8.3 (−5.2)	8.7 (−2.7)	0.29	0.32
USA	7.1 (−0.4)	6.0 (−1.5)	0.31	0.16
Canada	5.4 (−1.2)	8.1 (−0.2)	0.33	0.09
Germany	8.7 (+2.0)	4.3 (−)	0.34	0.18
Switzerland	4.1 (−3.9)	1.9 (+0.6)	0.42	0.61
Italy	6.2 (−2.8)	13.7 (−3.1)	0.23	0.23
France	8.3 (−0.6)	8.7 (−0.7)	0.31	0.11

[a]   Nominal interest rates shown without brackets, real interest rates in brackets (calculated as the average nominal rate over the relevant period minus the average rate of inflation).

[b]   Measured by the co-efficient of variation, a measure of dispersion defined as $\dfrac{100\sigma}{M}$, where σ is the standard deviation of the series and M the mean of that series.

records and no 'inflow problems' to justify this record—real interest rates have been negative on average throughout the period under consideration and have been unchanged or have fallen since the adoption of targets; indeed in the USA on the periods chosen *nominal* rates have also declined on average; while in Canada and the UK—the countries with the best target records—real and nominal rates have risen (albeit that the former has remained negative on average in both countries). Similarly, on the second test, the volatility of short-term rates has been unchanged or lower in the countries (except Switzerland) with poor target records; but the relevance of this test is doubtful, because only in the case of Switzerland has volatility been significantly greater since targets were adopted. Perhaps these figures can best be interpreted in a negative sense, to show that determination to keep to annual targets, as in the UK and Canada, does not necessarily require an increase in the short-run volatility of short-term interest rates.

VI. ASSESSMENT

Concern with inflation has been a principal preoccupation for most economies in the 1970s. By the middle of the decade, there was general agreement that counter-inflationary policies had to be stepped up, and, in the case of the countries discussed in this paper, one element in the firmer anti-inflationary stance which followed was the adoption of a monetary target.

In subsequent years, it would be a reasonable generalisation to say that inflation has been reined back; but only in Germany and Switzerland has anything approaching price stability been reached and even there the authorities remain very much aware of the risks of resurgent inflationary pressure. The central banks of target countries have found it difficult to reduce targets significantly and regularly and even to meet existing targets has often involved severe conflict with other policy aims (notably on the exchange rate and the level of interest rates). Further, while the instruments of monetary policy may not in many cases have ever been able to work sufficiently precisely or rapidly to ensure that targets were met, the intellectual basis of the approach has not been strengthened by continued evidence that over, say, a year the demand for money function for the target aggregate in the majority of countries is not necessarily stable.

The severest doubts among the authorities concerned about the practicability of persevering with monetary targets have been expressed in Switzerland and the United States. In the former, an exchange rate objective is now being given preference. In the latter, the authorities have been accused repeatedly by some observers of not trying hard enough to meet their targets and also of not trying to claw back excess growth in subsequent periods.[35] In so far as these accusations are justified, one suspects that the long-standing and well-documented instability of the demand for money functions in the United States go a long way to explaining disenchantment within the Federal Reserve System for monetary targets.

Other countries' pursuit of targets has encountered criticism too but nevertheless five of the six countries which freely adopted targets have continued with the experiment. In the cases of the United States and

Germany, however, and to a lesser extent France, it may fairly be asked how much longer the experiment will have meaning if success (in terms of setting non-accommodating targets and meeting them) continues to be limited in the extreme. As officials in both the United States and Germany have remarked, the central bank must retain its credibility in the eyes of financial markets for the operation of monetary targets to be of value.[36] Economists may differ over the value of monetary targets but most would agree that to set them up as a key policy aim and then persistently to overshoot them may, in a sense, afford the worst of both worlds.

NOTES

1. Over the previous few years, according to Wallich and Keir, the FOMC had set targets for money market conditions (and thus implicitly for interest rates) with the proviso that efforts to meet these targets should be modified if there were concurrently undesirable movements in the volume of bank credit and in the monetary aggregates.
2. Supranational interest in monetary targets is also worth noting. 'Already in late 1973 the EC Economic and Finance Ministers had agreed that over the coming year member countries should seek gradually to reduce the growth of money plus quasi-money to a figure corresponding to the growth of real GNP plus the target rate of increase of prices. In 1976 the EC Commission in its Annual Report recommended, for the first time, money targets as a means of fostering a convergence of economic conditions within the community, but these were subsequently deleted from the Commission's guidelines for economic policy in 1977.' Warren McClam (1978) p. 8.
3. Bank Rate was replaced by the very similar Minimum Lending Rate in October 1972.
4. 'In practice, the authorities do not know the current level of incomes in the economy. Therefore a reasonably comprehensive . . . picture emerges only some months after the event. . . . As interest rates are known from day-to-day and monthly data on the money stock are received quite quickly, the demand for money equations can be applied to discover what level of income would be consistent with the observed interest rates and money stock; this provides an early, if approximate, indicator of movements in income besides those already available.' L. D. D. Price (1972).
5. For a discussion of the evidence on this Keynesian transmission mechanism in the UK, see Price (1977).
6. 'Whatever else may need to be done to bring inflation under control, it is absolutely essential to keep the rate of monetary expansion within reasonable limits.' Governor G. K. Bouey (1975).
7. 'In the final analysis . . . the central banks that publish a monetary target have adopted the basic proposition that general price rises cannot occur in the medium-term, unless the money stock expands excessively.' Bockelmann (1977).

8. 'I would not claim that monetary policy can or should be left to figh inflation singlehanded.' Governor G. Richardson (Bank of England, 1978 p. 34).
9. '. . . monetary policy alone could not remedy the exceptionally wide-spread and persistent disorder typical of most national economics since 1974. Governor Clappier (1979).
10. However, we also can see here some good examples of the blurring noted above: 'But there is also a hard core of truth in the central theme of the monetarist school; over time, an excess supply of money contributes nothing to employment, nor to real income, nor to real wealth, but only to inflation.' P. Volcker (1977).

    'We have not, it is plain, adopted a wholehearted monetarist philosophy. But what we do is likely to give the monetarist a good deal of the prescription he would recommend.' Governor Richardson (Bank of England, 1978, p. 35).
11. '. . . the really new element in the publication of quantitative targets . . . [lies in the aim of avoiding] the costly process of learning by bad experience . . .' Bockelmann (1977, p. 21).

    'It will be said that those involved in wage bargaining pay no heed to the size of monetary targets. That may be so . . . Yet, over time, perseverance . . . will, I believe, have an increasingly pervasive effect.' Governor G. Richardson (Bank of England, 1978, p. 35).
12. '. . . the Federal Reserve has pointed out time and time again that it is neither possible nor desirable to attempt close control over the growth of the monetary aggregates during short periods of time, say a few weeks or even months.' P. Volcker (1977).

    'it was . . . realistic to expect that the path [set out by the monetary target] could be more or less followed over a period of 5 or 6 months.' Bockelmann (1977).

    'although the degree of short-run movements is not precise, the means available to the Bank [to keep monetary expansion within reasonable limits] . . . are broadly accurate.' Governor Bouey (1975).
13. '. . . these problems [e.g. the collapse of Franklin National Bank] had to be dealt with by techniques that cannot be encompassed by any simple monetary rule.' P. Volcker (1977).

    'However, the money supply growth target must not be the authorities' only policy aim.' Schürmann (1978).
14. '. . . it should be noted that at least eight definitions of narrow money and a still larger number of definitions of broad money can be proposed in Canada.' W. R. White (1976, p. 9).
15. 'This phenomenon of extended, dissimilar movements in [narrow and broad] monetary aggregates [found in Canada] has parallels in the UK, though perhaps not in the US.' W. R. White (1976, p. 36).
16. The subject of the monetary base deserves a paper in its own right. The base is defined as some set of the central banks' liabilities, over which the central bank is assumed—by proponents of base control—to have complete influence. Given such influence and a cash ratio requirement for banks, the argument then goes that the central bank can set a ceiling on the growth of the money stock, in principle on a day-to-day basis. The Swiss and Italians

have paid particular attention to movements in the monetary base but neither has attempted to exercise control over it in the very short run, presumably because of the fears, generally expressed by those against base control, that any short-run regulation may cause severe instability of interest rates, as banks, for example, sometimes find themselves short of cash. It is this same fear that argues against attempts to control any monetary aggregate closely in the short-run. White (1976, p. 100) and Ciccolo (1974) both for example found that such an attempt would lead to 'instrument instability'—i.e. potentially ever greater interest-rate fluctuations.

17. For an 'explanation' of central bank money see Bockelmann (1977).
18. Just such a doubt is one factor lying behind, for example, Courchene's criticism of the choice of M1 as the Bank of Canada's target variable (1976); more recently Congdon (1979) has made a similar point in the UK.
19. The asset counterparts of £M3 in the UK, for example, include the Public Sector Borrowing Requirement as a key item. The link between M1 and fiscal policy has been explicitly recognised by the Bank of Canada:

    'problems [of reducing the rate of growth of the money stock] will be much easier to avoid if governments manage to reduce the size of their borrowing requirements as the private sector . . . recovers.' (Bank of Canada, 1975, p. 13).
20. By contrast, the Bank of Canada's 1975 Annual Report contained the following rationalisation of its 10–15 per cent target. 'A growth rate of M1 of no more than 5% would probably be sufficient to accommodate a continuation of real growth . . . under conditions of price stability. On the other hand, a growth rate of 15% a year or more would probably involve accommodating in full a continuation of the recent pace of inflation.' (Bank of Canada, p. 18).
21. 'Firm deadlines can force one to try to adjust too fast to an unforeseen trend developing late in the period, or to appear to accept a failure to reach one's target.' Governor G. Richardson (Bank of England, 1978, p. 37).
22. See, for example, the first quotation in Courchene (1976).
23. This will not be possible, of course, if deposits in M1 receive interest at rates which vary in line with other market rates. In Italy, current accounts do bear interest, as does a small but growing element of M1 in the UK. In other countries too, notably the USA, the line between transactions and savings balances has become increasingly blurred.
24. This is a major question in its own right, encompassing, for example, the feasibility of influencing long-term rates of interest directly.
25. An excellent summary of the problems involved and a review of work in the United States up to 1973 is provided by Goldfeld (1973).
26. Unfortunately, Switzerland is not covered.
27. See, for example, the work reported by B. Friedman (1977) and the latest 'official' econometric evidence (Federal Reserve Bulletin, 1979).
28. In France, there is the long-established system of *encadrement du credit* recently described by the Governor of the Bank of France as 'barbaric but efficient' (Clappier, 1979). In Italy and in the Netherlands there are almost equally long-standing credit ceilings while the Japanese exercise so-called 'window guidance' (Bank of Japan, 1975).

29. The Italian record is in fact worse than it seems because Italy is the only country to have regularly *increased* its target during the target period.
30. This is a complex subject well discussed in Miles and Bull (1978).
31. Gross intervention amounted to over 21 billion Swiss Francs but this was partially offset by Swiss National Bank sales of dollars worth 12 billion Swiss francs under the capital export conversion requirement.
32. Thus, Professor Schürmann, Vice-President of the Swiss National Bank argued in April 1978: 'The money-supply growth targets must not be the authorities' only aim. In times of hectic foreign exchange rate movements, there is no alternative but to accept money supply growth faster than the target' (Schürmann, 1978). Similarly, in Germany 'factors [other than monetary targets] must, of course, also be taken into account in making credit policy decisions. If this were not so, we would hardly have been able to help in supporting the dollar to the extent that we did last year.' Pohl (1979).
33. See, for example, the bulletins of W. Greenwell & Co. in early 1979.
34. 'As long as the economy [Germany in 1978] was moving relatively slowly, overshooting of the monetary target could be tolerated; indeed it was actually desirable to help the economy along by means of favourable financing conditions.' Pohl (1979).
35. The Federal Reserve has been accused frequently of permitting 'base drift', i.e. of not reducing—as strict monetarist logic would automatically require—the next period's target to allow for overshooting in the previous period.
36. 'Without credibility that the Bundesbank is able to come close to the target and that it is determined to do it, the purpose of publishing the target, namely avoiding frictions between monetary policy and economic activity would be unattainable.' Bockelmann (1977, para. 22).

    'It is one thing to repeat . . . our dedication to the general proposition that, while encouraging growth, we also want to encourage a gradual return to price stability. It is quite another thing to present, defend and stick to specific numbers for monetary growth consistent with that objective. Obviously, credibility in that respect is crucial.' P. Volcker (1977).

REFERENCES

Banco Lar/Chase (1978), 'Trends and perspectives of the Brazilian economy', Numbers 19/20.
Bank of Canada, Annual Reports, various years.
Bank of England (March 1978), *Quarterly Bulletin*, pp. 31–7.
Bank of Japan (October 1975), Special Paper No. 60, 'Role of the money supply in the Japanese economy'.
Bockelmann, H. (1977), Deutsche Bundesbank, 'Quantitative targets for monetary policy', pp. 11–24 in Actes du seminaire des Banques Centrales et des Institutions Internationles, proceedings of a conference held in Paris in April 1977 and published by the Banque de France.
Bouey, G. K. (1975), 'Remarks to the 46th Annual Meeting of the Canadian Chamber of Commerce', Saskatoon, 22 September, 1975, reprinted in the *Bank of Canada Review*, October.

Boughton, J. M. (1979), 'Demand for money in major OECD countries', in OECD Economic Outlook Occasional Studies, January, pp. 35–57.

Ciccolo, J. H. (1974), 'Is short-run monetary control feasible?' in *Monetary aggregates and monetary policy* published by the Federal Reserve Bank of New York, October, pp. 82–91.

Clappier, M. (1979), Governor, Banque de France, speech to the Society of Political Economy in Zurich 17 January 1979, reported in *Le Nouveau Journal*, 19 January 1979.

Coghlan, R. T. (1978), 'A transactions demand for money', *Bank of England Quarterly Bulletin*, March, pp. 48–60.

Congdon, T. (1979), 'Why M1 should not be the Bank of England's target for the money supply', mimeograph, 9 March.

Cotula, F. and Micossi, S. (1977), 'Some considerations on the choice of intermediate monetary targets in the Italian experience', essay in the source quoted in Bockelmann (1977).

Courchene, T. J. (1976), 'Money, inflation and the Bank of Canada' (Montreal: C. D. Howe Research Institute).

Davis, R. G. (1977), Senior Economic Adviser at the Federal Reserve Bank of New York, 'Monetary objectives and monetary policy', *FRBNY Quarterly Review*, Spring, pp. 29–36.

Dimitrijevic, D. (1977), 'Targets of monetary policy in Yugoslavia', essay in source quoted in Bockelmann (1977).

Dragas, B. (1977), 'The effectiveness of monetary policy in Yugoslavia', essay in source quoted in Bockelmann (1977).

Federal Reserve Bulletin (1979), 'A proposal for redefining the monetary aggregates', January, pp. 13–42.

Friedman, B. M. (1977), 'Empirical Issues in monetary policy', in *Journal of Monetary Economics*, 3, 87–101.

Friedman, M. (1960), 'A program for monetary stability', The Millar lectures, No 3 (New York: Fordham University Press).

Frowen, S. F., Courakis, A. S. and Miller, M. H. (1977), 'Monetary policy and economic activity in Western Germany' (Surrey University Press).

Gebauer, W. (1977), 'Money stock control and economic activity: recent empirical evidence for Germany', paper presented at the Conference quoted in Bockelmann (1977).

Goldfeld, S. M. (1973), 'The demand for money revisited', Brookings Papers 3.

Gowland, D. H. (1978), 'Monetary policy and credit control' (London: Croom Helm).

Hacche, G. (1974), 'The demand for money in the United Kingdom: experience since 1971', *Bank of England Quarterly Bulletin*, September, pp. 284–305.

Haffner, F. (1977), 'Die einflusse der Zentralen geldunlaufplanung', *Kredit und Kapital*, 10(4).

Leutwiler, Dr Fritz (1979), President of the Swiss National Bank, interview reported in *The Banker*, February, pp. 15–17.

McClam, W. D. (1978), 'Targets and techniques of monetary policy in Western Europe', *Banca Nazionale del Lavoro Quarterly Review*, March, pp. 3–27.

Miles, C. M. and Bull, P. A. (1978), 'External and foreign currency flows and the money supply', *Bank of England Quarterly Bulletin*, December, pp. 523–9.

Pohl, K. O. (1979), Vice-President of the Deutsche Bundesbank, in a speech delivered to the Landeszentralbank, 16 January.

Price, L. D. D. (1972), 'The demand for money in the UK: a further investigation', *Bank of England Quarterly Bulletin*, March, pp. 43–55.

Price, L. D. D. (1977), 'Monetary objectives and instruments in the United Kingdom', essay in source quoted in Bockelmann (1977).

Schürmann, Professor (1978), Vice-President of the Swiss National Bank, in an article in *Handelsblatt*, 11 April.

Volcker, P. A. (1977), President of the Federal Reserve Bank of New York, 'A broader role for monetary targets', *FRBNY Quarterly Review*, Spring, pp. 23–8.

Wallich, H. C., Governor, Federal Reserve Board, and Keir, P. M. (1978), 'The role of operating guides in US monetary policy: a historical review', *Kredit und Kapital*, 1, 30–51.

White, W. R. (1976), 'The demand for money in Canada and the control of monetary aggregates: evidence from monthly data', *Bank of Canada Staff Research Study*, 12.

Appendix:
Country Summaries

1. UNITED KINGDOM

(a) Target aggregates

M3—target aggregate for 1976/77, first set in July 1976, comprising notes and coin in circulation plus all sterling and foreign currency deposits held by UK residents with UK banks.

Sterling M3—target aggregate for 1977/78 and subsequently, equals M3 less foreign currency deposits held by UK residents with UK banks.

A ceiling on *domestic credit expansion* was also set, as part of an agreement with the IMF, for 1976/77 and the two subsequent financial years.

(b) Targets/ceilings set and results achieved (seasonally adjusted)

	Target %		Ceiling £ billion	
	Set	Result	Set	Result
1976/77	12	10.7	9.0	4.9
1977/78	9–13	16.4	7.7	4.4
1978/79	8–12	8.6[a]	6.0	5.6[a]
October 1978/October 1979	8–12		N/A	

[a] Annual rate after 11 months.

2. UNITED STATES

(a) Target aggregates (one-year targets first announced in May 1975)

M1—comprises demand deposits at commercial banks (other than domestic interbank and US Government deposits) less cash items in

41

collection and the Federal Reserve float, plus foreign demand balances at Federal Reserve banks plus currency outside the Treasury, Federal Reserve banks and the vaults of commercial banks.

M2—equals M1 plus savings deposits, time deposits open account, and time Certificates of Deposit other than negotiable CDs of $100,000 or more at large weekly reporting banks.

M3—equals M2 plus the average of beginning and end of month deposits of mutual savings banks, savings and loan shares and credit union shares.

For a short time in late1978, a target was also set for M1+, defined as M1 plus savings deposits at commercial banks and 'checkable' deposits at thrift institutions.

(b) Targets set and results achieved (seasonally adjusted)

	M1		M2		M3	
	Target	*Result*	*Target*	*Result*	*Target*	*Result*
1975:II −1976:II	5−7.5	5.4	8.5−10.5	9.6	10−12	12.0
1975:III−1976:III	5−7.5	4.6	7.5−10.5	9.3	10−12	11.5
1975:IV−1976:IV	4.5−7.5	5.8	7.5−10.5	10.9	9−12	12.8
1976:I −1977:I	4.5−7	6.4	7.5−10	11.0	9−12	12.8
1976:II −1977:II	4.5−7	6.8	7.5−9.5	10.8	9−11	12.4
1976:III−1977:III	4.5−6.5	7.9	7.5−10	11.1	9−11.5	12.7
1976:IV−1977:IV	4.5−6.5	7.9	7−10	9.8	8.5−11.5	11.7
1977:I −1978:I	4.5−6.5	7.8	7−9.5	8.8	8.5−11.5	10.5
1977:II −1978:II	4.5−6.5	8.1	7−9	8.5	8.5−11	10.0
1977:III−1978:III	4−6.5	7.1	6.5−9	8.6	8.5−11	9.6
1977:IV−1978:IV	4−6.5	7.3	6.5−9	8.8	8−10.5	9.4
1978:I −1979:I	4−6.5		6.5−9		7.5−10	
1978:II −1979:II	4−6.5		6.5−9		7.5−10	
1978:III−1979:III	4−6.5		6.5−9		7.5−10	

As recorded in footnote *d* to Table 1.1, there have recently been particularly severe distortions to the main monetary aggregates and hence the latest results and targets are targets are not shown in the table above. The distortions, which have tended to reduce sharply the recorded rate of growth of money, have arisen for a number of reasons. For M1 at least, the major factor has been that, from November 1978, banks have been allowed to offer automatic transfer services; under these a customer can safely keep a low current account balance, in the knowledge that if the account goes into debit, the bank will transfer funds from his savings account. For further details of this and other developments, see Federal Reserve Bulletin (1979).

3. CANADA

(a) **Target aggregate** (first announced November 1975)

M1—comprises currency in circulation plus demand deposits (other than those of the Government of Canada) with chartered banks and denominated in Canadian dollars.

(b) **Targets set and results achieved** (seasonally adjusted)

	Target		% *Annual rate*
	Set	*Result*	
A/M/J 1975–F/M/A 1976	10–15	10.7	
F/M/A 1976–June 1977	8–12	8.9	
June 1977–June 1978	7–11	8.5	
June 1978–June 1979	6–10	9.1[a]	

[a] Annual rate June 1978–February 1979.

4. GERMANY

(a) **Target aggregate** (first announced December 1974)

Central Bank Money comprises all currency in circulation (since March 1978, excluding cash held by the banks) plus 16.6 per cent of residents' sight deposits plus 12.4 per cent of residents' time deposits plus 8.1 per cent of residents' savings deposits held with German banks. (These various percentages represent the required minimum reserves on those deposits as at January 1974.)

(b) Targets set and results achieved (seasonally adjusted)

	Target %	
	Set	*Result*
December 1974–December		
1975	8	10.1
1976 annual average[a]	8	9.2
1977 annual average	8	9.1
1978 annual average	8	11.5
1978:IV–1979:IV	6–9	

[a] Where the annual average equals the average of

$$\frac{January\ 76}{January\ 75} + \frac{February\ 76}{February\ 75} \cdots \frac{December\ 76}{December\ 75}$$

5. SWITZERLAND

(a) Target aggregate (first announced 1975: I)

M1—comprises notes and coin in circulation plus private and public sight deposits in Swiss francs held with banks and the postal cheque service.

Monetary base equals the Swiss National Bank's holdings of foreign currency reserves plus its open market portfolio of securities plus its refinance credits plus other assets less liabilities (including the minimum credit balances of banks).

(b) Targets set and results achieved

	M1		% Monetary base	
	Target	*Result*	*Target*	*Result*
1975 annual average[a]	6	4.3	6	5.4
1976 annual average	6	8.0	6	2.0
1977 annual average	5	5.4	—	
1978 annual average	5	16.2	—	

[a] as for footnote [a] in the piece above on Germany.

6. ITALY

(a) Target aggregates

General credit expansion (first announced March 1974) comprises bank lending in lire and foreign currency plus lending by the Special Credit Institutes plus bond issues by domestic firms plus the state sector's borrowing requirement (net of Treasury finance to the Special Credit Institutes).

Monetary base equals most of the liabilities of the central bank plus those Treasury bills held by the banks as part of their compulsory reserves.

(b) Targets set and results achieved (seasonally adjusted)

				lire trillion
	GCE		*Monetary base*	
	Target[a]	*Result*	*Target*	*Result*
March 1974–March 1975	21.8	19.3		
March 1975–March 1976	24.7	34.8		
1976	29.5	33.3		
1977	32.0	35.9		
March 1977–March 1978	30.0	39.4		
1978	46.0	50.0 (est)	7.5	8.9[b]

[a] Frequently, targets have been announced and subsequently revised: only the revised figures are shown here.
[b] For the year Nov 1977–Nov 1978.

7. FRANCE

(a) Target aggregate (first announced December 1976)

M2—(Care: this is not the M2 defined in French national statistics). Comprises notes and coin in circulation plus sight and time deposits (including certificates of deposit) in the banking and postal cheque clearing systems. External holdings by French residents are included as are certain non-resident and foreign currency deposits.

(b) Targets set and results achieved (seasonally adjusted)

	Target %	
	Set	*Result*
1977[a]	12.5	13.9
1978	12.0	12.3
1979	11.0	

[a] i.e. Dec 1976–Dec 1977.

Comments on Michael Foot's Paper

Patrick Minford
University of Liverpool

This paper by Michael Foot has many good points. First, it assembles the facts on monetary targets since 1972 usefully in one place. Second, it carries out some basic evaluation, did inflation drop after monetary targets were implemented? Were the targets 'achieved' or not? Third, it brings together a variety of views of different economists on the targets and their rationale. Fourth, it reviews experience with demand for money functions which is obviously relevant to the issue. The conclusion reached by the author is diplomatic, as one might expect of a Bank of England official with one eye on Charles Goodhart, another looking over his shoulder at Christopher Dow and a third warily directed at the Governor. It could be paraphrased: 'The demand for money functions shows instability, which perhaps is worrying. The results of implementing targets seem to have been quite good, though targets were perhaps helpful rather than necessary'. In its own terms this paper succeeds, i.e. as a judicious survey of the facts, without becoming too enmeshed in controversy. I begin with some general comments on the theory of targets and how one might test for their effect, an aspect I find lacking in the paper's exposition. Later, I will take up particular points made in the paper.

I. THE RATIONALE FOR MONETARY CONTROL

The first general point I would make is that Michael Foot does not underline the rationale for monetary targets under floating exchange rates though some passages could perhaps be considered to hint obscurely at it. The rationale is that if the exchange rate is floating then the money supply *must* be controlled, and interest rates must *not* because of problems of determinacy and stability.

If interest rates are controlled, then with adaptive expectations the price level and the inflation rate will be indeterminate in the long run and the model will almost certainly be unstable. (This is a point due largely to Friedman in his 1968 AEA Presidential address.) With rational expectations then the price level and the inflation rate will be indeterminate not only in the long run but also in the short run (a point due to Sargent and Wallace in their work in the early 1970s). Hence interest rate stabilisation implies failure to control the price level, either totally (rational expectations) or asymptotically (adaptive expectations).

If on the other hand the money supply is controlled then these problems are resolved. Under adaptive expectations the price level is determinate in the long run at the level given by the money supply and the model is (probably) stable. Under rational expectations the price level and inflation rate are determined in the short run by the money supply, subject to the effects of unanticipated shocks. So to reiterate, to control inflation it is necessary under floating exchange rates to control the money supply. This is the rationale for the whole philosophy of monetary targets.

Notice that this rationale is quite independent of:

(1) the stability of the demand for money function;
(2) whether there are short or long lags on interest rates in the demand for money function.

Both of these are points stressed by Michael Foot as necessary to the belief in monetary targets. They are not. Nor are some other issues that are frequently raised and are to some extent alluded to in the paper (e.g. the definition of money, the volatility of interest rates etc.). The argument merely requires that there *exists* a demand for money function, however 'shifting', and few would care to deny that, any more than knowing the problems with consumption function or investment functions they would deny the existence of those functions.

An alternative to control of the money supply that would in principle ensure determinacy of the price level is incomes policy. This of course ensures it by fixing wages and prices by law or by 'consent'. This ought to be mentioned but it is clear that there are considerable problems with such a course. First, no-one has yet in a democracy persuaded a majority of people to accept a *permanent* incomes policy. Yet this is needed to give a long-run determinacy to the price level (what determines it otherwise when the policy breaks down?). Second, even for periods of operation of the policy, a great deal of econometric work[1] (see Parkin and Sumner

1974); Henry and Ormerod (1978); and Minford and Brech (1979)) has
urned up no evidence that incomes policy succeeds in holding wages or
prices down except in one or two short episodes and even here the effects
have been found to be 'caught up' shortly after.

An implication of money supply control that is mentioned by the
paper, but not with appropriate emphasis, is the control of the budget
deficit. For while in the short run the budget deficit and the money
supply growth can go different ways, in the *long run* there cannot be both
a high deficit and a low money supply growth without ever-rising real
interest rates, which would be self-arresting and thus frustrating to the
combination. Thus with adaptive expectations you need long-run
control of the budget deficit to control long-run money supply growth.
With *rational* expectations a high expected long-run deficit will create
expectations of rapid money supply growth and so high inflation
expectations and high nominal interest rates. This will increase short-
run money supply growth and so it is that a necessary condition for
short-run monetary control under rational expectations is that long-run
budget deficit prospects be kept under control. This can, however,
permit some modest short-run fiscal stabilisation around this trend.

II. THE IMPLEMENTATION OF MONETARY CONTROL

These points relate to the underlying control of the money supply and
the budget deficit. However, we are then left with questions of
implementation. There are two main approaches possible here, provided one recognises that both presuppose a strong commitment to
some underlying growth of the money supply.

The one approach would be to emphasise the long-run control of the
money supply (with a target over three years for example) but to practise
short-run stabilisation policy around this underlying trend with respect
to selected targets (e.g. interest rates around their trend, whether real or
nominal, or output around its trend).

The other approach is to stick rigidly in the short run (e.g. over a one-
year horizon) to control of the money supply and to stabilise actual
monetary growth as closely as possible to this target, using interest rates
or the monetary base as a control instrument. Within this approach
there are more or less tight strategies of control possible in the very short
run (monthly, quarterly) and a wide variety of potential techniques to
achieve it.

Now this issue of how tightly you stick in the short-run to your long-

run money supply growth trajectory is one on which disagreement i
very easy and it is hard to reach a firm position. There are two mai
issues that need sharp distinction.

One is the extent to which the monetary authorities should react t
past events with a view to attempting to improve the future. These are s
called 'feedback' rules.

The other is the extent to which the monetary authorities shoulc
follow 'automatic response' rules to *current* events—such as som
intervention rule in the money market relating the supply of ban
reserves to changes in interest rates. Another example would be som
foreign exchange market intervention rule.

The criteria for judging the merits of these two sorts of rules ar
completely different. For example it may be impossible—as Sargent an
Wallace (1976) have argued—for monetary policy to affect *futur*
output through a feedback rule, but very likely within their model tha
any automatic response of monetary policy to current shocks will affec
output as well as inflation. A very useful discussion of this is to be foun
in Parkin (1979). This paper, incidentally, takes up the issues raised b
Poole (1970), which should be read as being a comment on automati
stabiliser rules and *not* on feedback rules.

Most of the literature of this subject, other than Parkin and Poole
relates to feedback rules. It includes of course the famous contribution
by Sargent and Wallace (1976) arguing that since monetary feedback
rules cannot affect output, only prices, the best feedback rule is a
constant growth rule because that is the one that minimises the varianc
of prices around their trend. With the same policy conclusion Friedmar
(1968), Brunner and Meltzer (1979) and Laidler (1979) have argued
from the uncertainty that exists about the dynamics of the economy t
the ill-advisedness of any sort of feedback rule; this is sometimes referre
to as 'pessimistic Keynesianism'. My own work with a rationa
expectations model of the UK suggests that monetary feedback rule
can do nothing useful for output stabilisation but there may be some us
in having a rule that tightens monetary growth in response t
accelerating inflation and vice versa. This arises because of th
possibilities of financial 'overshooting' in the system.

The general tendency of monetarists and also of the proponents o
monetary targets has been suspicious of monetary feedback rules, wit
the general view that any feedback rule should be modest and should no
interfere with the basic emphasis on the underlying monetary control

However, this is not true of automatic response rules, where ver
little work has been done on the relevant empirical magnitudes. In so fa

as there is an implicit view on the part of many monetarists it seems to be
that central banks should be left to the job of reacting to current
shocks—*if* they can identify them—in a pragmatic manner, much as
illustrated by the papers of George Freeman and Kurt Schiltknecht for
this conference (Chapters 6 and 8).

III. SOME DETAILED COMMENTS

'Success' of targets

Michael Foot's measures of 'success' are not right. The extent to which a
target is closely achieved is not strictly a measure of success precisely
because of this potential in-period automatic response to shocks. The
appropriate measure of success would be to fit some reaction function to
monetary policy and then evaluate first the size of the random
component in this function (the larger the variance of the error the more
the monetary policy adds to uncertainty) and second how well this
reaction function causes the system to behave relative to other potential
functions.

The reduction of inflation is a relevant measure of success, since the
need for control of the money supply reflects the problem of inflationary
control. However, comparison of successive periods is not a satisfactory
measure of this reduction; model simulation is the appropriate tool here.

Fixed v. floating rates

Michael Foot's discussion of the fixed/floating distinction is somewhat
inaccurate. He makes the points that monetary control is 'difficult'
under fixed rates and became easier under floating; secondly, that under
floating there is some *harsh* choice between 'exchange rate' and 'money
supply' targets.

On the first point it is simply the case that monetary control is
irrelevant under fixed rates as demonstrated by several models of fixed
rates (that of Jonson (1976), Laidler (1978), Minford (1979), the London
Business School etc.) while under floating rates as already discussed
monetary control became *essential*.

On his second point we need careful use of language. In particular we
must distinguish between targets for a period in the future and outcomes
in that period which will be influenced by unanticipated shocks. As far as

targets go any money supply target implies an exchange rate target under floating and vice versa. Thus there is no contradiction or harsh choice between targets. It is true that a tighter planned growth in the money supply will imply a higher exchange rate in *nominal* terms, but this is of no interest to a policy-maker since there will be no implication for the *real* exchange rate or 'competitiveness' which is presumably what disturbs policy-makers.

On the other hand, during the period actual money supply and exchange rate outcomes depend on the shocks hitting the system and the automatic response functions of the authorities, as discussed. Clearly, there is a variety of strategies that pragmatic central bankers can take in response to shocks and it is absolutely not the case that there is a stark choice between holding the exchange rate rigidly to the target and holding the money supply rigidly to the target. Any monetary system (whether it is the European Monetary System or any other) will allow for some flexibility in short-run responses, often where *both* variables react to the shocks.

As a postscript to this discussion I remark on the confusion that exists in many official minds between real forces affecting the exchange rate and monetary forces on it. With this confusion goes an apparent conviction that monetary policy can virtuously affect these real forces.

One wonders what these people have in mind as the reaction to the supposed upward pressure on sterling derived from North Sea Oil; would they like a period of rapid monetary expansion in order to cause rapid nominal depreciation in the rate? Or would they like to engineer (if they could) a severe shock to market confidence and cause the real exchange rate to drop like a stone in the short run, at the price of substantial impetus to the inflationary process and no long-run effect on the real exchange rate? I cannot believe they are really advocating such policies.

Choice of Monetary Aggregate

In discussing the choice of monetary aggregates Michael Foot says that M1 should not 'appeal to monetarists'; this is an obscure remark. But in general I agree with Gordon Pepper on this, that to fix just one aggregate is a risky process because of the stochastic errors affecting substitution and the temptation of the authorities to use cosmetics, as well as the problem that variables hitherto unimportant may come to exercise an important effect on the function (known in City circles as Goodhart's Law).

It must not be forgotten that the object of the monetary control is to pursue financial rectitude and to convince economic agents that this is being pursued. This is a way of life rather than a mechanical fixing of numbers. It involves keeping a spectrum of monetary aggregates within some tolerance ranges. Within this spectrum the important aggregates are the PSBR (the most important), the monetary base, M1, M3 and some broader measure such as M3 plus building society deposits.

But above all this pursuit should be carried out without cosmetics and not as a game played by clever Treasury and Bank of England officials with the object of fooling people into thinking they are pursuing monetary control when they are actually 'going for growth' etc. People will not be fooled and hence this game must be played straight. As an illustration, we should note the success of the Swiss and the Germans in reducing inflation. This even though their Central Banks 'broke the rules' frequently. The reason for their success is that they have engendered confidence that they mean business on inflation. It is this that the UK authorities should try to build up. They still have a long way to go.

REFERENCES

Friedman, M. (1968), 'The Role of Monetary Policy', *AER*, March.
Henry, S. G. B. and Ormerod, P. A. (1978), 'Incomes Policy and Wage Inflation: Empirical Evidence for the UK. 1966–1977', *NIESR Review*, August.
Jonson, P. D. (1976), 'Money and economic activity in the open economy: the United Kingdom, 1880–1970', *Journal of Political Economy*, September.
Laidler, D. A. (1978), 'A monetarist viewpoint' in *Demand Management*, M. V. Posner, ed. (London: Heinemann).
Laidler, D. A. (1979), 'The Monetary Theory of the Balance of Payments', mimeo, paper presented to Bank of England Seminar, April.
London Business School, *Economic Outlooks*. (Annual publication.)
Minford, A. P. L. (1979), 'A rational expectations model of the UK under fixed and floating exchange rates', forthcoming in *The State of Macroeconomics*, K. Brunner & A. Meltzer, eds, proceedings of April 1979, Carnegie-Rochester Conference on Public Policy.
Minford, A. P. L. and Brech, M. J. (1979), 'Wages and Rational Expectations', forthcoming in proceedings of AUTE Conference, March.
Parkin, J. M. (1979), 'The choice of monetary instrument under rational expectations', Manchester Business School.
Parkin, J. M. and Sumner, M. (1974), *Incomes Policy and Inflation* (Manchester: Manchester University Press).
Poole, W. (1970), 'Optimal Choice of Monetary Policy Instruments in a Single Stochastic Macromodel', *Quarterly Journal of Economics*.
Sargent, T. and Wallace, N. (1976), 'Rational Expectations and the Theory of Economic Policy, *Journal of Monetary Economics*, April.

Comments on Michael Foot's Paper Monetary Targets

F. Blackaby
National Institute of Economic and Social Research

I. INTRODUCTION

This paper gives a very interesting account of the rise of monetary targets—though not yet (except in the case of Switzerland) of their fall. I want to pick up for discussion here one main point—the question of the exact location of monetary targets in the taxonomy of economic policy—what kind of an animal is it?

Some people currently tend to identify monetary targets with monetary policy, and it is, I think, important to distinguish a whole range of monetary approaches to policy. At one end of the range there is the use of monetary indicators as one source of information about what is going on; then there is the use of monetary instruments for management, which is, of course, a very different matter. (The fact that one looks at monetary indicators carries no implication about whether or not one should use monetary instruments.) Then there is the use of a monetary rule (the Government or Central Bank do not need to announce this if they do not want to). Finally, there is the money supply target; the term 'target' implies an announcement. This note is particularly about money supply targets, and to a lesser extent about monetary rules. It is not concerned with monetary policy in general—it does not traverse the familiar argument that the use of monetary policy to bring down the rate of inflation is simply a special case of the general policy of attempting to deal with it by deflating the economy.

The standard taxonomy of economic policy is concerned with *objectives* and *instruments*. To quote one of the standard expositions: 'Economic policy is intended to further a number of general *aims*; these give rise to a set of more precisely defined economic *objectives*.

Governments, in attempting to achieve these objectives, employ a variety of instruments and take certain *measures*. The Government's main policy problem is to select, from a wide range of instruments, the ones which will, in its opinion, most nearly achieve its objectives' (Kirschen *et al.*, 1964).

The money supply is clearly not an objective of economic policy; objectives are outcomes desired for their own sake—such as expansion of production, full employment or stable prices. Nor is it an instrument: the term should be restricted to matters which are unambiguously under the government's control, such as the rate of VAT, or the standard rate of income tax. The money supply is not such an entity. It is an intermediate variable, lying between the set of instruments which the government can use and the final objectives which it is wanting to achieve. The instruments of monetary policy are such things as changes in the rate of interest offered on new issues of gilt-edged stock.

This, I think, immediately raises a conceptual question—what is the justification for a target for an intermediate variable of this kind? Targets for objectives have some economic justification—in that policy-makers can legitimately be asked what end result they are trying to achieve. (They may, of course, decline to·say—since the statement of targets for objectives gives hostages the fortune.) But what exactly is the rationale for a target for an intermediate variable—and for this intermediate variable in particular?

The proponents of money supply targets argue, in effect, that since the demand for money is stable the money supply can be treated as a proxy for national expenditure in money terms. However, they admit that the short-term movements of the monetary aggregates can be misleading; and indeed each time a new money supply figure is published it provokes intricate arguments in the city columns explaining that although the actual figure has gone down the 'true' figure has gone up (or conversely). If, then, the money supply is a proxy for money national expenditure, and if the month-to-month movements in the money supply are erratic, why not state the target in terms of money national expenditure? There are good quarterly figures, and early estimates can be made from the movement of output and prices. This leads on to a further thought. Governments are not indifferent to the output/price mix of changes in national expenditure: indeed, money supply targets are normally constructed from output and price targets. So why not just keep to targets for the final objectives—for output and for prices—and say that policy will be conducted accordingly?

I think I can illustrate that the concept of an intermediate variable as a target is a little odd by an analogy. Let us suppose you have a chauffeur-driven car, and you want the chauffeur to limit himself to 60 miles an hour on the motorway. There is a certain setting of the accelerator which, on a flat stretch and with no wind, will produce 60 miles an hour. You could make some kind of mark on the inside of the car, and instruct your chauffeur to put his foot down on the accelerator so far and no more. If you did this, your chauffeur would, I think, conclude that you were beyond the reach of rational argument; however, if he were prepared to reason with you, he would point out in the first place that since the car was equipped with a speedometer, it was really more sensible for him to be looking at that rather than to be peering down at his feet all the time. Further, since all motorways are not flat, and since the wind changes, keeping the accelerator in a fixed position would in fact result in variable speed.

I think this analogy is valid. There are two possibilities about the relationship between intermediate variables and final objectives. One is that the intermediate variable has a one-for-one relationship with some final objective. In that case the target might as well be stated in terms of the final objective itself. Or it does not have a one-for-one relationship— in which case the argument for a target for the intermediate variable is even weaker.

I know of no models which suggest anything like a one-to-one relationship. The Treasury paper in this volume (Chapter 4)—which, it is true, is not addressed to the question of relationships between intermediate targets and final objectives —nonetheless does incidentally provide some interesting evidence of dissonance. For example, a reduction of the PSBR by £1 billion by income-tax increases (admittedly on certain constrained assumptions) not only worsens the output figures for four years, but also the price figures as well, and even (under floating exchange rates) worsens the balance of payments in the fourth year. There is no simple relationship here from a reduction in the borrowing requirement to a reduction in the money stock and so to an improvement in the price trend.

There is always a danger that intermediate targets of this kind lead to silly economic policies. Obviously, once stated, they become objectives in their own right—that is inevitable. However, the government may then decide, because of changed economic circumstances of some kind, that it wants to avoid the 'normal' effects on the final objectives of economic policy of observing that target number for that intermediate variable. The consequence will be cosmetic economic policies: the government will look round for ways in which it can alter the intermediate variable without having any effect on the final objectives of economic policy. The best example is with the target set for the public sector borrowing requirement; we have seen the government persuading the joint stock banks to take over some of the burden of export financing, and the sale of part of British Petroleum. The economic effects of these policies are clearly quite different from the economic effects of reductions in current expenditure or increases in taxation. The same kind of difficulty arises with monetary targets. A particular definition of money has to be specified. The government then ceases to be concerned with increases in liquidity which fall outside that particular definition. As Charles Goodhart has pointed out, the very fact of making a particular series the object of control tends to make that series the inappropriate one for that purpose. Targets for intermediate variables tend to lead to cosmetic economic policies—to policies designed to affect that intermediate variable, and not to affect anything else.

The problem is made worse if, instead of having just one intermediate variable as a target, the Government has a number—target ranges for more than one monetary aggregate. The result is almost certain to be that, in order to meet the targets, the monetary authorities will dissipate their energies in monetary juggling.

What defence is left, therefore, for instituting a target for an intermediate variable such as the target for the money supply? I think there is only one. It is that it is a more credible way of influencing expectations than stating a target for a final objective. The argument is that if the government says it intends to bring the rate of inflation down to 5 per cent, it will not be believed. If it says that it intends to keep the increase in the money supply down to 8 per cent, it will be believed. This, so far as I can see, is the only argument that can be found for an announced monetary target. It is that it is a powerful instrument for altering expectations, and so altering behaviour. How valid an argument is this?

II. EXPECTATIONS

The world of expectations in economics is a weird and wonderful world, in which it is very rare for anybody to ask exactly who is doing the expecting; 'expectations' in economics tend to be rather like the Jungian collective unconscious, invisibly permeating the whole human race. There are three points I would like to make in considering the validity of the claim that the statement of monetary targets will affect expectations and so change behaviour.

The first point is a favourable one. For an implied doctrine to influence expectations and behaviour, it does not have to be true; it only has to be believed. Here the statement of monetary targets may have a certain advantage, in that many people do believe that the government can easily, simply and directly control the money supply, by ordering the printing presses to speed up or slow down. The idea that, in Doctor Dalton's phrase, inflation can be defined as too much money chasing too few goods, and therefore a reduction in the supply of money must deal with inflation, has a simple and popular appeal. If it were possible to find a way of phrasing the question so that it was understood, I think it would be found that the travellers on a typical Clapham omnibus believe in a stable demand function for money; not for them the complications arising from variable velocity, assets that could be turned liquid, or inflows from abroad.

For, of course, the question whether monetary targets influence expectations and behaviour is a separate question from the efficacy of the actual use of monetary instruments. It is perfectly possible to envisage that monetary targets might be efficacious, even if monetary policy itself did not do much; conversely, some people may take the view that monetary policy is powerful, but that there is no particular point in stating a target.

However, there are two other points less favourable to monetary targets. The first is the obvious one that, for any signal to be effective, it has to be received. A small research project which nobody will undertake because it is too simple would be to discover what proportion of the population—using a stratified sample—knew what the monetary target was, either in this country or indeed in any other country which has had a monetary target. I am reminded of a possibly apocryphal story which Sir Henry Phelps-Brown tells, of the occasion in Australia when the introduction of monetary targets was announced. There was at the time a strike of sugar-cane cutters in Northern Queensland, and a reporter at the press conference at which the monetary targets were presented asked how the new policy would deal with that. The Central Bank spokesman is alleged to have replied: 'They will call it off when they hear about M3'.

The second requirement for a signal of this kind, if it is to influence behaviour through changed expectations, is that the recipients of the signal should be clear precisely in what way they are expected to alter their behaviour as a consequence of receiving the signal. The difficulty of the simple exposition of monetary targets is that it does not appear that anybody else needs to do anything as a consequence. The government controls the money supply, and that is that. If the government then adds 'If you refuse to adapt your behaviour accordoingly, the consequences for the economy as a whole will be deflationary', this is too vague a threat to have much effect in changing behaviour. To take an analogy again, if I tell my five-year-old that if he continues to blow a trumpet in my ear, he may expect a reduction in his pocket money of 5p, that may be specific enough to alter his behaviour. If I tell him that, if he goes on doing it, the consequences for all children in general may be unfortunate, he would hardly be deterred. For a signal to be effective in changing expectations and behaviour, it has to be clear to the recipient of the signal exactly in what way his behaviour needs to be modified. I think monetary targets fail this test. Again, it could be investigated, by asking a wide range of people—'If the government announced a monetary target of 8 per cent in the coming year, would you alter what you intended to do, and if so in what way?'. To take a 1979 example, I do not believe that the announcement of an 8 per cent money supply target now would have much effect in altering the size of wage and salary awards in the wage round beginning September this year.

It is often argued that 'they will learn'. After a number of repetitions of wages pushing against a money supply ceiling, leading to pretty astronomical rates of interest, widespread bankruptcies, and severe cutbacks in private investment, trades unions will learn to behave rationally. This would be more plausible if trades unions negotiated *en masse*, rather than atomistically. In any case, there is the alternative possibility that they would draw a different conclusion from such events—that the economic system which produced such results was functioning so badly that it had to be changed.

III. EXPECTATIONS AND EXCHANGE-RATES

There is one approach to this question according to which there is no need to consider the effect of a money supply target on the expectations of businessmen or trade union negotiators; it is only necessary to consider the effects on operators in foreign exchange markets. Operators in these markets, it is argued, believe that exchange-rates are determined by the relative movement of money supply figures in different countries. Any given money supply target, therefore, will lead them to maintain a certain exchange rate. This in turn, by the law of one price, will

determine the rate of price increase. This in turn will determine the size
of the permitted rise in the national wage bill. So the money supply
target is a powerful weapon. By influencing the expectations of
exchange-rate operators it determines the rate of inflation in the
country.

It must be very flattering to those who operate in foreign exchange
markets to be told that it is their expectations which are all-important in
determining the short-term economic prospects for the country. I find a
certain intrinsic implausibility about this suggestion that the exchange-
rate tail wags the economic dog. It reminds me of the theory advanced by
a Cambridge history don in a college quadrangle late one night, when he
argued that the conquest of the West in America was dependent on the
supply of top hats from a factory in Burnley, England. The
'transmission mechanism' went something like this. The development of
the West depended on the railways. The railways were built on borrowed
money from the sale of railway bonds; this required the services of
railway bond salesmen who raised the money from gullible Easterners.
To be a railway bond salesman it was essential that one should be
elegantly dressed and equipped with a top hat. There was no factory in
America at that time which made top hats. Thus the supply of top hats
from the Burnley factory was essential for the conquest of the West in
America.

I think the transmission chain from the expectations of those who
operate in foreign exchange markets to the movement of the retail price
index also has its weak links. This is not the appropriate discussion
paper in which to go into them all. It is implied that manufacturers never
give a wage increase if it is likely to reduce their competitive power in
foreign markets. It is also implied that the wage awards in those sectors
of the economy which are immediately vulnerable to foreign competition set the pattern for the size of wage awards in the rest of the
economy. I doubt if UK experience bears out either of these
propositions.

In sum, I doubt whether the promulgation of a money supply target is
a powerful anti-inflationary weapon. Mr Foot's paper shows that a
person who studied the experience we have of such targets would be
sceptical about whether they were likely to be observed, and doubtful
whether their introduction radically changed the inflationary prospect.
But even if the announcement of a target did lead him to expect both that
the target would be observed and that it would bring down the rate of
inflation, I doubt whether this expectation would lead him to change his
behaviour (except possibly if he were a dealer in foreign exchange). For

the signal given by a money supply target is insufficiently specific, and its relevance to his own operations is too imprecise.

REFERENCE

Kirschen, E. S. *et al., Economic Policy in Our Time*, vol. I, *General Theory* (Amsterdam: North-Holland, 1964).

2 Choosing between Money Targets and Targets for Credit

Bruce Brittain
Bank for International Settlements

I. INTRODUCTION[1]

Central banks have an important potential role in stabilising the economic activity of modern economies. Exactly what the role entails, however, is a matter of debate. Whether monetary authorities should seek stable conditions in credit markets or whether they should stabilise economic activity by minimising fluctuations in the growth of the money supply is currently a point of controversy in most countries. The purpose of this paper is to explore some of the empirical evidence that bears on this issue.

The particular question that concerns me is whether monetary authorities should target the money supply or whether they should target some aggregate measure of credit available to the economy; that is to say, whether they should establish quantitative limits on the growth of these magnitudes. In the United States, for example, it has been suggested that the Federal Reserve System's Open Market Committee should add the so-called total debt proxy—all short-term financial holdings of the private non-financial sector—to its list of targeted variables[2] which already includes several measures of the money stock. In other countries similar suggestions have been made and in some, such as Italy, the monetary authorities actually target credit aggregates. In other countries hybrid systems of monetary targeting and credit control exist. In the United Kingdom and France, for example, the monetary authorities have explicit targets for measures of money supply growth. In the United Kingdom M3 is targeted to grow between 8 and 12 per cent over the four quarters between October 1978 and October 1979, and in France the target is a maximum of 11 per cent growth for M2 during the course of 1979. Evidently, these two monetary authorities have opted for control of the money stock. Yet when money growth has exceeded or threatened to exceed target in the United Kingdom, limits have been applied to the expansion of certain liabilities of the banking system. In France the monetary target is administered through the *encadrement du crédit* which is a system of quantitative controls on bank lending. In practice, then, the Bank of France and the Bank of England have had to resort to direct controls on components of the money stock or the quantity of credit in order to implement their monetary targeting strategies.

In Germany and Switzerland the monetary authorities have established numerical limits on the growth of the money stocks in their countries as well. After considerable debate, however, the Deutsche Bundesbank and the Swiss National Bank during 1978 allowed the monetary aggregates far to exceed previously announced target levels and the Swiss National Bank ultimately abandoned the policy of pursuing a publicly announced rate of monetary increase—for reasons related to changes in the credit markets.

The authorities pointed out that major multinational corporations domiciled in Germany and Switzerland had evidently accelerated additions of Swiss francs and Deutsche Marks to their portfolios at the expense of the dollar-denominated assets. Rather than let the Swiss franc and the Deutsche Mark appreciate to equilibrate the market for credit, the monetary authorities allowed the Deutsche Mark and Swiss franc money supplies to expand.

To summarise, in this paper I examine whether a monetary aggregate is preferable to some measure of credit as a potential instrument of monetary policy for the United States, Germany, Italy and Japan—four countries for which the necessary flow of funds 'stock' data are currently available.

I have not considered possible measures of credit conditions other than the total stock of credit. These other measures would include, for example, short-term interest rates which are often thought of as the best single indicator of conditions in the credit markets. But to justify using the total stock of credit instead, one can argue that credit may be a less ambiguous indicator of tightness or ease in the credit markets. This is because movements in short-term interest rates are affected by un-measurable shifts in the expected inflation rate and in the expected depreciation of the currency.

The tentative results of my inquiries so far[3] are that in the United States measures of money are better potential control variables than the measure of credit. Narrow measures of money should be excluded as potential control variables in Italy and Germany. In Italy the credit measure appears to be marginally superior to a broad measure of money while in Germany broad money satisfies the criteria for a potential control variable. No firm conclusion can be drawn from the Japanese evidence. In the paper's conclusions I summarise the rough correspondence between what central banks ought to be doing with respect to aggregate targeting, if these results are correct, and what they actually do. The correspondence is remarkably close.

II. CRITERIA TO BE SATISFIED BY POTENTIAL CONTROL VARIABLES

There are at least two criteria that one might apply in choosing among variables that could be used to stabilise economic activity. (I assume that stabilising economic activity means, roughly, stabilising nominal gross national product.) The first is the relationship between the control variable and the target variable. The second criterion is the exogeneity of the potential control variable with respect to nominal income.

The first criterion is straightforward. Unexpected shifts in the relationship between income and the control variable should be less—and therefore income more successfully stabilised—if the control variable is more closely related to income than the alternatives. The second criterion is somewhat more complicated. If a potential control variable is endogenous with respect to nominal income, then a stabilisation policy based on any statistical model that treats the control variable as exogenous will have unpredictable effects on the target variable. In the remainder of this section I shall discuss these two criteria in greater detail, suggesting specific tests for whether they are satisfied.

The closeness-of-fit criterion

Consider the first criterion, the closeness of the relationship between the control variable and the target variable. Let Y represent gross national product, X_i a potential control variable, E_i foreseeable disturbances to economic activity and summarise the relationship between Y, E_i and X_i as equation (1):

$$Y = f(X_i, E_i) + e_i \qquad (1)$$

where e_i is an unforeseeable random disturbance term. The variance of Y will be smallest if we choose to target the X_i associated with the smallest possible variance of e_i. For the sake of simplicity, suppose a set of simple regressions of Y on the various X_i provides a legitimate statistical model of the income determination process, then the standard errors of the regressions of Y on the various X_i provide an estimate of the standard deviation of e_i. Therefore, the closest relationship and thus the best control variable would be indicated by the smallest regression equation standard error.

This criterion is familiar from other questions in the formulation of monetary policy, in particular the question of which money supply variable is the most appropriately controlled in a regime of monetary targeting.[4] I shall not therefore dwell on it at length.

A preliminary step in applying the closeness-of-fit criterion suggested by equation (1) is to divide the value of GNP by each of the potential control variables and then to examine the variability of the resulting

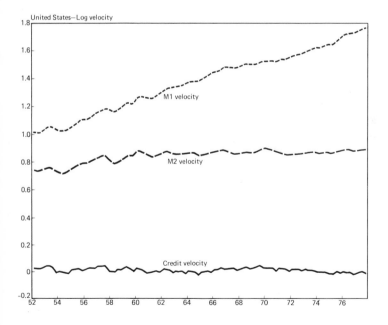

FIG. 2.1

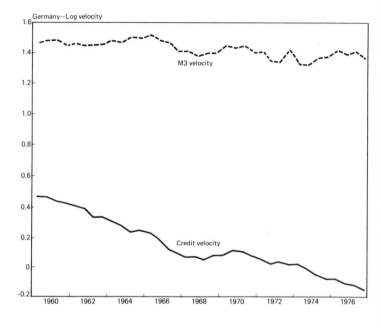

FIG. 2.2

velocity series. This procedure is also a simple first step in demonstrating the relative stability of demand for various types of money and it is the procedure that has been used to demonstrate the case for targeting the so-called total debt proxy in the United States. I have made the calculations for measures of money and credit for the United States, Germany, Italy and Japan. The results are plotted in Figures 2.1 to 2.4 as the logs of the income velocity of credit and money circulation.

I shall make no attempt formally to apply the criterion suggested by equation (1) but visually it would appear that for Italy and, possibly, for Germany and the United States credit is more closely related to income than money. The inference is that credit rather than money should be targeted in these countries.

Objections to this inference in the United States have been that credit data are not available frequently enough nor are the data timely enough for credit to be taken seriously as a potential control variable. Furthermore, by taking account of other arguments in the money demand function one can improve the closeness of the money-income relationship.

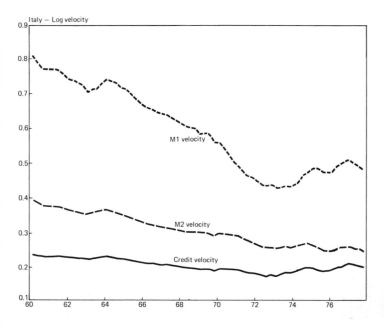

FIG. 2.3

The first objection is not tenable over the longer run since the timeliness and quality of the credit data are not fixed but can be improved. If it turned out that in the United States, for example, the total debt proxy were a better potential control variable than measures of the money stock, there would be a strong argument for improving the timeliness of the relevant flow-of-funds data.

The second objection is tenable but unconvincing, since improving the closeness of the money-income relationship involves using other variables that are endogenous to the system. These will be influenced by movements in the system's exogenous variables in a non-deterministic fashion. Hence, the expected variance of the money-income relationship will be greater than the error variance of the extended money-income model.

In my opinion, however, applying the first criterion in the simple way suggested by equation (1) is open to criticism on more serious grounds. Equation (1)-type representations of the economy are inadequate because slightly more complex models better capture the structure of

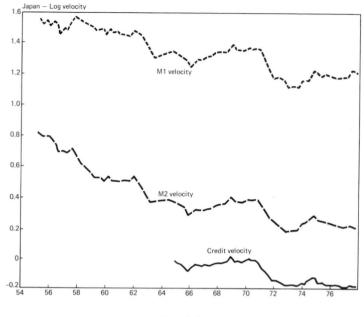

FIG. 2.4

income determination and perform better statistically.[5] If this is admitted, it follows that the relatively high correlation of income and credit in Italy, Germany and the United States—or, for that matter, the lower but still significant correspondence of income and money—may be due to strong mutual dependence on economic variables that are ignored in the simple graphs. For example, the rate of credit growth may be determined by the rate of growth of the money stock. Nominal income may also be determined by the stock of money in the way described by simple monetary models of income determination. In that case, credit and income will be closely related without the close relationship being evidence of causality.

Meeting this objection would involve the construction of full models of money income and credit in each of these countries and possibly simulating the path of income for various combinations of income and credit policy. Alternatively, stripping each of the income, credit and money series of the systematic dependence of current values on their own past values, and then relating the non-systematic components, comes close to achieving the same result.[6]

The point here is that all variables are assumed to be simultaneously determined. They are therefore all affected by random shocks and movements in the system's exogenous variables. In general the effect occurs after some period of time has elapsed. Lagged dependence ensures that current values of the series will be dependent on past realisations of the same series. Dependence on the same set of exogenous variables and random shocks means that these serial dependences will exist in all the endogenous variables. Thus, removing serial dependences in each of the series goes part of the way to avoiding the spurious inference of causality from high degrees of correlation. Removing serial dependence is not entirely adequate, however, if shocks and movements of the exogenous variables are felt instantaneously. This means that if the shocks and movements in the exogenous variables are not systematic themselves, the filtering procedure will not solve the problem of spurious correlation.

With these reservations in mind, I have derived non-systematic components of the money, income and credit series for the United States, Germany, Italy and Japan by estimating simple integrated auto-regressive, moving-average models for each. The specific forms of these models are reported in the Appendix A and as one application of the closeness-of-fit criterion, I have regressed the values of the non-systematic components of the GNP series on the money and credit series. The results are reported in Tables 2.1 and 2.1a, which show that in

TABLE 2.1   STANDARD ERRORS OF REGRESSION ESTIMATES (EXPRESSED IN PERCENTAGES) AND 'F' STATISTICS FOR THE SIGNIFICANCE OF THE REGRESSION[a]

| | *Country* | | | |
Regression	*United States*	*Italy*	*Germany*	*Japan*
GNP on MB	0.96 (1.61)			1.48 (2.27)
GNP on M1	0.95 (2.20)	1.71 (2.16)	2.14 (0.67)	1.56 (1.49)
GNP on M2	0.93 (2.39)	1.72 (1.84)		1.52 (1.70)
GNP on M3			1.95 (1.28)	
GNP on TC	0.95 (2.12)	1.74 (1.68)	1.84 (0.07)	1.56 (1.47)

[a] For regression time periods see footnote to Table 2.2.

TABLE 2.1a   STANDARD ERRORS OF REGRESSION ESTIMATES
(EXPRESSED IN PERCENTAGES) AND 'F' STATISTICS
FOR THE SIGNIFICANCE OF THE REGRESSION[a]

| | *Country* | | | |
Regression	*United States*	*Italy*	*Germany*	*Japan*
GNP on MB	0.94	2.07		1.47
	(0.56)	(0.04)		(11.39)
GNP on M1	0.87	1.97	1.63	1.02
	(6.19)	(3.78)	(0.84)	(0.02)
GNP on M2	0.90	2.04		1.67
	(3.73)	(1.11)		(0.37)
GNP on M3			1.48	
			(4.23)	
GNP on TC	0.86	2.04	1.65	1.66
	(6.96)	(1.19)	(0.40)	(0.91)

[a] For the period 1967:3 to 1978:4.

the United States, Germany, Italy and Japan monetary aggregates are
more often closely related to income than are credit aggregates.

It is interesting to note, however, that if this criterion were enough to
establish the best control variable and if all countries chose to target that
variable, income could be expected to be considerably more stable in the
United States than income in Italy, Germany and Japan.

The exogeneity criterion

The exogeneity of the potential control variable is an additional
criterion which I shall now discuss. To summarise the major point, any
potential control variable should also be exogenous with respect to the
target variable; otherwise, statistical models of the relationship between
the two would provide biased and unstable estimates of the true
relationship. Hence, any controlling action is likely to have unpredictable effects on the target variables.

To see in greater detail why exogeneity is an appropriate criterion to
impose on the choice of control variables, consider the stylised model of
income determination represented by equations (2) and (3):

$$Y = Y(C, M) + e_1 \qquad (2)$$
$$C = C(Y, M) + e_2 \qquad (3)$$

where Y is nominal GNP, C is credit, M is money and e_1 and e_2 are error terms. Suppose that money is truly exogenous and that income and credit are truly endogenous. What happens if one estimates a credit model of income determination where money is incorrectly assumed endogenous and credit incorrectly assumed exogenous? Assuming the system is linear in all variables, total differentiation (and setting dM to zero) yields a matrix representation of the system which is equation (4):

$$\begin{pmatrix} 1 & -Y'_c \\ -C'_y & 1 \end{pmatrix} \begin{pmatrix} dY \\ dC \end{pmatrix} = \begin{pmatrix} e_1 \\ e_2 \end{pmatrix} \tag{4}$$

solving for dY and dC functions of e_1 and e_2. Taking the ratio dY/dC (on the assumption that C is exogenous and dY/dC is being estimated), we obtain equation (5):

$$dY/dC = (e_1 - e_2 \times Y'_c)/(e_2 + C'_y \times e_1)$$

whose expected value is clearly different from Y'_c, the correct structural value of the relationship between income and credit.

The recently developed Sims test of causality (cf. Sims, 1972) is an appropriate application of the exogeneity criterion. By that test, money causes income and is therefore exogenous with respect to income if, and only if, future values of income contribute significantly to the statistical explanation of money but future values of money do not contribute significantly to the statistical explanation of income. The same test is clearly applicable to determining whether credit causes income and whether credit causes money.

By testing the significance of future values of the exogenous variable, the Sims procedure tests causality in the following way. Suppose that the true direction of causality is from X to Y, that the effects of any change in X take some time to be recorded in movements of Y and that values of Y are regressed on X. Past and current values of X will have a statistically significant effect on Y, while future values of X in the regression should not signficantly improve the explanation of Y. In a regression of X on Y, by contrast, future values of Y should contribute to the explanation of X. This is because X causes Y and changes in Y follow changes in X. Thus, future Y should be correlated with the current value of X. The Granger–Sims test therefore involves four regressions: one of Y on current and past X; one of Y on future, current and past X; one of X on current and past Y, and one of X on future, current and past Y. If future values of X are shown to be significant by the two regressions with Y as the left-hand variable, then we reject the hypothesis that Y causes X. If future values of Y are shown to be significant by the two regressions with X as the left-hand variable, we accept the hypothesis that X causes Y. If future values of both X and Y are shown to be significant by the two pairs of regressions, then we accept the hypothesis that X causes Y and that Y causes X–the hypothesis of joint causality.

For the same reasons as explained in my description of the first criterion for a potential control variable, the time series used to apply the second criterion ought to be stripped of systematic movements and only the non-systematic movements should be compared. The corrections to the series are as described above and in the Appendix.

I have calculated incremental 'F' statistics for four future values of the exogenous variable for regressions of money on GNP, GNP on money, credit on GNP, GNP on credit, money on credit and credit on money for corrected US, German, Italian and Japanese series. If an 'F' value is statistically significant, we can accept the hypothesis that the variable on the left-hand side of the regression equation 'causes' the variable on the right-hand side.

More precisely, I regressed all the potential endogenous variables on the current and on six past values of the potential exogenous variables and recorded the sum of squared residuals from the regression equation. Then I added four future values of the potential exogenous variable to the regression and recorded the new regression residual sum of squares. The incremental 'F' statistic is simply the difference between the first and second sum of squared residuals divided by the second residual sum of squares after correction for degrees of freedom.

The results, presented in Table 2.2, are mixed. All measures of money appear to be exogenous with respect to income in the United States. Further, one accepts the hypothesis that money causes income. US credit appears to be exogenous with respect to income but so does income with respect to credit. This ambiguity in the role of credit argues against its use as a control variable, as do the relatively high incremental 'F' statistics in the regression of total credit on money. These imply that money may cause credit. Despite the general superiority of money in the tests for the United States, we can reject the exogeneity of the narrowly defined money supply with respect to credit. Thus M2 and the monetary base are perhaps the best potential US control variables.

As far as narrowly defined money is concerned, similar results are obtained from the Italian and German experiences. The narrow aggregate appears to be endogenous with respect to GNP in both countries and with respect to credit in Germany.

Credit appears exogenous with respect to GNP in Italy, whereas the

TABLE 2.2 INCREMENTAL 'F' STATISTICS FOR FUTURE VALUES OF EXPLANATORY VARIABLES IN MONEY, INCOME AND CREDIT REGRESSION[a]

	Country			
Regression	*United States*	*Italy*	*Germany*	*Japan*
MB on GNP	1.88			0.36
M1 on GNP	2.33[c]	2.41[c]	1.39	1.02
M2 on GNP	3.47[b]	1.69		1.29
M3 on GNP			2.63[c]	
TC on GNP	0.95	2.45[c]	1.40	1.09
GNP on MB	0.73			0.68
GNP on M1	0.58	3.13[b]	3.58[c]	1.39
GNP on M2	0.67	0.90		1.17
GNP on M3			1.03	
GNP on TC	0.54	0.52	1.90	1.09
TC on MB	1.23			0.98
TC on M1	1.78	0.93	3.18[c]	2.66[c]
TC on M2	1.56	4.64[b]		0.79
TC on M3			1.32	
MB on TC	1.63			0.68
M1 on TC	2.99[b]	1.37	1.17	1.14
M2 on TC	1.56	3.48[b]		0.61
M3 on TC			1.19	

[a] Regression periods were: for the United States, 1951:2 to 1975:1,
for Italy, 1964:3 to 1976:4,
for Germany, 1960:2 to 1975:1,
for Japan, 1967:2 to 1976:1.

[b] Significant at the 5 per cent level.

[c] Significant at the 10 per cent level.

NB The hypothesis that the left-hand variable in the regression equation 'causes' the right-hand variable is accepted if the incremental 'F' statistic is significant.

evidence is ambiguous for M2. In addition, there is strong mutual interdependence between M2 and credit. Forced to choose, one might opt for controlling credit in the Italian case.

In Germany M3 appears to cause GNP. The reverse hypothesis can be rejected and there are no complications from mutual causation between M3 and credit. M3 appears to be the most suitable control variable in Germany.

In the Japanese case, narrowly defined money appears to be caused by total credit, but the results warrant no other firm conclusion.

III. RESERVATIONS REGARDING THE STATISTICAL TESTS

At this point I should like to discuss a major problem concerning the reliability of the tests of causality and closeness of fit. The problem is that the structure of the relationships among money, credit and income may differ between sub-periods in the overall sample. For example, in one sub-period money may truly 'cause' credit and income while, in a second, income may 'cause' the others. If this were true, the tests of exogeneity could give unclear or plainly misleading results.

I can imagine at least three changes occurring between 1960 and 1977 that might have altered the economic structure. First, and most important, is the shift from fixed to flexible exchange rates that occurred some time between 1971 and 1973. This argument is familiar from Frenkel and Johnson (1975) and is, simply stated, that under a regime of flexible exchange rates the central bank, in principle, controls the money stock. Furthermore, nominal income adjusts itself to the money stock so that money should cause income with flexible exchange rates.

By contrast, under a regime of fixed exchange rates, prices in an open economy may be determined by external considerations. Fluctuations in world prices will create temporary divergences between the stocks of nominal cash balances in existence and those demanded in the open economy. These divergences will be eliminated by expansions and contractions of the money stock through overall balance-of-payments surpluses and deficits. In a regime of fixed exchange rates, then, income may be said to cause money.

A second possible structural change associated with the turn of the decade has to do with labour unions, the effect they may have on wages or prices and, indirectly, on the behaviour of the monetary authority. A common argument in some countries is that labour unions have more or less autonomous control over the level of nominal wages. Seeking a wage increase in excess of marginal gains in labour productivity, the argument goes, labour unions will force an increase in final product prices as companies strive to maintain their profitability. This new, higher level of prices creates excess demand for cash balances—the existing quantity of nominal balances having been reduced in real value by the price rise—and forces hoarding and thus a decline in aggregate demand.

The central bank, according to this argument, can either validate the higher level of prices by expanding the money stock or it can leave the money stock unchanged. If it chooses to remain passive, wages and prices must fall before full employment output can be achieved. Thus a policy of accommodation will mean that tests of causality demonstrate that income causes money.

A quick review of events since 1971 shows that policies of accommodation may characterise the experience of such countries as Italy, France and the United Kingdom—higher wage demands and higher prices may have forced accommodative increases in the money supply. In the United States, Germany and Japan, however, during 1974 and 1975 the accommodative policy was, in fact, reversed. The authorities adopted more restrictive monetary policies in the face of the unanticipated rise in oil prices and the short-run increase in the inflation rate that it implied. Thus, policies of monetary accommodation probably vary significantly between countries and over time.

Finally, the growing body of literature on rational expectations (cf. Lucas, 1973, 1974 and Sargent and Wallace, 1975) suggests a third possible source of structural change. If prices are set by economic agents with a clear understanding of how the macroeconomy functions, changes in the money supply may be associated with an increasingly faster adjustment of the price level. Then the regression equations that test closeness of fit and causality will be mis-specified.

These three arguments are strong enough to indicate that a test for structural change is in order. Table 2.3 presents 'F' statistics that are the 'Chow' test of equality of regression coefficients in different linear regressions (cf. Chow, 1960). For the purposes of Table 2.3, the different

TABLE 2.3   CHOW TEST 'F' STATISTICS[a]

	United States	Italy	Germany	Japan
	(2, 36)[b]	(2, 36)	(2, 36)	(2, 16)
GNP on MB	0.304	1.973		0.805
GNP on M1	0.398	2.498	1.902	0.437
GNP on M2	0.100	1.830		0.045
GNP on M3			1.436	
GNP on TC	0.047	3.900[c]	1.773	0.594

[a] For the periods 1967:3 to 1971:4
                1972:1 to 1976:4
                1967:3 to 1976:4
and calculated as $((A - B - C)/\phi_1)/((B + C)/\phi_2)$
where A is the residual sum of squares from the regression equation estimated over the entire period; B and C are the residual sums of squares from the equations estimated over the two sub-periods; ϕ_1 and ϕ_2 are degrees of freedom.
[b] Degrees of freedom in brackets.
[c] Significant at the 0.05 level.

regressions are of nominal income on measures of money and credit in each of the four countries discussed in the paper for two different time periods. The two time periods are: from the third quarter of 1967 (second half in the German case) to the fourth quarter (second half) of 1971, and from the first quarter (first half) of 1972 to the fourth quarter (second half) of 1976.

It seemed reasonable to choose these sub-divisions, since the break corresponds roughly to the adoption of flexible exchange rates, the confirmation of labour union strength and a growing awareness of the role of money in the inflationary process. Except in the regression of GNP on credit for Italy, there is no evidence of structural change between these two sub-periods. Thus, apart from the qualification that caution should be exercised in choosing to target credit in Italy, I leave my interpretations of causality tests and closeness of fit unchanged.

IV. CONCLUSIONS

Perhaps the most interesting conclusion that one might draw from this paper concerns the behaviour of central banks. Central banks have been criticised, and there is ample evidence to support this criticism, for their handling of the choice between stabilising money and stabilising credit. Generally speaking, the criticism has been that they have too often opted for credit control at the cost of creating unduly expansive conditions in the markets for money. But there have been few attempts to explain why central banks behave in the way they do. After all, they draw on the same body of professional talent and the same body of information as do their critics. In what sense, then, have central banks made rational choices on the targeting issue?

I find it not entirely coincidental that in recent months the Federal Reserve System's Open Market Committee (in so far as it can be said to be targeting any monetary aggregate) has placed less emphasis on the narrowly defined money stock and more emphasis on the broader M2 aggregate. The Bank of Italy has targeted credit and the Deutsche Bundesbank the monetary base, which is very closely related to M3. The Japanese have yet to commit themselves on either form of targeting. Among other European central banks, those that have no information on the outstanding stock of credit occasionally reverse field—at some times emphasising the need to control credit and at other times emphasising the need to control the monetary aggregates.

NOTES

1. I should like to thank Dick Davis of the Federal Reserve Bank of New York, whose interest in the issue of credit targeting encouraged me to write this paper. My colleagues at the Bank for International Settlements made useful comments. The paper's remaining shortcomings are my own responsibility.
2. Letter from Henry Kaufman, General Partner, Salomon Brothers, to Senator W. Proxmire, Chairman of the Committee on Banking, Housing and Urban Affairs, 22 March 1978.
3. These results for the United States roughly correspond to those reached by Sims (1972), since they use a version of the Sims test for causality described in that article. Because of objections raised by Feige and Pearce (1978), I have not followed the Sims procedure directly. Rather than using the Sims arbitrary filtering procedure, I have used the procedure described in Nelson (1973) for pre-whitening money, income and credit series. I have not, however, extended my tests of independence to include the procedures suggested by Haugh (1976) and Pierce (1977) nor to that suggested by Pierce and Haugh (1977) as a direct test of causality in the sense of Granger.
4. See, for example, Lothian (1978).
5. See, for example, Barro (1977, 1978) and Sargent (1976).
6. This procedure is described in Sims (1972).

REFERENCES

Barro, Robert J. (1977), 'Unanticipated Money Growth and Unemployment in the United States', *American Economic Review*, 67, (March), 101–15.
—— (1978), 'Unanticipated Money, Output and the Price Level in the United States', *Journal of Political Economy*, 86, 4, (August), 549–80.
Chow, Gregory C. (1960), 'Tests of Equality Between Sets of Coefficients in Two Linear Regressions', *Econometrica*, 28, No. 3, (July), 591–605.
Feige, Edgar L. and Pearce, Douglas K. (1978), 'The Casual Causal Relationship Between Money and Income: Some Caveats for Time Series Analysis', Workshop series paper, (July), Social Systems Research Institute, University of Wisconsin, Madison.
Frenkel, J. A. and Johnson, H. G. (1975), *The Monetary Approach to the Balance of Payments* (London).
Haugh, L. D. (1976), 'Checking the Independence of Two Covariance–Stationary Time-Series: A Univariate Residual Cross Correlation Approach', *Journal of the American Statistical Association*, 71, (June), 378–85.
Lothian, James R. (1977), 'The Demand for High Powered Money', *American Economic Review*, 67, (March).
Lucas, Robert E. (1973), 'Expectations and the Neutrality of Money', *Journal of Economic Theory*, 4, (April), 103–24.
Lucas, Robert E. (1974), 'Econometric Policy Evaluation: A Critique', *JMCB*, Supplementary series No. 1.

Nelson, Charles R. (1973), *Applied Time Series Analysis for Managerial Forecasting* (San Franscisco: Holden Day).

Pierce, D. A. (1977), 'Relationships – and the Lack Thereof – Between Economic Time Series with Special Reference to Money and Interest Rates', *Journal of the American Statistical Association*, 72 (March), 11–22.

Pierce, D. A. and Haugh, L. D. (1977), 'Causality in Temporal Systems: Characterizations and Survey', *Journal of Econometrics*, 5, (May), 265–93.

Sargent, T. J. (1976), 'A Classical Macroeconomic Model of the United States', *Journal of Political Economy*, 84 (April), 207–37.

Sargent, T. J. and Wallace, Neil (1975), 'Rational Expectations, the Optimal Monetary Instrument, and the Optimal Money Supply Rule', *Journal of Political Economy*, 83, No. 2, (April), 241–54.

Sims, Christopher A. (1972), 'Money, Income and Causality', *American Economic Review*, 62, (September), 540–52.

Williams, D., Goodhart, C. A. E. and Crowland, D. H. (1976), 'Money, Income and Causality: The UK Experience', *American Economic Review*, 66, (June), 417–23.

Appendix

TABLE 2.4 THE STRUCTURE OF THE ARIMA MODELS USED TO
DERIVE SERIALLY UNCORRELATED TIME SERIES

		ND^a	P^b	Q^c
United States	MB	2	4	4
	M1	1	3	1
	M2	1	6	1
	TC	1	2	1
	GNP	1	2	1
Germany	M1	1	1	1
	M3	2	1	0
	TC	1	0	0
	GNP	1	0	0
Italy^d	MB	1	1	1
	M1	1	1	1
	M2	1	1	1
	TC	1	1	1
	GNP	1	1	1
Japan	MB	1	1	0
	M1	1	1	0
	M2	1	1	0
	TC	1	1	0
	GNP	1	0	0

[a] ND = degree of differencing.
[b] P   = number of auto-regressive parameters.
[c] Q = number of moving average parameters.
[d] All Italian series were seasonally adjusted, using first degree seasonal differences, one auto-regressive parameter and one moving average parameter.

A. THE DATA (see Table 2.4)

Money and nominal GNP data are taken from conventional national sources. The German credit series is 'Household and enterprise holdings of negotiable assets less equities and trade credits' from the Deutsche

Bundesbank's 'Zahlenübersichten'. This series is half-yearly. I therefore aggregated German GNP and money data into half-yearly series, using simple averages, and conducted the German analysis on the basis of a half-yearly frequency. The Japanese and US credit data are acquisitions by households, personal trusts, non-profit organisations and non-financial business of demand deposits, currency, time and savings accounts at commercial banks and savings institutions and credit market instruments. Both are from national *Flow of Funds* publications. The Italian credit data are 'Total internal credit', the financial obligations of the private sector and of state enterprises, from the Bank of Italy's *Bulletin*.

Comments on Bruce Brittain's Paper: On Monetary Targets

Roy A. Batchelor
The City University, London

Michael Foot's survey paper shows that the practice of targetting (see note on p. 85) monetary aggregates is spreading, but that the precise aggregate chosen has varied both across countries and in some cases, across time within individual countries. Much popular debate has focused on the month-by-month performance of these chosen aggregates *vis-à-vis* their targetted values. Less attention has been paid to the fundamental questions of whether the economic structures of different countries demand different targetting strategies, and if so, which aggregate it is most appropriate to target in each country. These fundamental questions are addressed in Bruce Brittain's paper. His perspective is also commendable. He is concerned with the relationships between measures of money, credit and nominal income in four countries quarter by quarter through the last two decades. His results are encouraging for the monetary authorities of these countries. The figures suggest that, at least in the United States, West Germany and Italy, the authorities have rapidly moved towards targetting the variable which best anticipates changes in nominal income.

It is important that the statistical basis for engaging in targetry, and for choosing particular measures of money or credit growth as targets, be well understood. None of my criticisms of this paper is directed at its motivation. My comments are instead intended to elucidate the theoretical and econometric background to such work in a constructive way. My conclusions are, however, rather negative. I doubt whether the statistical tests employed in the paper are robust enough to discriminate among the alternative candidate target variables; and I doubt whether we have sufficient experience of targetry to permit any strong inferences to be drawn about their effects from aggregate data on money and income growth.

My comments fall into two sections. In the first I want to try to fit the various aggregates investigated by Brittain into the semantic framework of monetary control, and suggest that some do not fit the role played by 'targets'. My second set of comments relate to the power of the statistical tests which form the core of Brittain's paper.

The semantics of monetary control were developed in the United States in the 1960s. A useful dictionary is provided in an article by Thomas Saving. The economic variables involved in the process of control can be assigned to one of four classes—instruments, indicators, proximate objectives and ultimate objectives. Instruments are variables under the direct control of the authorities; indicators are variables which are functionally related to instruments in a way which makes it possible for the authorities to assess whether on balance their actions have been expansionary or contractionary; proximate objectives are variables which give an early and unambiguous reading of the way in which ultimate objectives will move in response to policy, and to other disturbances in the economy. This terminology overlaid the older and more bald distinction between instruments and objectives; but has itself been overtaken by further concepts borrowed from engineering control theory, and from the political hard-sell of monetary discipline. The idea of a monetary 'target' grew out of the last development. The word first appears formally in Saving's dictionary, where it is made clear that a monetary target is a proximate objective by another, punchier, name.

Now let us consider the status of the variables involved in Bruce Brittain's study within Saving's framework. A first point is that the terms 'control variable' and 'target variable' are used throughout Brittain's paper in a rather confusing way. By 'control variable' is meant the monetary target or proximate objective: by 'target variable' is meant the ultimate objective, in this case nominal national income. The second point is more substantial. When in the 1960s modellers came to fill out Saving's conceptual boxes with economic variables, they ran into the problem that in their small expository models there were not enough independent variables to go round. One or more of the boxes remained empty. Today, however, Bruce Brittain is inviting us to choose among an embarrassment of candidates for the role of proximate objective– base money, narrow money, two versions of broadly defined money, and total credit. This makes me uneasy, and closer inspection of the variables suggests why. Base money, for example, looks more like an indicator than a proximate objective: the authorities have control of its domestic sources, but not of its foreign sources and inspection of movements in the base as a whole lets the authorities know whether their open market and sterilisation operations have been sufficient to offset the effects of undesirable balance of payments flows. At the other end of the spectrum the total credit measure is liable to blend into an ultimate rather than a proximate objective. The broader the measure of credit chosen the closer it approximates the value of the economy's stock of wealth and—with stable real rates of return or high rates of inflation— the more correlated it is liable to be with the income stream associated with that wealth—namely, nominal national income. In short, I think that the behaviour of the monetary base contains a message for the authorities which is different in kind from the message they should read into measures of the money stock proper; and that the value of targetting credit aggregates may easily be overstated because of their inevitable, almost definitional, correlation with nominal income.

The mainstay of Bruce Brittain's argument is a set of statistical tests designed to establish first the closeness of the relation between the proximate monetary objectives and the ultimate, nominal national income, objective, and second, the extent of feedback between each intermediate objective and nominal national income. The closer the first relation, the more informative is the intermediate objective as a barometer of economic conditions. Similarly, the less feedback there is from nominal national income to some monetary aggregate the more confident we can be that movements in that proximate target presage movements in the ultimate target.

The first criterion is investigated in two ways. To start with, the income velocities of the various monetary aggregates are plotted over time, and compared. The relative constancy of the ratio of total credit to nominal national income is taken to signify its superiority as a proximate objective. In view of our comments above on the near-definitional association between total credit and income, this constancy is unsurprising and certainly cannot be used to infer that credit is a useful proximate objective. Conversely the fact that the other velocities are trended does not rule them out as intermediate targets. What matters is whether the velocity is *predictable*, not whether it is *constant*. For example, if the ratio of nominal income to narrow money has increased regularly by about 6 per cent per annum, as seems to be the case in the United States, an ultimate objective of 10 per cent expansion in nominal income can be realised within narrow limits by meeting a $10 - 6 = 4$ per cent proximate target for growth in the narrow money stock.

The second approach to analysing the closeness of proximate and ultimate targets is in principle much more satisfactory. This involves regressing unexpected changes in nominal income on unexpected changes in the alternative monetary and credit aggregates. The approach to the second criterion of the feedback from ultimate to proximate targets also follows current best statistical practice in seeking unambiguous lagged relations between unexpected movements in pairs of data series.

The reason for removing predictable movements in these series is simply that *anticipations* of, say, monetary growth might cause nominal income to rise as workers demanded and were paid higher money wages so that velocity temporarily rose. Income growth would then lead monetary growth in time, but would in no sense be causing the eventual monetary growth. Unfortunately, the method of removing predictable components of monetary and national income growth is not foolproof. By fitting pure times-series models to each data run it is implicitly assumed that all parties efficiently exploit past systematic movements— trends and cycles—in forming expectations. It is easy to argue that agents might be more or less 'rational' than this. They may, for example, have advance warning of certain shocks to the economy and modify their expectations accordingly. In particular, the very process of setting monetary targets may affect expectations. Indeed, unless the targets are used simply as a discipline on the monetary authorities, it is essential that the private sector believe that the targets will be observed for them to be in any way beneficial. In periods when credible monetary targets are in force expectations errors should be measured by the deviations of outcomes from targets, and not by the residuals from a pure time-series model based on past behaviour of the series. On the other hand we may well have agents in the economy who act 'irrationally' or have interpretations of the past history which differ from the models estimated here.

A particularly difficult problem arises if the monetary authorities themselves cannot distinguish between permanent and transitory movements in the economy. If, for example, money actually causes most nominal income movements, but the authorities decide to make money available to accomodate a rise in nominal income which is in truth merely transitory, then the chain of causation between unsystematic money and income movements will appear at best ambiguous, and at worst perverse. Equally seriously, experience with the sort of time-series models chosen here—ARIMA, autoregressive integrated moving average processes—has shown that a variety of alternative specifications will explain any given series equally well, but will yield quite different estimates of the residual 'unexpected' components of the series. This problem is exacerbated by the fact that Bruce Brittain's paper utilises runs of data which are too short to discriminate among the many alternative ways we might imagine the private sector forming its expectations.

That said, it seems to me that the exercise performed in the paper has not been bled of every drop of useful information. A comparison of the structure of the time-series models—set out on Table 2.4—as well as their residuals is interesting. In particular we know that if two variables are simultaneously determined within the same economic model, their time series should display the same autoregressive properties: that is, the parameters ND and P of Table 2.4 should be the same. This is clearly true of total credit and nominal income in the United States, Germany and Italy. In Italy it is also true of the other, monetary, aggregates: but in Japan it is true of none. This does not establish whether money causes income or vice versa in the United States and Germany, but it certainly makes it unlikely that total credit can be relied upon as a proximate target, since credit may be determined simultaneously with nominal income. This rather weak and negative conclusion, rather than the more intricate and encouraging interpretations given by Bruce, seems the only safe statement which we can make on the basis of the statistics presented. It is no less important for that.

REFERENCES

Saving, T. R. (1967) 'Monetary-Policy Targets and Indicators', *Journal of Political Economy*, 75 no. 4, supplement August.
Wallis, K. F. (1975) 'Testing Dynamic Specification from the Final Form', Econometric Society World Congress, Toronto, August.

NOTE

The use of 'target' as a transitive verb is not recognised in most dictionaries. The Oxford English Dictionary does, however, cite its use in the form 'targetted' albeit in a quotation from 1843. The spelling 'targeted' has the special intransitive meaning of 'being furnished with a "target" ' (i.e. a shield), OED XI, p. 94. Two 't's should probably therefore be used in forming participles—cf. conjugation of 'rivet'.

Comments: On Monetary Targets

Max Corden
The Australian National University

This paper and the discussion at the conference raise a number of issues which should be distinguished from each other. To summarise my argument, there are really four issues.

(1) Should there be some target growth rate in nominal terms—such as for nominal GNP or for a monetary aggregate—to which the labour market would then have to adjust appropriately? In my view this is by far the most important issue.

(2) If it is agreed that there should be a nominal target, what is the case for an intermediate target—such as a monetary aggregate or an interest rate—rather than for targeting nominal GNP directly? I should like to suggest that directly targeting nominal GNP might be preferable to the indirect approach of aiming at one of the possible intermediate targets.

(3) If there is to be an intermediate target, should it be in price or quantity terms—in other words, should it be an interest rate or a monetary aggregate target?

(4) Finally, if it is agreed (i) that there should be *some* target in nominal terms, (ii) that this should be an intermediate target, and (iii) that the intermediate target should be in terms of the rate of growth of a monetary aggregate rather than an interest rate, what particular monetary aggregate should be chosen? Much of the discussion at this conference and in this paper has been concerned with this last issue, and one aim of my taxonomy is to put this discussion in perspective.

To limit these comments I shall assume a floating exchange rate regime. The money supply is thus within the control of the authorities.

There is no significant difference between a domestic credit expansion target and a money supply target.

I. THE LABOUR MARKET AND MONETARY TARGETING

The Keynesian demand management approach that was widely accepted in the 1950s and '60s was to aim at some *real* target—such as the level of employment or output, or their rates of growth—and then to adjust (or 'fine-tune') the various instruments of policy so as to achieve the target or set of targets. Thinking in terms of manipulating nominal GNP through fiscal and monetary policies, the idea originally was to ratify any cost-inflation due to 'wage-push' or supply shocks, these being seen as determined exogenously. This approach came to be modified by 'Phillips-curve thinking'. The curve was thought of as exogenously given (and perhaps shifting for exogenous reasons), and the aim was to attain an optimal point or target range on it.

The new monetary-targeting approach implies that there is not such a *given* rate of nominal wage increase, or a given non-vertical Phillips curve, but rather that nominal wages are determined endogenously, at least after allowing for lagged responses in the labour market. Nominal wages are determined such as to attain a desired level or structure of real wages, the latter of course changing over time and depending on real features of the economy, such as the strength of trade unions and degree of unionisation, as well as on the amount of unemployment associated with any particular real wage structure. The rate and pattern of productivity growth affect the extent to which a particular real wage structure generates unemployment. The success with which nominal wage decisions lead to the desired levels of real wages and levels of unemployment depends on the correctness of expectations by the actors in the labour market about prices, about demand and about productivity.

Is there then a case for having a firm nominal GNP target, whether achieved directly or indirectly? It must first be noted that a target set for six months or a year, and subject to revision after that, is not a 'target' in the sense in which I am using the term here. A short-term target is just a guide to an old-fashioned Keynesian fine-tuning policy. Wage increases will not be significantly inhibited if it is known that a wage increase this year may lead to an increase in the nominal GNP target next year. The target has to be of a fairly long-term nature. In any case, what considerations should influence one's view as to the desirability of a nominal GNP target in preference to Keynesian fine-tuning? There seem to be three.

(1) The first consideration is the institutional situation in the labour market. One has to have a view about how wages are determined in the particular country. It is here that so many differences of opinion arise. Above all, do demand conditions in the labour market and—even more important—expected demand conditions have a significant influence on wage demands and on the readiness of employers to grant these demands?

(2) The second consideration is the credibility of the targets. This has to do with expectations. Can expectations of nominal demand for goods and services be influenced by a nominal target? Essentially one is concerned here with the credibility of the political authorities and with the firmness with which the general public in a democracy would stand behind the politicians should they try to maintain the targets in a 'crunch' situation. It is here that the situation seems at present to differ so much between Britain and Germany.

(3) Finally, the willingness of the authorities temporarily to accept an increase in unemployment is crucial. It must be remembered that they do not know in advance how long this painful period might last. The establishment of credibility takes time, and the reluctance of governments to adhere firmly to targets can be explained rather obviously by the concern with unemployment.

Before leaving this first topic, one additional point might be added. Even though nominal wages may be determined endogenously, an absolutely rigid nominal GNP target is not necessarily appropriate. Granted that nominal wages cannot actually be expected to fall absolutely (though the rate of growth of nominal wages can fall), there may be a case for adjusting the target in response to various changes that are exogenous from this point of view, notably changes in the rate of productivity increase and in the terms of trade. Of course, if prices and nominal wages were thought to be completely flexible both upwards and downwards such a qualification would not be needed. But even the most ardent 'targeteers' would, I think, concede some downward rigidity or sluggishness in nominal wages.

II. WHY HAVE AN INTERMEDIATE TARGET?

I come now to the issue of the choice between targeting nominal GNP
and targeting some intermediate variable, such as M1,M3, or an interest
rate. It is certainly possible to conceive of a situation where a
government announces a firm target for the rate of growth of nominal
GNP, making it quite clear that it will not alter this target in response to
changes in the rate of increase in nominal wages. It would then try to
'fine-tune' its monetary and fiscal policy instruments so as to attain the
target. For example, decreases in velocity resulting from a rise in the
household saving ratio might be deliberately offset by measures leading
to an increased money supply. Complete structural models, with lags
and so on—of the kind used by the Treasury and presented in Chapter
4—would be used in the 'fine-tuning' process so as to attain the desired
nominal GNP target.

The question then arises why it should be desired to target some
monetary aggregate or an interest rate, rather than aiming directly at
nominal GNP. I can think of two possible reasons.

(1) The main aim of the target is to establish credibility so as to
    influence wage determination. Therefore the target must be
    clearly understood by the general public. A successful public
    relations exercise is required. But it can be argued that the concept
    of 'nominal GNP' or 'money national income' cannot be readily
    understood.

    Real magnitudes can be understood, but the crucial message is
    that the authorities fix a nominal magnitude and the forces in the
    labour market then determine what real magnitudes—notably
    real GNP—result from this. What *can* be understood is 'Money'.
    This is a possible argument for announcing a money target rather
    than a nominal GNP target. Nevertheless, it needs to be
    remembered that the true object is to aim at nominal GNP.

(2) A second reason for preferring an intermediate target to a
    nominal GNP target has to do with lagged effects. The authorities
    must first adjust the basic instruments of policy; after a lag the
    intermediate target responds; after a further lag the nominal GNP
    growth rate target responds; and after a further lag, that one
    hopes is not too long, wage determination responds. An in-
    termediate target is needed if it is to be known fairly quickly
    whether the instruments have been set correctly. Thus a crucial
    quality of the desirable intermediate target is that it responds

fairly quickly to the instruments. Hence it should be easier to achieve than a nominal GNP target. In terms of the concepts used below, the *controllability* of a well-chosen intermediate target should be greater than of a nominal GNP target.

The argument *against* targeting on an intermediate variable, such as money supply, is essentially that there may not be a clear predictable relation between the intermediate target and nominal GNP. *The predictability* of the intermediate target may be low. I shall come to the issue of *controllability* versus *predictability* again when discussing different possible intermediate targets.

III. INTEREST RATE VERSUS MONETARY AGGREGATE AS INTERMEDIATE TARGET

Given that there is to be an intermediate target—even though the real aim is to stabilise the rate of growth of nominal GNP—the first question is whether the target should be expressed in terms of an interest rate or a monetary aggregate.

The monetarist approach has involved two distinct ideas, namely (i) that nominal GNP growth should be stabilised to keep nominal wages under control, nominal wages being assumed to be endogenous, and (ii) that a monetary aggregate should be used in preference to the interest rate both as a short-term indicator and as the longer term intermediate target. The case of jettisoning the nominal interest rate in favour of a monetary aggregate rests on two separate arguments or issues. The first appears to carry most weight.

(1) When inflationary expectations are positive, nominal and real interest rates diverge. Nominal interest rates may then give false signals as to what is happening in the real economy. A rise in the nominal interest rate may result from an increase in the money supply because it feeds inflationary expectations. In the old days it would have been a signal to raise the money supply; now it may be a signal to lower the money supply. With inflationary expectations depending either directly on monetary growth or on the current level of nominal GNP in relation to potential output, the nominal interest rate gives ambiguous signals and hence is no longer a useful intermediate target. The intermediate target may be to keep the real interest rate constant, but the change in the

nominal rate is no longer an indicator of the change in the real rate.

(2) If the demand for money shifts about while the various factors determining demand other than the interest rate remain constant—in other words, if the LM curve shifts while the IS curve stays put—stabilising nominal GNP requires the money supply to be varied to meet the changing money demand. The LM curve will then be stabilised and the real interest rate fixed. With zero inflationary expectations, the best policy is then to choose the nominal interest rate as the intermediate target. But if there may be expectations of inflation, one can only say that the *real* interest rate would have to be the target, thus implying an appropriately changing nominal interest rate. On the other hand, if the IS curve shifts about (perhaps because of changes in savings propensities or in the desire to invest), stabilising the real interest rate would destabilise demand further. For example, a fall in savings would, with a given money supply, both raise the real interest rate and increase nominal GNP. If the money supply were then raised so as to bring the real interest rate down again, nominal GNP would rise even further. The common argument in favour of a money supply target is that there are greater instabilities on the real side than in the demand for money so that it is better to stabilise the money supply than the interest rate.

It must be noted that if the money supply is stabilised (say with a constant rate of money growth policy), nominal GNP will still be unstable if the IS curve is unstable. Only in the extreme case where the demand for money is unresponsive to the interest rate (the LM curve being vertical), will an unstable IS curve with a stable LM curve not lead to instability in nominal GNP. But econometric work has shown that the demand for money is responsive to the interest rate. Hence stabilising the money supply will not perfectly stabilise nominal GNP. But it will stabilise it relatively more than would a policy that aims to stabilise the real interest rate.

IV. THE CHOICE OF MONETARY AGGREGATE

Given that a monetary aggregate is to be the intermediate target, which aggregate is it to be? This issue has been much discussed at the conference, and is a principal question of Bruce Brittain's paper. There are two distinct issues here, namely *controllability* and *predictability*.

Controllability concerns the ability of the original policy instruments to influence the monetary aggregate with some degree of certainty and speed. It is likely that most reasonable monetary aggregates would measure up better in this respect than nominal GNP itself. No one would doubt, for example, that it is easier to regulate Ml than nominal GNP. This is one reason, mentioned earlier, for preferring an intermediate target to aiming at nominal GNP directly. As to which monetary aggregate is best chosen from this point of view, it is likely to differ between countries and depend on various institutional considerations. The difference between countries emerges clearly from the paper under discussion. A broad measure is likely to be more appropriate in countries that control credit expansion rather than operating through open market operations. The monetary base must rate high as a controllable target—presumably highest—once other kinds of credit controls are abandoned.

Predictability concerns the stability of the relevant income velocity, or at least stability around a trend. While *controllability* asks how the intermediate aggregate moves with the original policy instruments, predictability asks how nominal GNP moves with the intermediate aggregate. Here there are again two issues.

(1) The first issue concerns the stability of the demand function for the particular kind of money (M1, M3, etc.,) that is being considered as the intermediate target. Some kinds of monetary aggregates appear to have more stable demand functions than others in any given country. Furthermore, different aggregates come out relatively better in one country than in another. But I have the impression that it is not unreasonable to formulate policy on the basis of a reasonably stable demand function for at least one monetary aggregate in any country.

(2) The second issue concerns the interest elasticity of the demand for the particular monetary aggregate.

Even when the demand for money function is stable, the IS curve is not stable, so that with a given money supply or money growth rate, the interest rate and nominal GNP would still fluctuate, the interest rate moving pro-cyclically. Velocity is thus not stable even when the demand function for money is stable. The higher the interest elasticity of the demand for money the greater this effect. If there is to be complete reliance on targeting a monetary aggregate, that aggregate will have to be chosen which not only has a stable demand function but also where the interest elasticity is low.

V. NOMINAL GNP VERSUS MONETARY AGGREGATE TARGET . . . ONCE AGAIN

It is clear that the aggregate with the maximum predictability in its effects on nominal GNP is nominal GNP itself. The argument against choosing an intermediate target is that, if it were chosen, some degree of unpredictability—i.e. variation in income velocity—would be unavoidable. This argument has to be set against the two arguments in favour of an intermediate target given earlier—namely that 'money' is more easily understood than 'nominal GNP' (the public relations argument) and that because of lagged effects, an intermediate target may be needed to signal whether the instruments are being adjusted appropriately. The more difficult 'fine-tuning' is thought to be the stronger the case for a 'controllable' intermediate target rather than a less controllable target which is closer to the ultimate purpose of economic management. Nevertheless, it seems to me that the case for targeting directly on nominal GNP—assuming that there is to be targeting of a nominal aggregate at all—is quite strong.

One other point should be noted here. It is possible to reconcile a nominal-GNP target with a nominal money supply target by the use of a counter-cyclical fiscal policy. As pointed out above, with a given money supply and fluctuations in the IS curve—that is, fluctuations in investment demand, savings propensities and external demand factors—nominal GNP would still fluctuate. It is possible to offset this with fiscal policy—assuming the usual 'fine-tuning' difficulties can be overcome—and thus obtain a stable nominal GNP. Hence it *is* possible to reconcile an intermediate monetary target with a nominal GNP target by having a 'fine-tuning' fiscal policy. But in that case the intermediate monetary target has little meaning, and a nominal-GNP target policy is really being adopted.

VI. COMMENTS ON BRITTAIN'S PAPER

I have not so far made any specific comments on Bruce Brittain's paper. This is not meant to imply any criticisms. Rather, his paper stimulated me to set out the issues in the way I have, even though my points are unlikely to be new to the *cognoscenti* and many of the ingredients are in his own very interesting paper. It seems to me that his econometric work is very valuable though I am not competent to make any detailed comments.

The only minor criticism I have is that he seems to suggest that the existence either of 'cost-push' inflation or of 'rational expectations' might affect his principal arguments, which concern the stability of various income velocities, and hence the appropriateness of a monetary or a credit aggregate. It seems to me that the degree of cost-push or of rationality of expectations will affect the change in output or in prices that results from a given change in nominal GNP—in other words, the split-up between P and Q when MV changes in the equation $MV = PQ$. But it need not affect the stability of V in any particular way. One issue is whether a change in M will affect MV predictably and a distinct issue is whether a change in MV will affect P or Q more. In the extreme cost-push model, P is given and changes in nominal GNP manifest themselves wholly in changes in Q; while in the extreme rational expectations model Q is given, and all the changes are in P.

3 Problems of Monetary Targeting in the UK

J. R. Sargent
Midland Bank Limited

I

The first problem of monetary targeting is why we need it. Here and now the question may seem a trifle *démodé* or even daring, like asking why we need unions at the Trades Union Congress; but it is not otiose. It may be useful to reach for an answer by standing on a proposition with which almost everyone can agree; that the economy cannot be safely and successfully driven without keeping an eye on the monetary dials. By these I mean the ones which record the relationship between the current stock of money, variously defined, and the flow of spending at current prices, or if preferred, the real stock of money and the current flow of spending at constant prices. What the monetary dials indicate is unlikely to be fundamental for long-run growth, either way, and in the short run readings of the state of the 'real' economy deserve equal attention. But to ignore what is on the monetary dials is like keeping a car's engine in good shape while failing to replace defunct windscreen wipers and worn tyres. Such a driver might claim that he 'had his priorities right' but can hardly be regarded as a safe user of the road.

There is, of course, some way to go from these neutral propositions to positive and public commitment to monetary targets, carrying a presumption of action to be taken if the needles on the monetary dials move to certain limits. One justification for taking this further step is that the ratio of money stock to GDP represents an overhang of potential purchasing power which could be released against the current level of real output. Whether it actually would be released in specific circumstances, and how much of it, is bound to be debateable, but the probability must increase as the size of the overhang grows. The inflationary danger

95

this brings is obvious enough when there are supply-side constraints on expanding real output, which have been detected by real as well as monetary indicators. They are not always easy to detect, and have probably become narrower in recent years, although I shall argue later that monetary policy itself bears some responsibility for this. But they are not crucial to the argument; the potential danger of a relatively large overhang of purchasing power is more general. Even if the economy is currently operating below its productive potential in a genuine sense, a sharp acceleration of the growth of demand is liable to create bottlenecks and opportunities for wage drift which will cause the increased demand to dissipate itself in a wage-price lift (or in imports) rather than generating increased output and employment. To be successful a reflationary policy needs to attend not simply to the degree of underutilised capacity, but also to the rate at which it can be brought into use without side-effects which undermine the policy, including that on expectations. Setting this rate involves judgements about the real economy; translating it into a growth rate of nominal GDP has to take a view about the rate of inflation of costs already 'in the system' as a result of contracts agreed by the start of the target period; and these things may be amenable to control by non-monetary instruments. But to the extent that the rate of growth of nominal GDP thus arrived at is exceeded by that of the nominal money stock, the risk of loss of control grows. This is the minimalist case for fixing an upper limit to the growth of the money supply. To include it among the safeguards against loss of control of an expansionary process is perhaps particularly desirable at present when there is a joker in the pack in the form of the personal savings ratio, whose behaviour we lack confidence to predict. When an unmanageably large acceleration of the demand for consumers' goods could come from this direction, there is all the more reason for keeping a close watch on all sources from which it could be financed.

The argument so far is for an upper limit on the growth of the money supply which is quite permissive. Its real component is not limited to the growth of productive potential (except when this is judged to be fully employed), and it accepts the inflation already 'in the system'. I have described it as minimalist, and as such it is hardly monetarist at all. It stands much less upon confidence that people behave in a stable and predictable way with their money balances, than upon lack of confidence, and upon a precautionary attitude to the vagaries of human behaviour, seeking to limit the scope for them which exists in the form of immediately available spending power. It is, therefore, likely to commend itself to pragmatists who suspect, not without justification in the history of economics, that this decade's stable function will be de-stabilised in the next. I number myself among them. The pragmatic approach, however, specifically does not allow for the active use of monetary targets to squeeze the inflation out of the system, and having done so to prevent its reappearance by permanently aligning the growth of the money supply as closely as possible to the growth of productive capacity. Action along these other lines may be advocated on the grounds that overriding priority must be given to eliminating, or at least (since many who propose it are also practical men) to reducing the rate of, inflation. But what has added enormously to its attractions in recent years is the particular piece of monetarist analysis which suggests that there is no long-run trade-off between inflation and unemployment, so that those who resist the use of monetary targets to bring down the inflation rate on the ground that the penalty in terms of unemployment would be too high, seem to have that ground cut from under their feet.

Nevertheless, there may still be some to stand on. The controversy may be looked at through the two equations below. The first relates the rate of change of money wages ($\dot{w}$) in a conventional way to the unemployment percentage (u) and the rate of change of prices ($\dot{p}$), the latter being taken as the best approximation to the expected inflation rate. The second equation draws on a neo-classical labour-demand function and states that unemployment rises or falls according as the rate of increase of the real wage exceeds or falls short of that of the productivity of labour ($\dot{\pi}$), or in other words according as there is a rise or fall in the real product wage. Evidence from UK manufacturing since the late 1960s in Figure 3.1 appears to support the existence of a relationship of this kind. Thus we have:

$$\dot{w} = a - bu + c\dot{p} \qquad\qquad b > 0 \qquad\qquad (1)$$
$$\dot{u} = k(\dot{w} - \dot{p} - \dot{\pi}) \qquad\qquad k > 0 \qquad\qquad (2)$$

The line labelled 'real product wage' in Figure 3.1 attempts to approximate how much it effectively costs the employer in real terms to take on labour. First, an index of average wages, salaries and employers' contributions (for National Insurance and superannuation) is divided by an index of 'value-added' prices (selling prices less unit cost of fuels, materials and services bought in). This measures the real cost of a unit of labour to the employer. But since the productive effectiveness of a unit of labour changes over time, the result is further divided by an index of output per employee, to obtain the 'real product wage' shown. The upward trend of the 'real product wage' mirrors that of the share of

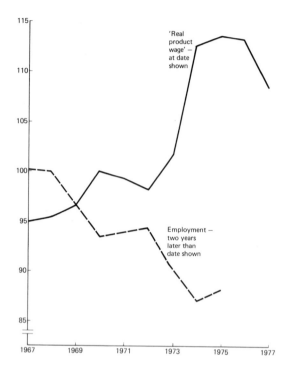

FIG.3.1 UK manufacturing (1970 = 100)

employment income in value-added. The productivity of labour, π, we regard as exogenous. It will keep things simple and give no offence to the monetarist opinion we are probing, if we regard $\dot{p}$ in the same way, imagining it to be directly and uniquely linked to the growth of the money supply. (Actually, the link will be complicated by whether u and therefore real output is rising or falling.)

Thus we have two variables to find, $\dot{u}$ and $\dot{w}$. Substituting (1) into (2) we have:

$$\dot{u} = k(a - \dot{\pi} + (c - 1)\dot{p}) - kbu \tag{3}$$

and the solutions are:

$$\dot{u} = \bar{u} + (u_o - \bar{u})e^{-bkt}$$

$$\dot{w} = \overline{\dot{w}} + (\dot{w}_o - \overline{\dot{w}})e^{-bkt}$$

where:

$$\bar{u} = \frac{a - \dot{\pi} + (c-1)\dot{p}}{b} \qquad (4)$$

$$\bar{w} = \dot{\pi} + \dot{p} \qquad (5)$$

Evidently both variables converge upon these long-run equilibrium values. A necessary condition to ensure the plausibility of $\bar{u}$ is that $a > \dot{\pi}$, but this is not difficult to suppose.

Evidently, from (4), if monetary targets are set with the object and the effect of lowering the inflation rate, the level of unemployment will remain unaffected in the long-run if $c = 1$; that is, when a change of one percentage point in the rate of increase of prices is fed back whole to the rate of increase of money wages. Positively benign effects are theoretically possible; if $c < 1$, lower inflation will actually lower unemployment, because the size of the feedback of prices onto money wages sets the real product wage falling. The unfavourable trade-off, which descends from Phillips, occurs when money wages respond only sluggishly to the rate of inflation. This is hardly news; but its relevance here is that whatever the econometricians may tell us about the average size of the c coefficient in some sample period, it would be wise to reckon that it will tend to be rather small when restrictive monetary targets are imparting a downward twist to the rate of increase of prices; that is, unless something is done to see that it is not. Thus the first problem of monetary targeting, if it is to be promoted from the minimalist position to an active role in cutting down inflation, is to ensure that there is sufficient feedback on to money wages to keep the rise in unemployment within tolerable bounds. It seems highly unlikely that the problem can be left to solve itself, and the implication is that, as they erect their monetary targets, the authorities will at the same time have to devise ways and means of influencing the attitudes of trades unions and wage-earners generally. A system of indexing might help to move c closer up towards unity. As an alternative, in the face of an immoveably low c, an incomes policy might do something to lower a. There are also $\dot{\pi}$ and b to be considered, although the means of levering up productivity growth remain elusive and measures designed to increase the deterrent effect of unemployment are likely to prove difficult. The main point is that if monetary targets are operated as an isolated tactic rather than within the context of a general anti-inflation, anti-unemployment strategy, they may achieve their immediate objective only at the cost of disillusionment with the consequences and an urge to be done with them.

A feature of the simple model used above is that the rate of increase of money wages is in stable equilibrium at $\bar{u}$. In this sense it differs from the monetarists' 'natural' level below which inflation accelerates. It is, therefore, better to call it the equilibrium level, noting that, even when c = 1 and there is no trade-off either way, it is at least theoretically amenable to alteration by working on wage earners' attitudes through the constant a. The stability of the equilibrium is ensured by the neo-classical equation (2) of the model, for which I have claimed empirical support from Figure 3.1.

The removal of the instability of the monetarists' model also removes a source of nervousness about the inflationary consequences of re-flationary policies which push unemployment below its putative 'natural' level. Can we be bolder, then and argue that, when unemployment is high, some reduction in it can still be bought by a lift in the rate of monetary growth relative to that of productive capacity, if we are prepared to pay for it by a somewhat higher inflation rate? The question itself risks provoking cries of 'defunct economist!'. The difficulties are quickly apparent from equation (4). Although in the face of a fall in the rate of increase of prices, money wages may react with considerable inertia (c well below unity), they may react with more alacrity to a rise. It could even be that they overcompensate ($c < 1$), so that unemployment begins to rise. Short of this, it may be that an irreversibility or ratchet of this nature has caused the alternating bouts of reflationary and deflationary policies since the war to have as their net result the upward trend in unemployment. Although it may be possible initially to contain the feedback of prices onto money wages through some kind of incomes policy, this is liable to come under increasing strain to the extent that the reflationary policy is successful and unemployment actually falls. Thus it may be difficult, though it still deserves effort, to find policies which will ensure that employment and output respond positively to monetary expansion (or to fiscal action supported by it). But it does not follow from this that they will remain unaffected by monetary constraint.

This discussion may be summarised by saying that the trade-off between inflation and unemployment has not so much disappeared as dis-solved into a more complex pattern of relationships. There is clearly a trade-off between unemployment and real wages (as Pigou argued some 50 years ago), and real wages are not necessarily invariant to the rate of increase of prices. If monetary targets are set to press the latter down, and the feedback to money wages is weak, then monetary targets will also depress employment and output. This may partly account for the disappointing performance, in the recent now decelerating expansion, of the 'supply-side' of the economy, resulting in large imports of manufactured goods which home producers lacked the profit incentive to meet the demand for themselves. Part of the blame lies elsewhere, of course. Recent experience suggests that in exchange for unions' co-operation in pay restraint, administrative restraints on prices, operated through the Price Commission for example, had to be accepted to a degree which actually aggravated the problem of unemployment. This has turned inside out the argument that pay restraint buys more employment than would otherwise be available; recently it was bought by measures which helped to make less employment available. There is a sense in which the Price Commission acted in a bureaucratic and piecemeal way towards an effect which is generalised by restrictive monetary targets, although it also claimed to influence productivity.

Thus the main problem of monetary targeting in the UK lies well outside the technical issues of defining, measuring and influencing the money supply itself, which are apt to dominate discussions within the City of London. It is the problem of making sure, once a target is set, that wage negotiators appreciate the adverse effects of excessive settlements on output and employment and settle so as not to provoke them. Although the mind boggles somewhat at the vision of anguished committees of shop-stewards conning the latest estimates of the income and interest elasticities of the demand for money, and so on, in order to translate a 10 per cent limit on the growth of sterling M3 (or Mi, where $i = 0 \ldots 100$) into a maximum wage increase attainable without loss of local employment, I would not write off the capacity of wage negotiators to learn to read the signals transmitted by a firm money supply constraint. The Governor of the Bank of England has himself referred to the plain man's ability to perceive, on occasions, more clearly than the sophisticated. But the learning process will take time unaided, and more perhaps than can be afforded. A major effort of education, propaganda and cajolery is likely to be required, if monetary targets are not to be blown away in the wind but are to stand up and be effective.

To this end some purpose may be served, despite the yawns of the cynics, by the annual tripartite discussions copying the German model, which the Labour government proposed, and the Conservative Manifesto mentioned. It is possible, of course, that the unions are so disenchanted with the tribulations of actively agreeing and operating an incomes policy that they would actually prefer to acquiesce in a monetary constraint which leaves them some degree of freedom individually—if not collectively—to get what they can. Also we have had comparatively little experience yet of operating the economy under a money supply constraint and could gain some which will cast light on its relationship with real expansion. But signs are that the real is the loser, and that downward pressure of monetary constraint on the increase of prices relative to wages is weakening the responsiveness of supply to demand. Nevertheless, I conclude that while it would be undesirable to accept money supply limits set to squeeze the inflation out of the system, it remains desirable to keep one which at least makes it difficult to have more of it.

II

Having thus pinned my colours to the minimalist position, I turn to some particular problems which can complicate the decision to enforce the upper limit of a target range, even if it is set in the minimalist sense, allowing for inflation of costs already 'in the system', and for some feasible increase in the utilisation of capacity within the level at which 'overheating' occurs. It may be asked, of course, why there should be any question over its enforcement; a limit is a limit is a limit, and needs to be clearly seen to be if it is to carry conviction as a signal. I have much sympathy with this view; it is implied by the concern I have expressed above about the effectiveness of the feedback from monetary targets to collective bargaining decisions, and while preferring the targets to be relatively permissive in the sense defined above, I also prefer them to be inflexible, even to the extent of doubting the wisdom of allowing the authorities six-monthly opportunities to roll them forward. Nevertheless, enforcement does create problems, although they will seem larger to those who are minimalist or less, and smaller to those who are more committedly monetarist. Thus this section is addressed more to the former.

An upper limit on the growth of the money supply carries with it the risk that, as a result of certain speculative forces which can temporarily inflate the demand for bank credit, the 'real' economy will be subjected to disturbance. There are three cases which have been particularly relevant. The first is speculation against sterling in the form of leads and lags, such as developed from March to October 1976. Earners of foreign exchange, expecting a fall in sterling, hold on to it longer than usual within the limit allowed; they are therefore short of sterling for their domestic business and borrow more from the banks. If there is a limit on the money supply and this is in danger of being exceeded, credit will have to be restrained and interest rates rise, thus adversely affecting non-speculating borrowers and the economy at large. Would it not be better if the money supply could simply 'roll with the punch'? It is by no means clear that it would, since this would effectively be financing this form of speculation and allowing it to drive the exchange rate lower than would otherwise happen, with adverse effects on import costs. I am not wholly converted to the fashionable view of the speed with which these feed back to domestic inflation. This surely depends upon the state of demand in the domestic economy, and econometric results which support the fashionable view rest upon the experience of a past in which there was often an inappropriate combination of a lower exchange rate and expansionary policies. Nevertheless, speculative influences un-doubtedly caused the exchange rate to move well below its equilibrium level in 1976, and contributed to reversing the decline in the inflation rate at a time which turned out to be crucial for wage restraint. Thus lack of freedom to absorb this kind of speculative influence by an expansible money supply is not necessarily a disadvantage.

The second kind is more problematical. It is the kind of 'go slow' in the gilt-edged market which recurs from time to time, and has sometimes been characterised as a 'strike'. If the managers of pension funds and other large institutional investors take it into their heads—and their heads are usually quite close together—to withhold their large flows of funds from the gilt-edged market, either expecting that interest rates will rise or hoping to encourage them to, the public sector may have to turn to the banks to meet its borrowing requirement. If there is no limit on the money supply to prevent more bank lending to the public sector, it has the option of outfacing the institutions and waiting until the sheer weight of uninvested funds forces them back into the gilt-edged market. The existence of a limit, on the other hand, enforces higher rates of interest. It is not clear how far the redistribution of income and wealth which this causes from taxpayers to the beneficiaries of pension funds and others can be criticised as socially unjust; but the disturbance to the cost of borrowing and confidence in general may have contributed to setting back the expansion of the economy in early 1977, and possibly in late 1978. Nevertheless, the alternative of leaving the institutions to stew in their own liquidity and allowing the money supply to expand accordingly, is not without its own dangers. It would be untrue to say the institutions have nowhere else to go. They can buy property, or stocks of commodities, giving a direct inflationary twist to prices in general. Finding the government broker's prices for going tap stocks too high, they can buy existing gilt-edged securities from other private sector holders, providing the latter with capital gains which might take the process further. Moreover, the institutions' expectations about interest rates are unlikely to be entirely self-generated. They may be based at least partly on evidence. They may have observed a rapid growth of bank lending to the private sector, in which case a parallel expansion of the public sector's bank borrowing would raise the money supply at a rate to make almost anyone nervous. Or the institutions' expectations of rising interest rates may be based on their having observed inflation accelerating; and in that case they would not sit stewing in their own liquidity but move more into real assets or commodities with inflationary effects. Or again, if their expectations derived from a falling exchange rate, they might help finance the firms whose leading and lagging was behind it. Thus, in the face of this type of speculative behaviour, the danger in outfacing the institutions with an expansible money supply has to be weighed against the necessity of giving in when it is limited.

The third instance of speculative pressure affecting the domestic economy through the agency of a limit on the growth of the money supply is the capital inflow which occurred in 1977 and subsequently. Given the possible adverse effects on exports and economic activity of letting the exchange rate rise, the inflow has to be absorbed into the reserves, and the sterling needed to finance this is added to the sums the public sector requires to borrow (though not, through a curiosity of the statistics, to its Borrowing Requirement). The public sector may then borrow more from the banks, and as this threatens the limit on sterling M3, the authorities are forced to accept an upward shift in interest rates in order to stay within it. This particular story suggests good material for Britons to indulge their instinctive insularity. Under a money supply limit we are slaves to the whims of foreigners, even when they seem to approve of us. After cutting us to pieces with the arrows of 1976, they smother us with the ointment of 1977, and suffocate us in 1979. Nevertheless, although the capital inflow may be the origin of an upsurge in the money supply, it is not itself the sole cause of it. In the first place, the provision of sterling bank deposits to non-residents against currencies taken into the reserves does not itself increase the money supply as measured by sterling M3. The increase occurs when those non-resident deposits are transferred to the domestic private sector, in consideration for assets sold by the domestic private sector, and the latter prefers to stay liquid rather than reduce its bank borrowing. Thus the expansion of the money supply in this case is due as much to decisions within our own economy as to decisions outside it. It is not simply a reflection of irrelevant foreign influences but a symptom of a build-up of domestic liquidity. As such it is a case for treatment in terms of the general arguments advanced earlier for controlling the scale of monetary overhang.

This throws some light on the relevance of DCE as a monetary target. When a capital inflow seeps into the domestic private sector and raises sterling M3 in this way, DCE may well be unchanged. The counterpart to the rise on the lending side is an increase in bank lending to the public sector, as the authorities issue more Treasury Bills to provide themselves with the sterling they need to offer to non-residents in exchange for foreign currency if the exchange rate is to be held. But the increase in the official exchange reserves enters the statistics as a net reduction in the overseas financing of the public sector—in effect, it is public sector financing of the overseas sector—and DCE is calculated by adding overseas financing of the public sector to the increase in sterling M3, with some other items. The fact that it is liable to be unchanged in these circumstances, despite an increase in domestic liquidity reflected in sterling M3, suggests that DCE should not be seen as a measure of monetary expansion as such; that is, as something which, set against the flow of goods and services at current prices, monitors the extent of inflationary potential. The relevance of DCE lies elsewhere. A limit on it is an operational device for ensuring that a balance of payments deficit of more than a certain size, broadly defined to include autonomous capital items, will force the authorities to make a corresponding reduction in the growth of sterling M3. Thus a limit on DCE may serve its own purpose but not that of a monetary target as such. There is, however, one exception to this conclusion, in that DCE does include the increase in sterling deposits held by overseas residents, which does represent a potential, if less probable, augmentation of the purchasing power overhanging the supply of goods and services.

Thus although the monetary targets may lay the economy at large open to disturbances due to passing speculative movements, and preclude these being accommodated in the way which might be possible in a less excitable environment, this is a matter for regret rather than a reason for their rejection. At the end of the day it has simply to be accepted, if targets are to be enforced with the degree of inflexibility that is required to make them credible and effective. You cannot make an omelette without breaking some eggs, although the number needlessly broken might be less if only the heat in the kitchen were to simmer down.

III

There is no point in wasting time setting up the target if the bows and arrows are weak or inaccurate. In this section I turn to this question, but concentrating primarily on the latest model, namely the Supplementary Special Deposits scheme, or 'corset'. If sterling M3 is the definition of the stock of purchasing power which the monetary authorities have as their prime target, it would be logical to expect that their major weapons of monetary control would be directly trained on it—or at least on that part of it which, disregarding notes and coin, consists of sterling deposits of UK residents with the UK Banking Sector. In point of fact this is not the case. The minimum Reserve Asset ratio and calls for Special Deposits are aimed at a rather different aggregate, namely the Eligible Liabilities of UK Banks; and the 'corset' is applied to the interest-bearing component of these. Between the Eligible Liabilities of UK Banks, which are the object of the authorities' controls, and the sterling deposits of UK residents with the Banking Sector, which are a major objective of those controls, there are two differences, illustrated in Table 3.1.

The difference between the Banks and the Banking Sector is

TABLE 3.1

£	16 November 1977 £m	Change to 17 May 1978 £m	%	Change to 15 November 1978 £m	%
Eligible Liabilities of UK Banks	40209	+4293	+10.7	−176[a]	−0.4
Domestic deposits component of Sterling M3	36263	+3115	+ 8.6	+1350	+3.4
of which estimated contribution of UK Banks	35490	+3231	+ 9.1	+1208[a]	+3.1
Interest-bearing Eligible Liabilities of UK Banks	26656	+2442	+12.9	−1393[a]	−4.6
Interest-bearing sterling M3	23996	+2244	+ 9.3	+ 178	+0.7
of which estimated contribution of UK Banks	23566	+2342	+ 9.9	+ 133[a]	+0.5

[a] Excluding effect of inclusion of National Girobank at the end of September 1978. See Table 3.2 for detail.

comparatively trivial as far as the deposits components of sterling M3 is concerned. The Banking Sector includes the Discount Market and the Bank of England Banking Department in addition to UK Banks, and even before the National Girobank, always a part of the Banking Sector, was reclassified in September 1978 among UK Banks, the latter accounted for all 2 per cent of the deposits included in sterling M3; the figure is now all but 1 per cent. The difference between Banks and the Banking Sector is far from trivial on the lending side, as we shall find, owing to the activities of the Discount Market; but as far as deposits are concerned we can ignore the fact that sterling M3 is an aggregate applying to the Banking Sector and concentrate on the banks' overwhelming contribution to it.

The second difference which Table 3.1 brings out is between the banks' contribution to sterling M3, on which the authorities presumably intend to exert leverage, and their Eligible Liabilities, which are the fulcrum. No statistics are published of the banks' contribution to sterling M3 as such but the total can be estimated with a fair degree of accuracy. The main unknown is the amount of CDs held by the private and public sectors, but those held by banks and the Discount Market can be identified, as can the small number known to be held by overseas residents. The residue of the total issue is assigned to the private sector in Tables 3.1 and 3.2.

The main point which emerges from Table 3.1 is the loose leverage between changes in the banks' Eligible Liabilities, interest-bearing and non-interest-bearing, and their contribution to sterling M3. The two periods chosen to compare these changes are the six months from 16 November 1977 to 17 May 1978 when the 'corset' was not in place, and the subsequent six months when the banks came under notice of its reapplication by reference to the August–October average of their Interest-bearing Eligible Liabilities. Between the two periods it required a turnround of £4835m in the banks' IBELs (from an increase of £3442m to a decrease of £1393m) to effect a reduction of £2210m in the growth of their contribution to interest-bearing sterling M3 and of £2023m in their contribution to total sterling M3. Table 3.2 throws some further light on this, and shows that £2842m, or nearly 60 per cent of the turnround in IBELs, was accounted for by transactions involving the rest of the Banking Sector. As the official definition of Eligible Liabilities says:

Inter-bank transactions and transactions with the discount market (other than reserve assets) and sterling certificates of deposit (both

TABLE 3.2

UK banks	16 November 1977	Change in six months to 17 May 1978	Change in six months to 15 November 1978
1. Sterling deposits of domestic non-bank sectors:			
(a) private sector sight deposits[a]	14551	+ 1285	
			+ 478
(b) public sector sight deposits	527	− 21	
(c) public sector time deposits	391	+ 48	
			+ 730
(d) private sector time deposits[b]	20221	+ 1919	
Total 1 = Contribution to £M3	35490	+ 3231	+ 1208
of which estimated interest-bearing	23566	+ 2343	+ 133
2. Sterling deposits from overseas			
(a) sight	2234	− 38	+ 29
(b) time	2728	− 59	+ 211
Total 2	4962	− 97	+ 240
3. Sterling deposits from banking sector			
(a) sight deposits	1285	+ 298	+ 635
(b) time deposits *less* market loans to UK banks	−952	+ 57	− 868
(c) CDs held by Discount Market	458	+ 620	− 720
(d) *less* market loans to Discount Market	−566	+ 519	− 395
Total 3	225	+ 1494	− 1348
4. *TOTAL 1 + 2 + 3*	40677	+ 4628	+ 100
of which estimated interest-bearing[c]	27451	+ 3691	− 1037
5. *Eligible Liabilities*[d]	40209	+ 4293	− 176
of which interest-bearing	26656	+ 3442	− 1393

[a] Adjusted for transit items.

[b] Includes CDs other than held by banks, Discount Market and overseas residents.

[c] Excludes change in October 1978 due to inclusion of National Girobank among UK Banks (but not changes between October and November for Girobank).

[d] Differences between 4 and 5 are mainly due to exclusion from Eligible Liabilities of deposits with an original maturity over two years.

held and issued) are taken into calculation of individual banks'
liabilities on a net basis, irrespective of the term.

For the banks collectively, therefore, line 3 of Table 3.2 represents their
net borrowing from or lending to the Discount Market other than in
forms which qualify as reserve assets. It is worth noting the contrast
between the small amount of outstanding net borrowing on 16
November 1977 and the large swings either side of this which took place
in the two subsequent periods of six months, in which the banks first
anticipated the 'corset' and then adapted to it. The two periods
compared in Tables 3.1 and 3.2 are very recent, but my colleauge John
Dorrington has studied the whole period since the end of 1973, when the
'corset' was first introduced, although it has not been continually
activated since then. Among his results is the following relationship
between the banks' IBELs and their contribution to sterling M3,
excluding notes and coin, both being measured in one month percentage
changes:

$$\%\Delta \pounds M3 = 0.580 + 0.335 \quad \%\Delta IBEL$$
$$(4.67) \quad (5.56)$$

$\overline{R}^2 = 0.3255$ S.E. $= 0.935$ D.W. $= 2.12$ (November 73–January 79)

Thus the 'corset' involves disproportionate action for uncertain
results. Yet in one sense it is surprising that the action has any results at
all, since it is possible to imagine a situation in which the banks' IBELS
are collectively reduced in response to a threat of 'corset' penalties
without any effect whatsoever on their contribution to sterling M3. This
could happen in the following way. Imagine that the reduction of IBELS
required to avoid penalty is £500m and that the banks effect this by
increasing their deductible market loans to the discount market by this
amount, or alternatively by not replacing CDs maturing in the Discount
Market's hands. A reduction of £500m in their total ELs allows a
reduction of (say) £65m in reserve assets, to maintain a 13 per cent ratio,
and this could take the form of reduced money at call with the Discount
Market. Special Deposits, assuming these to be at 3 per cent of Eligible
Liabilities, would be reduced by £15m. The remaining £420 m may be
able to be found by reducing market loans to local authorities or sales of
short-dated gilts. The Discount Market meanwhile is in possession of
£435m extra to be invested, and the Bank of England of £15m less. It is
convenient to assume for the time being that the Discount Market is up
against the maximum of its Undefined Assets Multiple. In that case the

whole of the £435m will have to go into public sector debt, and this will
exactly replace the withdrawal which the banks have made to the extent
of £420m and the Bank of England of £15m from lending to the public
sector. Thus the Banking Sector's lending to the public sector is
unaffected in total, and nothing has occured to disturb its lending to the
private sector or its net lending overseas. The total of sterling M3 as
calculated from the lending side is therefore unchanged, and correspondingly the deposits of public and private sectors which contribute
to sterling M3 are unchanged, while IBELs have come down by £500m.

However, the disappearing trick performed by IBELs may not reach
its completion without effects being felt on the structure of short-term
interest rates. The initial change is that, at any given level of interest
rates, the banks want to do more deductible lending to the Discount
Market, or to issue fewer CDs to it, and correspondingly to do less
lending of other kinds. Unless they happen to be flush with reserve assets
and can simply lend less money to it at call, the Discount Market has to be
persuaded to add to its liabilities to the banks and to take on more public
sector debt, or alternatively to substitute the latter for CDs. But the
incentive to do this will be provided by the banks' redistribution of their
portfolios, which leads on the one hand to downward pressure on
interest rates in the interbank market, and on the other hand, in so far as
they switch out of public sector debt, to upward pressure on the yields
from it. Given the close substitutability of the assets concerned, the yield
differential which develops may not have to be a very large one to induce
the shift required to accommodate the banks' requirements, although
the heavier these are the larger it will become. Whatever differential does
the trick, however, will also affect the decisions of non-bank financial
institutions and large non-financial companies which appear as lenders
in those markets. Their reactions can take a number of possible forms,
some of which will lead to a decline in sterling M3:

(1) They may decide that the lower level of money market rates does
    not justify keeping so much of their funds in the form of wholesale
    interest-bearing bank deposits, and will prefer to increase their
    liquidity by shifting some to non-interest-bearing sight deposits.
    In this case IBELs fall further, ELs are unaffected, and M1 rises,
    but sterling M3 remains unchanged. Money market interest rates
    move back up somewhat towards their original level and the
    liquidity of the private and public sectors is enhanced.
(2) Non-bank wholesale depositors with the banks may shift into
    short-term public sector debt, such as certificates of tax deposit,

Treasury Bills, short gilts and deposits with local authorities. In so far as these are available on tap, the non-bank take-up of public sector debt increases and, with the public sector's borrowing requirement, the overseas take-up of its debt, and bank lending in foreign currency to the public sector at given levels, sterling lending by banks to the public sector falls. Thus sterling M3 falls on the lending side, and domestic deposits fall correspondingly; so do IBELs. If there is a short gilt on tap but overpriced, the pressure of demand may raise market prices until the flow out of the tap is resumed. This may in turn influence expectations about prices in the medium and longer reaches of the gilt market, and lead to greater sales of tap stocks already available there or new ones which the authorities will take the opportunity to introduce. Thus the reduction in bank lending to the public sector and in sterling M3 will be pushed further. The general effect of the desire of non-bank wholesale depositors with banks to shift them into public sector debt will be to lower the rates of interest on the marketable components of that debt, and thus narrow the margin which originally opened up over wholesale money-market rates. Although there will have been a reduction in sterling M3, domestic liquidity will not necessarily have been reduced if account is taken (in a more Radcliffean mood) of the capital gains accruing to holders of gilt-edged generally, which would increase the flow of spending. Moreover, some of the switch will be from deposits with banks to deposits with local authorities, and leave their owners not much less liquid on balance, despite the fall in sterling M3 which occurs when local authorities in turn reduce their borrowing from the banks.

(3) The transactions described in (2) involve a flow of funds to the public sector, out of which it can reduce its bank borrowing, from private sector wholesale deposits seeking a better return following the depression of money market rates by corset-induced bank lending there. In so far as these deposits are used to buy existing public sector debt from other private sector holders, there is no flow of funds to the public sector and sterling M3 is unaffected, although there may be some transfer from its interest-bearing to its non-interest-bearing components (not necessarily to M1, however). But at least some of the private sector wholesale deposits will buy existing public sector debt from overseas holders, and this transfer from domestic to overseas deposits will reduce sterling M3. The corresponding fall occurs on the lending

side if bank lending overseas is reckoned net of deposits from overseas. It is possible that the overseas residents concerned will wish to repatriate the proceeds of their sale of public sector debt, and if sterling is supported by the Exchange Equalisation Account, the movement will become a flow of funds to the public sector and the fall on the lending side of sterling M3 will turn out to be as in (2) above, in bank lending to the public sector rather than overseas.

(4) A fourth possibility is that private sector holders of wholesale funds will seek out other potential borrowers in the private sector to whom they can lend directly, offering rates of interest somewhat between what they are now getting from the banks through the wholesale money markets and what they were getting before the increase in the banks' desire to lend in these markets pushed rates down. A fringe of unsatisfied borrowers may simultaneously have emerged to the extent that the banks' switch to deductible lending to the discount market has been at the expense of their advances to the private sector. They may facilitate the direct flow of funds within the private sector through the medium of acceptance credits, feeling that if companies are beginning to lend and borrow between themselves without bank intermediation, it is better to have some stake in the business rather than none. To the extent that private sector borrowers are thus able to satisfy their requirements directly from elsewhere in the private sector, bank lending to the private sector will fall and sterling M3 with it.

The fall which occurs through this mechanism, however, seems likely to be somewhat limited. In the first place, the number of private sector holders of bank deposits who are prepared to undertake the trouble and risk of finding non-bank borrowers elsewhere in the private sector to lend their deposits to directly, is probably not large, given the absence of an organised market in commercial paper in the UK. Secondly, a number of the large companies which might be borrowers in an intercompany market may well already have available to them the opportunity to borrow from their banks at money-market-related rates of interest which will have been lowered by the immediate impact of the 'corset'. These companies can get the benefit of the lower rates without having to borrow from non-banks. So far as bank lending to the private sector does fall, it will be because the flow of credit to the private sector is being met to a correspondingly greater extent outside the banks; the fall will denote disintermediation rather than constraint.

Although the direct effects of the 'corset', working through bank lending to the private sector, may thus be limited for the reasons outlined above, they do not take into account indirect effects which may be felt from the decline in bank lending to the public sector described in (2) above, and its influence on the Reserve Assets available to the banks. Initially, of course, the banks' demand for Reserve Assets falls in line with the reduction in their IBELs which they have to make. But the amount they can get may fall by more. In the first place, the Discount Market will be bidding for Treasury Bills, other eligible bills and gilt-edged stock with less than a year to run, all of which the banks use as Reserve Assets, and will be funding them from market loans rather than money at call from the banks. In addition the competition for these assets will be intensified from outside the Banking Sector by the switch of private sector wholesale deposits into them, as rates on these deposits fall. Thus the banks may find it difficult to keep their stock of Reserve Assets from falling faster than their need for them; and since their holdings of non-reserve-asset public sector debt will also have fallen in the process of adjustment, they may be compelled to restore their Reserve Asset Ratio by restraining their lending to the private sector. Pressure of this sort on Reserve Assets occurred during the summer of 1978 when the downward adjustment to the 'corset' was beginning and became at times intense enough for the authorities to relieve it by temporary releases of Special Deposits. On other occasions they might make use of such pressure to sustain the general level of short-term interest rates.

This discussion of the impact of the 'corset' on lending to the private sector has been concerned with the banks rather than the Banking Sector as a whole. This is because we have assumed hitherto that, when the banks seek to adjust to the 'corset' by increasing their deductible market loans to the Discount Market, the latter is compelled to channel the additional resources made available to it into public sector debt, being already at the permitted maximum of its Undefined Assets Multiple. But this is not necessarily the case; and its absence has been an important feature of the experience of the last year. On 16 November 1977 the Undefined Assets Multiple stood at 15.6. Not only was this well below the permitted maximum of 20, but over the turn of the year the capital and reserves of the Discount Market, to which the Multiple is applied, increased by about one-fifth or £25m. Thus the Discount Market was in a position to add considerably between 16 November 1977 and 17 May 1978 to its holdings of assets other than public sector debt. Its undefined assets in fact increased by £877m over these six months, and the Undefined Assets Multiple to 18.9. Thus the Discount Market was able, within the controls applicable to it, to use its extra resources from the banks to effect a considerable expansion in its lending to the private sector and to a lesser extent to overseas. In this way the restraints which fell via (4) above on lending to the private sector by the banks were substantially, though not entirely, offset by increased lending to the private sector by the Discount Market. Lending to the private sector by the Banking Sector as a whole was thus redistributed within it, flowing in greater volume through the Discount Market and in lesser volume through the banks, rather than being significantly curtailed in the aggregate.

This is illustrated in Table 3.3. The published statistics do not permit identification by sector of all the items in the balance sheets of the banks and the Discount Market, and some assumptions have to be made about this; they are set down in the notes to Table 3.3. The estimated distribution by sector of changes in the liabilities and assets of the banks and Discount Market taken together is in columns A(3) and B(3). For comparison the published figures for the Banking Sector as a whole— including the Bank of England Banking Department and the National Girobank, whose sectoral asset/liability breakdown is known only to a limited extent—are set down in columns A(4) and B(4) to provide a check. The table shows that between the first six-monthly period and the second—the latter representing the period of adjustment to the 'corset'—the contribution to the growth of sterling M3 of the banks and Discount Market together was reduced by £1777m or 57 per cent (from +£3108m to +£1331m), while the growth of their combined lending to the private sector was down by only £289m or 11 per cent (from +£2555m to +£2266m). But while the increase in lending to the private sector was cut by £771m (31.3 per cent) for the banks, it rose by £482m (6½ times) for the Discount Market. Of the total increase in lending to the private sector by the banks and the Discount Market together, the banks accounted for 96.5 per cent in the first period and only 74.8 per cent in the second. Thus a significant reduction in the growth of the sterling M3 was associated with a minimal reduction in the expansion of credit to the private sector as a whole from the Banking Sector as a whole, although within the Banking Sector there was a sizeable shift of its origin away from the banks.

It is clear that the 'corset' is a method of monetary control which is troublesome for the banks. Because its leverage is loose, the changes it produces in the balance sheet are large in proportion to the effects the authorities intend. Some of these changes will be to the banks' disadvantage, such as the loss to the Discount Market of some of their more profitable lending, or even to a more limited extent outside the Banking Sector altogether. Moreover, it inhibits competition between banks, since the penalties are applied to them individually, although this disadvantage is reduced by lifting the 'corset' periodically to allow adjustment of market shares between banks. It could be further reduced if a method of trading IBELs were available, and this would certainly be required if the 'corset' were to be a permanent method of monetary control. On the other hand, it has some advantages for the authorities. One is that it provides them with a weapon which works, albeit loosely, on their target variable in a way which is associated with downward pressure on interest rates in the wholesale money markets; and although there may also be upward pressure on some other rates, there is no presumption of an increase in the general level of interest rates such as Special Deposits, or operations in the open market to exert pressure through the Reserve Asset Ratio, will tend to bring about. Thus with the inclusion of the 'corset' the authorities dispose of an armoury which allows them an appropriate degree of pressure on interest rates, while moving at least towards their quantitative targets at the same time. Thus they may have found the philosopher's stone which crushes the tiresome logic of the economists who are always saying that you cannot fix both supply and price.

Secondly, the 'corset' has the advantage of effecting its leverage upon the money supply rather than upon the flow of credit from the Banking Sector to the private sector. Although the latter may be marginally curtailed by the application of the 'corset', the total flow of credit available to private sector borrowers may be restored from outside the Banking Sector. This effect is likely to become more significant if continued monetary controls, through the 'corset' and other means, breed a more vigorous commercial paper market in the UK along the lines of that in the USA.

Thus it may be said that the 'corset' is a useful device for keeping down the blood pressure which rises with sterling M3, while leaving the Banking Sector as a whole relatively free to get on with its business of meeting the needs of trade and industry. This is not as cynical as it may

TABLE 3.3

£m, not seasonally adjusted	A. Changes, 16 November 1977 to 17 May 1978				B. Changes, 17 May 1978 to 15 November 1978			
	(1) Banks	(2) Discount Market	(3) Banks plus Discount Market	(4) Banking Sector	(1) Banks	(2) Discount Market	(3) Banks plus Discount Market	(4) Banking Sector
Liabilities								
1. Banks' sterling deposits from public and private sectors (contribution to £M3)	+3231		+3108	+3115	+1208		+1331	+1350
Discount Market's borrowed funds from UK other than banking sector		−123				+123		
2. Intrabanking-sector borrowing in sterling (net of lending) from								
(a) banks	+518	−754	−236	0	−623	+667	+44	0
(b) discount market	−184	−	−191		+131	−	+131	
(c) Bank of England		−7				0		
3. Banks' non-deposit liabilities (net)	−242		−269	−831	+191		+209	+258
Discount Market's capital and other funds (net)		−27				+18		
4. Total 1–3	+3323	−911	+2412	+2284	+907	+808	+1715	+1608
Assets								
5. Lending in sterling to public sector	−120	−1036	−1156	−968	−314	+94	−220	−318

6. Lending in sterling to private sector	+2466	+89	+2555	+1695	+571	+2266	+2157
7. Lending in sterling to overseas sector	+977	+36	+1013	−474	+143	−331	−231
8. Total 5–7	+3323	−911	+2412	+907	+808	+1715	+1608

The column headed 'Banks' is derived from the *Bank of England Quarterly Bulletin* Table 2.1, and that headed 'Discount Market' from Table 5; for further detail see below. The column headed 'Banking Sector' is from the same source, Tables 6.3 and 11.3.

Banks
Line 1 is identical with line 1 of Table 3.2.
Line 2(b) is line 3 of Table 3.2, *less* money at call with the Discount Market.
Line 2(c) consists of Bankers' Deposits and Special Deposits.
Line 5, lending to the public sector, comprises notes and coin, Reserve Assets in the form of Treasury Bills, local authority Bills and British Government Stocks with 0–1 years to maturity, market loans to local authorities and public corporations, advances to the public sector, and investments in British Government and other public sector stocks.
Line 6, lending to the private sector, consists of Reserve Assets in the form of money-at-call with listed brokers and 80 per cent of commercial bills, market loans and advances to the private sector adjusted for transit items, 80 per cent of bills other than Reserve Assets, and investments other than in public sector stocks.
Line 7, lending to the overseas sector (net), consists of the remaining 20 per cent of commercial and non-eligible bills, together with market loans and advances to overseas, *less* sterling deposits of overseas residents.

Discount Market
Line 2(a) equals funds borrowed from UK banking sector other than the Bank of England *less* funds lent to UK banking sector including CDs held.
Line 3 is the residual item.
Line 5 consists of Treasury Bills, other public sector bills, funds lent to local authorities, and investments in British Government and local authorities' stocks.
Line 6 consists of 80 per cent of bills other than those of the public sector, funds lent to UK borrowers other than the public sector and investments other than in public sector stocks.
Line 7 consists of 20 per cent of bills other than those of the public sector, plus funds lent overseas. *less* borrowed funds from overseas.

Banking Sector
In addition to the banks and discount market this includes the Bank of England Banking Department and the National Girobank. The effect of the inclusion of the National Girobank in UK Banks in September 1978 has been taken out of the figures in section B of Table 3.3. Thus the differences between columns A(3) and A(4) and between B(3) and B(4) should in principle reflect the transactions of the Bank of England Banking Department and the National Girobank, about whose distribution by sector there is only limited knowledge. But the differences will in practice also reflect errors in the estimates for the banks and the discount market. These seem rather evident in Section A of Table 3.3, lines 2 and 3. In line 2 a rather large increase in net interbank borrowing by the Bank of England and the National Girobank is implied if the transactions of the banking sector as a whole are to net out to zero. In line 3 a rather large decline is implied in the net non-deposit liabilities of these two institutions. It is possible that these discrepancies may be due to the mysterious misclassification of 'certain public funds placed temporarily with banking institutions through the interbank market' referred to in the current footnote to Table 6.3 of the *Bank of England Quarterly Bulletin*.

sound. Certainly the 'corset' is not well adapted to the exercise of monetary constraint upon an economy which is currently overheated and where the immediate objective is to cut back the flow of spending in the private as well as the public sector. But there are occasions, with which the UK has become familiar in 1976–78, when the economy is clearly not overheated (or at any rate not clearly overheated) currently, but nevertheless the overhang of immediately available purchasing power in the form of bank deposits is growing in a way which threatens overheating at some future date. On such occasions monetary control needs to be precautionary, not punitive, and it may be a positive advantage that it should work to reduce the purchasing power immediately available in the form of bank deposits, while allowing some disintermediation through which the impact on the private sector's credit-financed demand for goods and services is moderated. The 'corset' appears to have this property. On occasions when overheating is present or imminent, this will be less than is required; on others it will be exactly right.

IV

The history of economic management is littered with policy-weapons which the authorities have felt bend in their hands. Given the fallibility of economic forecasting and the likelihood of errors of judgement, it is not necessarily or always disastrous that the authorities should fail to achieve the objectives they set themselves. Nevertheless, by setting them they create expectations, and confidence is liable to be undermined if they are manifestly not fulfilled. Moreover the failure to fulfil is apt to lead to a burdensome multiplication of controls. Thus it was the apparent looseness in the controls intended to be exerted through the Reserve Asset Ratio as defined by Competition and Credit Control that led to the invention of the 'corset'; and looseness in her 'corset' is no doubt turning the Old Lady's mind to new ways of tying us up. All this has given weight to the argument that the system should be simultaneously simplified and tightened by operating exclusively through the monetary base.

I refer to the 'apparent looseness' of control through the Reserve Asset Ratio because I am less than convinced that the system itself bears a major responsibility for the breakdown of monetary control when it has occurred, rather than the pressures put upon it in the early stages in 1973–74, and subsequently the reluctance to come to terms with the fact that, in a conflict between monetary control and the level of interest rates, the latter have to give. It is worth noting that in one respect the Reserve Asset Ratio defined by Competition and Credit Control tightened things up by restricting to 2 per cent of Eligible Liabilities the extent to which commercial bills could be held as Reserve Assets. Thus one route through which banks are alleged to 'manufacture' Reserve Assets, by leaning on customers to borrow through the medium of commercial bills rather than advances, was truncated. Nevertheless, other possibilities remain. One is that banks may increase their Reserve Asset lending to the Discount Houses in the form of money at call, and off-load to them gilt-edged securities with 1–5 years to run, which are not Reserve Assets to the banks but which the Houses can absorb without adding to their Undefined Assets Multiple. Another is that there is a reservoir of market Treasury Bills held outside the banks which banks may be able to buy in to supplement their existing Reserve Assets.

To the extent that these leakages are significant, rather than multiply the number of thumbs in the dyke, with side-effects which might distort the operation of financial markets, it would be simpler to create a single reserve asset which banks would be required to hold as a certain minimum proportion of their deposits, and whose quantity would be wholly within the authorities' control. This required property of the reserve asset would not be satisfied by reverting to something like the old 8 per cent cash ratio, consisting of notes and coin in tills plus bankers' deposits at the Bank of England. As was the case when this operated, the banks would be carrying a secondary liquidity reserve which would include some assets, such as Treasury Bills, convertible into cash with minimal delay. If these can be bought in from outside the banks, their cash base is not under the authorities' control, although they are still able to operate on interest rates in such a way as to make non-banks unwilling sellers of these assets. The fundamental property of the reserve asset which constitutes the monetary base is that it must be available for holding only by banks and by no-one else. This means segregating the liabilities of the Bank of England to the commercial banks into two classes; one in the form of bankers' ordinary deposits, which will rise or fall for individual banks with their position in the clearing and for banks collectively with the balance of transactions between the public sector and the private sector, and with changes in the note circulation, and the other in the form of bankers' reserve deposits which for banks individually will be adjusted by transfers to and from bankers' ordinary deposits as required to maintain the required ratio to deposits, but otherwise only as decided for banks generally by the Bank of England.

One might call these latter bankers' Special Deposits, since the system could be introduced by the Bank of England directly taking over an appropriate quantity of the banks' existing Reserve Assets in exchange for Special Deposits. The latter would then replace the former as the fulcrum of control.

Provided that the new reserve asset which constitutes the monetary base is one which can only be held within the banking system, so that the banks collectively cannot obtain it except from each other or the Bank of England, it would provide the most simple and logical method of control. It does not follow, of course, that the authorities would always eschew the temptation to add to the supply of the reserve asset when the public sector's borrowing needs were difficult to satisfy by sales of gilt-edged securities to non-banks at 'reasonable' rates of interest. But given their commitment to a monetary target, the enforcement of it could be tighter; and the argument that it would further increase the volatility of interest rates has worn a trifle thin. Nevertheless, there is a case against overegging the pudding. The major problem of monetary targets, to revert to the theme with which I began, is not so much whether they can be accurately enforced as how they can ensure that there is a sufficient feedback from the constraint they imply upon prices to the constraint required upon wages. This is the fundamental problem; and until it is within sight of solution, it may be positively dangerous to pile tighter enforcement of a given monetary target on top of a tighter monetary target itself. If the latter can be made effective without significant damage to output and employment, because organised labour can be brought to take the point, I shall be persuaded of the advantages of reforming the system of control to concentrate upon the monetary base. Meanwhile, although I am against sin, I am conscious of the advantages of not overzealously pursuing the path of virtue.

Comments* on Professor Sargent's Paper

Alan Budd
London Business School

I am concerned, in this comment, mainly with the first part of Professor Sargent's paper in which he argues for the 'minimalist approach' to monetary targeting. He bases his argument on a simple macroeconomic model and particularly emphasises the possible long-term costs in terms of unemployment arising through a failure of money wages to adjust rapidly to lower prices. There are a number of slightly strange features both about the model and about the conclusions he draws from it. I shall suggest an alternative model which is in the same spirit as Professor Sargent's. The key issues, I suggest, are concerned not with the long-term properties of the model but with its short-term dynamics. Experiments with the London Business School model do not support Professor Sargent's fears. I conclude that as far as the macroeconomic effects are concerned, there is a strong case for observing monetary targets and severe dangers in operating the minimalist approach espoused by Professor Sargent.

Since Professor Sargent's arguments are presented in so reasonable (and entertaining) a manner, it is difficult to challenge them without appearing villainous or arrogant or both. Villainous because it will look as if one does not care about unemployment, arrogant because one will be claiming to know things which Professor Sargent modestly says he is unsure about. Nevertheless, in spite of the risks, I do challenge the arguments. I believe that it is reasonable to use monetary targets to

---

* This discussion expands points made at the Conference. The discussion at the Conference was based on a necessarily hurried reading of Professor Sargent's paper. I am grateful to Mr A. Gosling for assistance with the simulations on pages 125–127.

squeeze inflation out of the system and thereafter to stabilise prices. Under flexible exchange rates in particular, the minimalist approach can readily become an accommodating policy with grave dangers of loss of control of prices.

I. SARGENT'S MODEL

The paper presents a two-equation model in wages and unemployment.
    The first equation

$$\dot{w} = a - bu + c\dot{p} \qquad b > 0 \tag{1}$$

is a conventional disequilibrium equation representing wage adjustments in response to excess demand in the labour market. As a long-run equation it is difficult on *a priori* grounds to believe that c can be anything but unity; but, as will be seen, Professor Sargent attaches much importance to the assertion that c may be less than unity, especially when prices are falling.
    The second equation

$$\dot{u} = k(\dot{w} - \dot{p} - \dot{\pi}) \qquad k > 0 \tag{2}$$

is, presumably, derived from supply and demand equations for labour. It has been expressed in difference form for algebraic convenience.
    Sargent derives a dynamic equation for $\dot{u}$

$$\dot{u} = k(a - \dot{\pi} + (c-1)\dot{p}) - kbu \tag{3}$$

and two equilibrium equations

$$\bar{u} = \frac{a - \dot{\pi} + (c-1)\dot{p}}{b}. \tag{4}$$

$$w = \dot{\pi} + \dot{p} \tag{5}$$

Sargent interprets this system in terms of a somewhat confusing mixture of long-term and short-term properties. As mentioned, he emphasises the question of the value of c; but the dynamics of the system, as equation (3) shows, depends on the value of the coefficient bk which determines the relationship between the current level of unemployment and its rate of change.
    It is not true, as Sargent argues, that his system removes the problem of the 'Phillips knife-edge'. It is correct that in this system, as in all versions of the 'natural' rate of unemployment, the system is self-

stabilising if there is an autonomous shift away from equilibrium. But attempts by the authorities to move and keep unemployment below $\bar{u}$ by expansionary monetary policy will generate ever-accelerating inflation.

II. AN ALTERNATIVE MACROECONOMIC MODEL

Sargent seems to be overstating his case in attempting to argue from the long-run properties of a macroeconomic model. Apart from anything else it seems inconsistent with normal usage to describe as 'equilibrium' a system in which wages may be growing permanently less (or more) rapidly than prices. Also the argument as he has presented it seems to have little to do with the questions usually raised in connexion with monetary targeting. If an economy wishes to choose ever-accelerating inflation in an attempt to hold unemployment below its equilibrium level that can be regarded as a legitimate political choice (if a highly risky one) but it will (on Sargent's generous concessions about the effectiveness of monetary policy) still require monetary targets. The questions surely, are whether monetary targets will affect inflation, and, if they do, what is the *short-run* cost in terms of unemployment.

These questions could be considered in terms of the following model, which would seem to be the smallest possible which could capture the relevant aspects of behaviour:

$$M = P + kY \tag{2.1}$$
$$\dot{w} = a - bu + \dot{P} \tag{2.2}$$
$$u = L^s - L^d = \alpha_1(w - P) + \alpha_2 Y \tag{2.3}$$
$$\dot{P} = \beta_1(Y - \overline{Y}) + \beta_2 \dot{w} \tag{2.4}$$

All variables are in logs. Equation (2.1) expresses the demand for money as a function of prices and output. Equation (2.2) is equivalent to Sargent's equation (1) but it is assumed that wages respond completely to price changes. Equation (2.3) is related to Sargent's equation (2) but here it is expressed in terms of levels rather than changes. It incorporates the same neo-classical assumption of a market for labour in which supply and demand depend on real wages. However it differs from Sargent in assuming that the demand for labour also depends on the level of output.

Equation (2.4) completes the system by explaining inflation in terms of demand-pull ($\overline{Y}$ is a measure of capacity output) and cost-push.

If the money supply (M) can be taken as exogenous, the system solves for the four endogenous variables Y, U, P and w. No attempt is made to portray the dynamics. In equation (2.1), for example, neither P nor Y will necessarily respond instantly to changes in Y. In equation (2.2), wages will not necessarily respond instantaneously to changes in prices. In this system it is quite possible that, in the short run, an attempt to reduce inflation by controlling the money supply will result in an increase in unemployment through equations (2.2) and (2.3). Professor Sargent relies on this to support the 'minimalist' approach to monetary targeting which would not use monetary policy to squeeze inflation out of the system and which would accommodate inflation already in it.

How large are the unemployment costs likely to be? This will depend on how serious the wage inflexibility problem is and on how strongly the employers react to excessively high real wages. Is it reasonable to assume that, as Sargent's model seems to imply, firms react rationally to changes in the money supply but employees react irrationally? Also, why should one believe that the problem is likely to be more serious when price inflation is slowing down? If Sargent is right one would expect to see low real wages when inflation is accelerating and high real wages when inflation is decelerating. Casual empiricism, as presented in Sargent's chart, seems to suggest the opposite. The years of high real wages were 1974 and 1975, the periods of explosive inflation. Real wages fell thereafter as the inflation rate fell. Of course a lot of other things were going on at the same time, including the kinds of administered wage/price distortion described by Professor Sargent.

In terms of economic modelling this will, indeed, be a very difficult area since we are dealing with expectations and with learning. It might be reasonable to expect that, as time goes by, the response of earnings to prices becomes more rather than less rapid and the evidence with regard to exchange rate changes certainly suggests that this happens. It would seem wrong to base a policy strategy on the assumption that people will continue to make mistakes even though the evidence—through unemployment and profit shares—will reveal the results of these mistakes.

There is a further objection to Sargent's analysis. He omits the level of output from his labour market equation. Output is surely needed to capture the dynamics of employment. Thus even if the real wage effect is tending to reduce the demand for labour directly there may be other effects tending to raise it indirectly through an increase in output. One of these, which used to be stressed in policy circles, is the demand effect of high real wages. Thus if wages do not adjust rapidly to prices there may be some effect on output and employment to offset the direct effect on labour demand. In addition there are the demand effects likely to accompany a reduction or stabilisation of the inflation rate. The effect on consumption of a fall in the inflation rate is now well recognised and one can also expect an increase in investment in response to greater price stability.

On *a priori* grounds therefore one may be less anxious than Sargent about the short-run costs of using monetary targets to control inflation.

III. POLICY SIMULATIONS

It is possible to explore some of the arguments in Professor Sargent's paper using a macroeconomic model. The LBS model incorporates the ideas embodied in equations (2.1) to (2.4). The following simulations are based on the version of the model used to generate the forecasts published in *Economic Outlook*, July 1979.

The main transmission mechanism from money to prices operates via changes in the exchange rate. A reduction in the money supply *ceteris paribus* raises the exchange rate. This reduces consumer prices and wholesale prices directly. It also reduces them indirectly via the fall in world prices in sterling. There is a short-run effect of consumer prices on earnings. The long-term effect on earnings comes through changes in wholesale prices. There is an implied demand for labour as a function of real wages. It is thus possible for unemployment to rise, for a given level of output, if real wages rise. There is also a transmission mechanism via domestic demand and a Phillips curve.

Three simulations are shown. In simulation I, there is a cut in the money supply (sterling M3) starting in 1979:2 which cumulates to a 2 per cent cut by 1980:1. Thereafter the money supply is permanently 2 per cent below what it would otherwise have been. In simulation 2 the cut cumulates to 4 per cent by 1981:1. Thereafter the level is permanently 4 per cent lower. In simulation 3, the cut cumulates to 6 per cent by 1982:2. Thereafter the level is permanently 6 per cent lower. The results are shown below. All figures represent percentage differences from the control forecast.

Simulation 1

	M3	Consumer prices	Wholesale prices	*Average earnings in manufacturing*
1979:4	−1.5	−0.1	−0.2	
1980:4	−2.0	−0.5	−0.4	−0.5
1981:4	−2.0	−0.9	−1.3	−1.1
1982:4	−2.0	−1.1	−1.3	−1.5

Simulation 2

	M3	*Consumer prices*	*Wholesale prices*	*Average earnings in manufacturing*
1979:4	− 1.5	− 0.1	− 0.2	
1980:4	− 3.5	− 0.6	− 1.2	− 0.4
1981:4	− 4.0	− 1.5	− 2.3	− 1.5
1982:4	− 4.0	− 2.1	− 2.7	− 2.5

Simulation 3

1979:4	− 1.5	− 0.1	− 0.2	
1980:4	− 3.5	− 0.6	− 1.2	− 0.4
1981:4	− 5.5	− 1.6	− 2.6	− 1.5
1982:4	− 6.0	− 2.7	− 3.7	− 3.0

In each case GDP is either virtually unchanged or slightly higher by the end of the period. That result is possibly somewhat optimistic since the change in the money supply has been imposed without any corresponding increase in interest rates. Also the direct effect on expenditure of the fall in the real money supply is muted by comparison with the expansionary effect on consumption of the reduction in the inflation rate.

However, although those results are somewhat worrying for a model with neo-classical aspirations, they are not at issue here since Professor Sargent has concentrated on the issue of movements in real wages. As the simulations show, wholesale prices, which are more closely related to world prices, adjust more rapidly than consumer prices. Earnings tend to adjust less rapidly than prices. In the long run, the model has the property that earnings adjust fully to wholesale prices; however, as discussed earlier, the case for the 'minimalist' approach to monetary policy lies in the short-run response of earnings. In simulation 1, where there is a 2 per cent cut in the money supply (achieved by the first quarter of 1980), the adjustment of earnings to wholesale prices is complete within $2\frac{1}{2}$ years. The relative increase in earnings at its peak raises unemployment by 4000. The effects appear to be approximately linear over a feasible range of policy changes. A reduction in the money supply by 4 per cent causes a peak increase in unemployment of about 10,000. The speed of adjustment is unchanged and earnings are in line with wholesale prices by mid-1982. Simulations 2 and 3 are designed to show the effects of extended reductions in the money supply. Not surprisingly, since inflation is still being reduced, the effect of higher relative earnings persists for longer, though in simulation 2 the adjustment is almost

complete by the end of 1982. For the economy as a whole the LBS model
suggests that the unemployment effect is little different from simulation
1. In simulation 2 the peak effect on unemployment is an increase of
5500. In simulation 3 unemployment is 6000 higher by the end of 1982.
The link between inflation and consumption offsets the real wage effect.

Although the LBS model rules out the possibility of long-run costs of
reducing inflation via the money supply it does support the idea that
there are short-run costs. It also suggests that the costs are greater the
more savage the cuts in the money supply and the longer the cuts
continue. There is nothing surprising in that. It should always have been
recognised that the attempt to reduce the money supply rapidly is likely
to cause an increase in unemployment and that this should be taken into
account in monetary targeting. However, over the range examined here
the cost seems to be quite small and transitional. If economic agents have
learned from past experience and have speeded their reactions, the cost
may now be even smaller. Given the costs—especially in terms of
unemployment—of accelerating inflation, the permissive approach to
monetary control would seem far more dangerous than firm adherence
to monetary targets.

To argue, after what happened in the mid-1970s, that policy should be
based on a long-run trade-off between inflation and unemployment does
represent to a quite remarkable degree what Dr Johnson described as the
triump of hope over experience.

IV. THE GRAND OLD DUKE OF YORK

In Section II of his paper Professor Sargent refers to the occasional
problem of the 'go slow' or 'strike' in the gilt-edged market. The
institutions are said to hold back from buying gilts. The result can be an
increase in government borrowing from the banks with a resulting
increase in the money supply. This, it is said, makes matters worse
because the institutions can now justify their behaviour on the grounds
that the money supply is 'out of control'. This leads to the familiar
increase in interest rates until eventually a tap stock is sold and everyone
appears to make vast profits as interest rates come back to where they
were before.

I wish to make some deliberately naïve comments on this phenomenon. First, a market in which the largest operator (apart from the
Authorities) has a share of 2 per cent and in which hundreds of
institutions take part would seem to have the basic properties of a perfect

market. One would expect such a market to operate as an efficient market in financial assets. Yet the Grand Old Duke of York experience suggests that the institutions are enjoying a sure prospect of success. They refuse to buy gilts today in the confident belief that they will be able to buy them more cheaply tomorrow. That can only be true on average if someone helps them, and that someone can only be the Authorities.

Faced with a 'go-slow' by the institutions, based presumably on the idea that prices will be lower tomorrow, the Authorities can do one of three things.

(1) They can ignore the market view and sell gilts steadily according to their monetary targets. There will be some market price at which the necessary sales will be possible.
(2) They can accept the market view, in which case as sellers they will try to sell an exceptional amount today since they believe the price will be lower tomorrow.
(3) They can take the opposite view to the market and delay sales in the belief, presumably, that the price will be higher tomorrow.

The Authorities appear to do (3) but they lose regularly since the tap stocks are sold at what prove to be exceptionally low prices. It is very hard to see why this problem has been allowed to rise (and it does not, incidentally, appear to have much to do with the question of 'tap versus tender'). It is sometimes said that it arises because the government announces both a PSBR and a money supply target. But all that that does (subject to considerable uncertainty) is to establish the equilibrium price of gilts. It does not allow the institutions to choose another equilibrium price and to impose this choice on the Authorities. If competitive financial markets are left to operate freely, 'bear' raids cannot succeed. If they do succeed this is because the taxpayer is being made to act as a victim. (The same argument applies to exchange rate markets.) Such self-inflicted problems should certainly not be part of the case against monetary targets.

Comments on Professor Sargent's Paper

C. A. E. Goodhart
Bank of England

It is as well for anyone working in a central bank to keep in the forefront of his mind the fact that commercial bankers are not in being just for the convenience of us central bankers. Indeed the ingenuity of commercial bankers, and the innovations that they introduce, ensure that the monetary system is never static, is never fixed, but continuously evolving. Moreover, that ingenuity is often brought prominently into play in order to get around some particular controls that we central bankers set in order to control our monetary target. In the United States, for example, where most emphasis has been placed by the authorities on controlling M1, it is forbidden to pay interest on current accounts and the reserve ratio imposed on such current accounts is both high, very high compared with this country, and non-interest-bearing. Is it therefore particularly surprising that there are a number of structural developments that have occurred in that country to switch demand deposits into other interest-bearing forms, and that, in so far as demand for money (M1) functions have malfunctioned, they have tended to overestimate the growth of M1? In this country, on the other hand, the authorities have introduced controls on *interest*-bearing eligible liabilities. Surprise, surprise, in the last year in which we have had such controls the rate of growth of *non-interest*-bearing eligible liabilities has been much higher than previous equations would have suggested. Although Professor Sargent does not specifically mention it, some large part of the technicalities that emerge in his survey of the working of the 'corset' in section III reflect the age-old interaction between gamekeeper and poacher. So, when considering the problems of monetary control, from our point of view I must say to Professor Sargent that he and his innovative and ingenious colleagues in the commercial banks also form

129

a part of the problem itself. Moreover, despite his being kind enough to proffer some advice to us gamekeepers in the final section of his paper, I myself would be inclined to wonder, among a whole series of reservations about the Duck – Sheppard proposals which he there appears to espouse, whether this scheme would not generate, indeed even necessitate if the monetary system was to work at all efficiently and flexibly, a whole series of major consequential structural changes in the financial system to an extent that would subsequently call into question the whole exercise.

But let me turn back again to the first section and try briefly to make four points. First, how minimal is Professor Sargent's minimalist approach? In particular what would he do if the forecasters said that they expected there to be an acceleration in the rate of growth of wages and prices in the course of the next year? Would he then accommodate it by budgeting for a higher monetary target? In which case, to what extent, if any, would his monetary target provide some contra-inflationary support or guarantee against the price level instability and indeterminacy that Patrick Minford was talking about? On the other hand, if he would seek to hold the line with an unchanged monetary target against a prospective upsurge in wages and costs is not then his approach more than purely minimal? [Subsequently Professor Sargent said that he would himself choose the second alternative, if only to test whether the prospect would become a reality, and might in the end find himself sticking to it.]

Secondly, Professor Sargent suggested that the natural rate hypothesis was a monetarist concept, part of the monetarist armoury: I think that that can be challenged. Although Keynesians are more inclined to stress market imperfections, the absence of monetary illusions and the belief that you cannot fool all the people all the time is something that many Keynesians would accept, and that really is about all that is needed for the natural rate hypothesis. Indeed Franco Modigliani, who is perhaps about as Keynesian as can now be found in the US, has shown in a number of articles specifically that, even when you accept the natural rate of unemployment hypothesis, you can still aim for a particular non-inflationary rate of unemployment (NIRU) related to the natural rate. The real division in my view is between those who feel that they know exactly where the Phillips' curve is, the exact position of the wage inflation/unemployment trade-off, and those who believe that these relationships are very volatile and uncertain, so that it is not possible to observe a stable and predictable natural rate of unemployment.

I was glad to see in this same section that Professor Sargent suggests that unemployment might be related to real labour costs. The old hypothesis contained in most UK models simply relating the level of unemployment with the gap between actual and trend output has failed fairly miserably in recent years. However, while this new hypothesis, which intellectually I welcome, is an attractive one, the empirical evidence has not yet been studied sufficiently to make it a clear frontrunner.

Finally, I share Professor Sargent's general pessimism, and welcome him to the ranks of pessimists. For example, Frank Blackaby's comments about the difficulties and disadvantages of monetary policy and monetary targetry are so much more persuasive than his comments about why incomes policy should work. Equally I find Patrick Minford's comments about why incomes policy will not work much more persuasive than his arguments why monetary policy, monetary targets should work efficiently. In this case Professor Sargent's pessimism is exhibited in his suggestion that there may be asymmetry in the reaction of wages to inflation. Thus the coefficient relating wage increases to price inflation may tend to be lower when the authorities are trying to introduce contra-inflationary restrictive policies, but much higher when they go for reflationary policies. Alas, this is only too plausible. What one needs in the realm of policy-making is innovative pessimists who assume the worst and try to think how to deal with it rather than conservative optimists who believe that everything will come right in the event.

Let me now turn to the second part of Professor Sargent's paper, where he describes three problems that may arise in the process of maintaining or enforcing monetary targets. In fact two of his problem cases are really mirror images of the same internal-external dilemma, and I will address myself to this problem. The authorities, of course, always face the general problem of what weight, if any, to give to exchange rate objectives. The worldwide experience of recent years, especially 1978, with particular reference to the US, which once thought itself to be virtually a closed economy, Switzerland and Germany, has shown in practice just how difficult it is to maintain a hands-off policy in respect of exchange rates. But if the authorities do have certain aims for exchange rates, where does that leave monetary targetry and in particular the choice of emphasis within monetary targets between DCE targets, or limits, on the one hand and monetary targets on the other?

Technically, however, I thought that Professor Sargent's exposition of the internal-external dilemma was slightly flawed, because he put too much weight on the direct effect of flows over the exchanges on to the money stock, as compared with the more significant secondary indirect effects working through interest rates and liquidity within the banking system. Although such flows over the exchange rates can be large and can have a large direct effect on the money stock, as occurred in this country for a few months in the autumn of 1977, its impact is more generally much exaggerated; this is so for two reasons which have particular relevance for the UK. First, some of the more speculative flows over the exchanges represent non-residents moving into sterling money balances and shifts in the banks' switched position: these do not affect the £M3 monetary definition which has been adopted. This aggregate was, in my view absolutely rightly, so defined as to exclude such non-resident balances on the grounds that fluctuations in them were largely speculative, and would have little effect on the domestic economy. Second, the inflows over the exchanges tend quasi-automatically to generate offsetting movements in domestic credit: thus, for example, the news that Japanese buyers of gilts have been sighted in Lombard Street often unleashes a stampede of domestic buyers. Now, for those members of the gilt-edged market here present, I should warn you that, as an instrument of monetary control, I am thinking of hiring a troupe of Japanese actors in the coming year.

Indeed, conditions conducive to large-scale inflows frequently, as in the first half of 1977, are propitious for a cutback in the rate of growth of domestic credit expansion. Thus, at the time of such inflows in the first half of 1977 there was no great expansion in £M3. Instead, the greater problem that such flows cause for monetary controls is indirect. Such exchange flows, *especially* when domestic credit does quasi-automatically tend to fall back to offset those flows, produce conditions that put pressure on the authorities to vary interest rates in a countervailing manner. Since the response, both of capital flows and of domestic credit, to interest rate changes is muted in the short run with long lags, the resulting interest rate fluctuations can be very considerable and thereby lay up the seeds for future difficulties. Let me give two examples. The growth in the German money stock in 1978 was primarily to be found in credit expansion to the private sector rather than directly as a counterpart of external flows, with such credit expansion to the private sector being encouraged by low interest rates and easy availability of credit. Second, the problems of monetary management in the UK in the first half of 1978 sprang largely from the extremely low levels to which interest rates had been pushed in the autumn of 1977 in the vain attempt to deter inflows.

Finally, let me turn to section III which largely consists of a detailed and technical analysis of the workings of the 'corset'. As an aside, I should note that some enjoyment is often to be found from the metaphors that can be conjured up from the 'corset', my own favourite being the occasional reference to a 'corset with teeth in it'. Although the terminology can be fun, the details are intricate and time-consuming but perhaps not quite as complicated as Professor Sargent makes them in his paper. Let me try to simplify. The key is to understand that the workings of the 'corset' can only be analysed in conjunction with, and in interaction with, the pressure being contemporaneously applied via the reserve asset ratio.

Let me take three cases of varying reserve asset pressure, starting with a situation of ease. In this case a sizeable proportion of the total (and excess) reserve assets will be held by banks in the form of money at call with the discount market. If a bank then shifts money at call with the discount market into money *not* at call with the discount houses, it moves funds out of reserve assets into a form of lending to the discount houses which counts as interbank lending, which is treated as an offset to its interest-bearing eligible liabilities. So, with excess reserve assets, all that the banks have to do in order to get their IBELs down within the 'corset' is simply to shift funds from one form of holding with the discount market to another, with no effect on anything at all.

One starts getting an effect via the 'corset' only when the reserve asset ratio begins to tighten; indeed the switch of funds from money at call into money not at call, discussed above, destroys reserve assets, and begins to tighten the reserve asset ratio. As the banks find their reserve assets becoming short, the first step will be to run off their near reserve assets, which will tend to cause an interest rate differential between near reserve assets, such as local authority short-term instruments which banks would otherwise have taken up, and the rate offered on wholesale money. In exactly the manner described by Professor Sargent this will induce disintermediation which is largely cosmetic or optical in nature. But there are, of course, limits to that disintermediation process, depending on the existence and the availability of near reserve assets and liquidity. If the authorities squeeze yet further on the liquidity position, on the reserve asset position of the banks, then the banks will become caught in a position where they have no alternative but to cut back on their lending activity.

This interaction between the pressure placed on the reserve asset ratio and the 'corset' does entail some advantage to the authorities, in that they can to an extent vary the way in which the 'corset' is actually affecting the banking system, by adjusting the pressure placed on the reserve asset ratio. That is another aspect of a general advantage of the 'corset', that it does have considerable flexibility. On the other hand, these interrelationships are sufficiently complicated that trying to estimate the effect on £M3, as Professor Sargent notes, of a given degree of 'corset' pressure is very difficult. I would, however, emphasise that it is the predictability of this relationship, rather than the question of its statistical looseness, that matters and we can certainly predict rather better than the looseness that Professor Sargent shows in his tables might suggest. Rather I would end by noting that I am not all that greatly worried by the complications and slippages, particularly with the discount market, on which Professor Sargent puts a lot of emphasis, because they are limited and to some large extent predictable.

Instead I am much more worried by two other developments, one of which he plays down, the other which he does not mention at all. The one that he plays down is the tendency when 'corset' pressure is put on the banking system for the banks, in effect, to off-load their lending outside their balance sheet through the development of a commercial bill market outside the banking system; this developed noticeably this last autumn, and it might grow considerably further if severe 'corset' pressure occurred again. The other problem, which he did not mention, is that the 'corset', of course, bears on the banks' *interest*-bearing eligible liabilities. In so far as banks can provide a notional yield, an effective return, on non-interest-bearing eligible liabilities and thereby control to some extent the proportion of their funds which go into one pigeon-hole rather than another, this would tend to undermine the rationale, and the basis, on which the 'corset' at present depends.

4 Monetary Targets and The Public Sector Borrowing Requirement*

P. E. Middleton, C. J. Mowl, J. C. Odling-Smee and C. J. Riley[1]
HM Treasury

I. INTRODUCTION

The objective of this paper is to explore the relationship between the Public Sector Borrowing Requirement (PSBR) and the growth of the money stock in the short to medium term. If the government sets itself a monetary target, it is naturally interested in what fiscal policies, and what associated PSBRs, are consistent with the target. Of course, this is only one of the many ways of looking at the PSBR but it is an important one. The discussion refers mostly to £M3, the aggregate in terms of which the UK government's monetary target is expressed.

Following a general introduction, which sets both monetary targets and the PSBR in their wider economic and policy contexts, there are two main sections. The first explains how we see the determination of £M3, and the second discusses the changes in £M3 associated with PSBRs of different size and composition. Both are illustrated by simulations using the Treasury model complete with its recently published financial sector.

The Policy Context

The publication of a monetary target establishes the authorities' commitment to adjust the various instruments and policies at their disposal, so as to keep the growth of the money stock within the

---

* This article is reproduced by permission of the Controller of Her Majesty's Stationery Office.

published range. But monetary targets should also be related to the achievement of final objectives for prices, output, employment etc., and this paper considers some of the implications of this.

With a wide aggregate such as £M3, the public has a yardstick against which to judge the overall mix of a whole range of policies. There are direct links with fiscal policy through the size and composition of the PSBR; with exchange rate policy and capital flows; with open market operations and the level and structure of interest rates; and with policy towards the banking system. When deviations from the target seem likely to persist, the government can operate in any of these areas in order to bring the growth in £M3 back towards the stated range and has in fact done so.

In arriving at its decision on the target range and on how to deal with deviations from it, the government has to be able to analyse the implications of all the main elements in its macroeconomic policy for monetary conditions. It also has to consider the implications of different combinations of policies with a given target, and of different targets for its final objectives. An important part of the assessment is the role of fiscal policy, to which we now turn.

Fiscal Policy and the PSBR

It is tempting to regard the PSBR as a measure of fiscal policy, but discretionary changes in fiscal policy and changes in the PSBR are not always closely related. There can be changes in fiscal policy instruments (that is, tax rates and public expenditure plans) which affect the economy in various ways but do not change the PSBR. The textbook balanced budget multiplier is a simple example.

On the other hand, the PSBR can change without there being any change in fiscal policy instruments as just defined. Financial transactions, such as the sale of financial assets (e.g. BP shares in 1977), provide one example. Another is the change in the PSBR that results from changes in activity and prices in the economy. These may cause changes in revenues from income and expenditure taxes and earnings-related national insurance contributions, the trading surpluses of public enterprises and corporations, unemployment benefits and, in the absence of rigorous enforcement of cash limits whatever the rate of inflation, all public expenditure on goods and services.[2]

Thus there is no simple equation between discretionary fiscal policy and the PSBR. If fiscal policy were to be based on a target for the PSBR, perhaps because it was thought to be a good way to achieve a monetary target, there would not be any straightforward rule which would indicate what changes in discretionary fiscal policy were necessary to keep on target. For example, no change in target PSBR would not necessarily require no change in fiscal policy instruments. It depends on what autonomous changes in the PSBR are anyway taking place, and whether the balance between various fiscal policy instruments, each of which affects the PSBR differently, is being changed. In practice, the best way to proceed would probably be to estimate the likely PSBR on the basis of no change in policy, and then to construct a package of fiscal policy measures which filled the gap between the projected and the target PSBR and which also came nearest to satisfying other criteria.

£M3 and the PSBR

Much of the discussion about the relationship between the PSBR and £M3 starts off from the identity which links the two. The traditional form of the counterparts of £M3 is:

Public Sector Borrowing Requirement

- − Sales of Public Sector Debt to the Non-bank Private Sector
- + the increase in Banks' Lending in Sterling to the Private Sector
- − External Finance of the Public and Banking Sectors
- − the Increase in the Banks' Non-deposit Liabilities
- = the Change in Sterling M3.

(These accounting relationships are set out in detail in Table 7.3 of *Financial Statistics*).

This identity reflects the fact that the PSBR provides a rough measure of the public sector's need for finance—though it is not a complete measure of the total amount that the public sector has to borrow: by convention the financing of the Exchange Equalisation Account is excluded as is the refinancing or repayment of official debt. That part which cannot be financed by the non-bank private or overseas sectors has to be financed, along with private sector demand for credit, from the banks.

It is, however, wrong to conclude from this that there is a simple arithmetical relationship between the PSBR and the money stock. There is certainly not a one-for-one relationship such that changes in the PSBR bring about changes of the same size in £M3. Table 4.1 shows the absence of any close link year by year.

TABLE 4.1   THE PSBR AND THE GROWTH OF £M3

| | PSBR | | Growth of |
	£bn	% of GDP at market prices	£M3 (%)[a]
1972–73	2.5	3.8	25.2
1973–74	4.4	6.1	24.0
1974–75	7.9	9.1	8.4
1975–76	10.6	9.8	6.9
1976–77	8.5	6.8	8.4
1977–78	5.5	3.8	14.5

[a] Growth of seasonally adjusted stock between the ends of successive first quarters.

Source Financial Statistics, Tables 7.1 and 7.3, Economic Trends.

The main explanation for the absence of a simple relationship is that things which change the PSBR also affect most of the other elements in the conventional table shown on p. 137. Furthermore, in the short to the medium term at least, the composition of the PSBR can be as important—or more important—than its size. The same nominal PSBR made up of high expenditure and high taxation will have a different effect on monetary conditions from one made up of low expenditure and low taxation. And differing compositions of the tax and expenditure sides of the public sector's accounts will feed through in different ways to the money supply.

This suggests that the best way to trace the effects on the stock of money of the factors which go to make up PSBRs of various size and composition might be by the use of a sophisticated structural model. We develop the argument in this paper in terms of the relationships in the Treasury model, and we present the results of simulations on the model. The model of the financial sector is fairly new and we are still examining its properties. Research is continuing into all important aspects of the complete model; most importantly in the present context into the transmission mechanism between the monetary and income/expenditure components. The results on which this paper draws are therefore of a preliminary nature, though we do of course believe that the size and direction of the various effects are plausible.

Alternative Models

The paper focuses on the association between the PSBR and the monetary aggregates over the short to medium term. There are also two additional ways of looking at the association which might be mentioned here.

First there is the simple textbook theory of the money supply. This relates the outstanding stock of bank deposits to the quantity of reserve assets available to the banking system and the legal reserve ratio. Provided the banks' desired reserve asset holdings are below the legal minimum, an increase in the supply of reserve assets to the banks will increase the supply of bank deposits by a multiple equal to the reciprocal of the reserve ratio. If reserve assets are the residual source of finance for the government, their supply is given by the PSBR minus the supply of other forms of public sector debt. If cash is not a reserve asset, and assuming some simple rule for the demand for cash by the banks, the supply of cash and bank deposits combine to imply a money supply function in terms of the PSBR, the legal reserve ratio, the supply of non-reserve asset public sector debt instruments and the supply of cash. If cash is the reserve asset, a similar relationship can be obtained by assuming that the demand for cash by the non-bank private sector is rigidly linked to their holdings of bank deposits.

This model has been criticised by Tobin[3] as being too mechanistic. In addition it clearly ignores the possibility that reserve assets may be acquired by the overseas sector. Also relevant in the UK context is the criticism that it does not describe the UK banking system. Banks hold reserve assets in excess of the legal minimum and to a degree that varies over time. Non-banks exchange reserve assets with banks in response to movements in interest rate differentials, and the discount market can expand the supply of reserve assets with no change in public sector asset supplies. Given these institutional arrangements a simple linear model of money supply determination would seem to be inappropriate.

Secondly it is sometimes argued that an entirely bond-financed increase in the PSBR is impossible. If this is so, part of any increase in the PSBR has to be financed by expanding money and thus the relationship between the PSBR and monetary growth must be positive. The argument is based on the familiar hypothesis that the stock demand for bonds is a function of the level of interest rates. To persuade investors to accept a continuing shift in the balance of their portfolios away from money and towards bonds requires a continuing rise in interest rates. But this will be anticipated by rational speculators, creating expected capital losses and thus a *fall* in the demand for bonds. The situation is unstable and so the bond-financed increase in the PSBR is impossible.

This analysis bears a close resemblance to the arguments in the fiscal policy literature that a bond-financed increase in the public sector deficit could be unstable in practice as a result of different wealth and interest rate effects in the money and goods markets. It extends the argument to include the effect of changes in interest rates on wealth, and, more importantly, by allowing for the possibility of a collapse in the market in long-term fixed interest bonds. Ultimately, of course, whether the system is unstable can only be resolved by empirical work. Our analysis does not deal explicitly with this issue and in the simulations reported later in the paper we assume unchanged interest rates. While we would recognise that the scope for continually changing the structure of private sector portfolios is limited we are concerned in this paper with the short and medium terms over which changes in portfolio structure are possible.

II. THE DETERMINATION OF £M3

This section discusses the determinants of £M3 and how they are handled in the Treasury model. £M3 comprises notes and coin in circulation with the non-bank private sector and sterling bank deposits held by both the public sector and the non-bank private sector. Within bank deposits it is useful to distinguish 'retail' deposits which offer a zero rate of return or one related to base rate, and 'wholesale' deposits, including certificates of deposit (CDs), which offer a market-related rate of return. The narrow definition of money, M1, comprises notes and coin and sterling sight deposits held by the non-bank private sector.

Demand, Supply and Market Clearing

The stock of £M3 is determined by the interaction of demand and supply. All general references to the quantity of money will be in terms of the *stock*. The word *supply* will be used only in the sense of supply as opposed to demand. The main factors which influence the demand for money by the non-bank private sector are real income, financial net wealth, prices and interest rates. Expected capital gains or losses on fixed interest securities such as gilts should, of course, be included in the rate of return on those assets. Real income is a major determinant of the transactions demand for money and of bank lending. Both financial net wealth and bank lending have a major influence on the asset demand for money, but one would expect to find a relatively stronger link between

M1 and real income than between M1 and wealth. Prices act as numeraire. It is mainly the level of interest rates which is relevant to the demand for M1 because it represents the yield forgone by not holding interest-bearing assets and most of M1 is non-interest-bearing. As well as the level, the structure of interest rates is relevant to the demand for £M3, because much of £M3 is interest-bearing.

Banks supply all the components of £M3 except notes and coin which are supplied by the Bank of England and the Royal Mint. The latter are supplied on demand so that there is no independent supply side determinant. The components of £M3 supplied by banks can be ranged from liabilities such as sight deposits which are also supplied on demand, to liabilities such as CDs, the supply of which is a function of balance sheet considerations and interest rates. In the latter case the market clears through changes in interest rates. Between the two extremes are retail time deposits, other interest-bearing sight deposits, and wholesale deposits other than CDs. In these cases the banks supply however much is demanded at the ruling interest rate, but they change the interest rate and hence quantity supplied in response to changes in market rates and balance sheet considerations. (The rate on other wholesale deposits changes daily or at shorter intervals.)[4]

Thus, apart from interest rates, the main factor affecting the supply of £M3 is the structure of banks' balance sheets. This in turn is affected by many things, including the amount of bank lending, the operations of the Bank of England in the gilt-edged and money markets (these may also affect the stock of £M3 through changing interest rates), the SSD scheme in so far as it is a binding constraint, and variations in the calls for special deposits.

Although the market for £M3 always clears in the sense described above, there are three reasons why it can be said that it is not generally in equilibrium: non-clearing of other financial markets, non-clearing of non-financial markets, and lagged adjustment. The credit market is probably the most obvious case of a potentially non-clearing financial market. Before the introduction of Competition and Credit Control (CCC) in 1971, bank lending was subject to quantitative restrictions and, particularly in the case of lending to persons, the banks frequently had to resort to non-price rationing. Since 1973 the SSD scheme has occasionally been imposed in order to achieve control over banks' interest-bearing eligible liabilities in part by influencing the volume of bank lending. Although the extent of its influence through this channel is debatable, it is probably the case that some degree of non-market clearing has been induced. In so far as the credit market fails to clear—

and in particular in so far as the non-bank private sector goes short—
the demand for £M3 and other financial assets is affected. Excess
demand for credit by the non-banks implies that, *ceteris paribus*, their
total liabilities are below desired levels and thus asset demands
conditional on the available supply of credit are less than if there had
been no excess demand. It would be wrong, however, to view credit
rationing as affecting money solely through the demand side. Supply-
side effects are of course being observed in so far as banks' interest rates
and/or their CD issues change.

Spill-over effects from non-clearing of non-financial markets also
influence the stock of £M3. Non-clearing of the labour market, for
example, is likely to affect, *inter alia*, personal incomes and saving and
hence the demand for both credit and money. Likewise non-clearing of
the market for capital goods is likely to affect company net saving, etc.

Neither the demand for £M3 nor its supply adjust instantaneously to
changes in their determinants because of the existence of adjustment
costs, perception lags and expectational effects. Thus in general the
stock of £M3 would not be in long-run equilibrium even in the absence
of non-market clearing in other markets and without anyone in the
market going short. Dynamic disequilibrium of this sort probably also
affects other variables in the economy, including real expenditure.[5]

The Treasury Model

The Treasury model comprises, for the purposes of this paper, the
income-expenditure model which is described in the technical manual[6]
and the domestic monetary and external capital flows models described
in a recent working paper.[7] The model of the financial sector comple-
ments the income-expenditure model with a set of equations describing
monetary flows. Given the exchange rate and domestic monetary
variables, the income-expenditure sector determines the current price
surpluses and deficits of the main sectors of the economy. The models of
the domestic monetary system and external capital flows allocate these
surpluses across the financial markets. In the process, the exchange rate
and interest rates can be determined if intervention policy and a
monetary target are specified and they of course feed back on to
expenditure decisions. Interaction between the models produces a fully
consistent solution of both real and financial markets.

The Treasury model is therefore a structural model of the expenditure
and financial relationships which are explicitly identified. It differs from

a reduced form model, such as those of the St Louis type, which attempt to explain nominal incomes and prices directly in terms of the stock of money and perhaps other variables such as fiscal policy. A structural model is definitely preferable when the objective is to explore the channels which link the PSBR and £M3.

The determination of £M3 in the Treasury model starts from the net financial saving decisions of the various sectors of the economy. The identity which relates these sectoral surpluses and deficits is as follows:

$$\text{Private sector financial surplus} = \text{Public sector financial deficit} + \text{Overseas sector financial deficit}$$

The public sector deficit is not quite equal to the PSBR since the latter includes certain financial transactions, such as net lending to the private sector (e.g. by local authorities for house purchase) and the difference between accruals and receipts of the revenues, but again for expositional purposes this distinction can be ignored. Similarly, the overseas sector deficit is generally, though not always, equal to the balance of payments current account surplus. Thus after allowing for the effects of changes in long-term interest rates on the market value of existing fixed-interest securities, the PSBR and the current account surplus together measure changes in private sector financial net wealth:

$$\text{Change in private sector net wealth} = \text{PSBR} + \text{Current account surplus} + \text{Asset revaluation effects}$$

This is an identity, not a behavioural relationship. The PSBR and the current account surplus do not determine the private sector surplus. Rather, all three are affected by the same factors, such as fiscal policy, the growth in world trade and so on. Asset revaluations directly affect net wealth, but not necessarily on a one-for-one basis since they may also affect the other two items on the right-hand side of the identity.

Demand and Supply in the Treasury Model

The demand for money is not determined directly as a function of real income, wealth, prices and interest rates in the Treasury model. It is identified indirectly, essentially as the result of decisions by the non-bank private sector on the accumulation of financial net wealth (as embodied in the financial surplus), bank lending and investment in non-monetary assets such as gilts. The advantage of modelling it this way round is that the speculative factors which influence the demand for bonds, and net wealth which affects the demand for all assets but which is often not included explicitly in direct money demand functions, influence the demand for money.

The indirect demand for money is derived from the non-bank private sector's budget identity as the difference between total liabilities (financial net wealth, sterling bank lending to the private sector, net foreign currency liabilities, and others including overseas sterling liabilities) and non-money assets (gilts, National Savings, Certificates of Tax Deposit, local authority short-term debt and Treasury bills). Taking liabilities first, the change in financial net wealth is described above. Net foreign currency liabilities and miscellaneous liabilities are handled judgementally in the main, although some flows on balance of payments capital account directly affect the latter. Sterling bank lending in real terms is mainly demand determined, depending on real incomes (with an elasticity of rather less than unity), and interest rates. However, bank lending to the personal sector also reflects supply factors and the possibility of credit rationing: demand factors are given a weight of around two-thirds in the determination of the stock of lending to persons under present circumstances.

Turning to non-money assets, holdings of gilts are related with a long-run elasticity of almost unity to total asset holdings and the difference between the rate of return on gilts, measured by the yield on twenty-year gilts (the 'long rate') plus expected capital gains, and the rate on competing (mainly short-term) assets, measured by the three-month interbank rate (the 'short rate'). Inflows into National Savings depend on the personal sector financial surplus, and Certificates of Tax Deposit are exogenous to the model. Holdings of these three assets are deducted from total asset holdings to yield holdings of liquid assets, which are then allocated between local authority short-term debt, Treasury bills and £M3.

The allocation process is complicated. Relative holdings of Treasury bills, of 'parallel money' (comprising local authority temporary debt and CDs), and sterling retail deposits depend on the Treasury bill rate, the 'short rate' and the rate on bank deposits. Parallel money has to be broken down further, because holdings of LA temporary debt are not in £M3 but CDs are. This is difficult because they are assumed in the model to be perfect substitutes in non-bank portfolios and the rates on them are both assumed to equal the 'short rate'. The allocation depends on the total supply of LA temporary debt and the portfolio behaviour of the banks. A further disaggregation of retail deposits into time and sight deposits is necessary in order to identify M1 separately.

It was noted above (pp. 140–141) that the banks will supply sight deposits and retail time deposits in the quantities demanded without changing the interest rate paid on these deposits. The banks have complete discretion over the CD issue, however, and the supply of this item—and hence £M3—will reflect balance sheet considerations. Given the size of balance sheet items such as retail deposits, bank lending, required reserve asset holdings and special deposits, over which they have relatively little discretion, at least in the short run, the CD issue is determined in the model by the cost to the banks of such issues (defined as the CD rate plus an allowance for the cost of holding the reserve assets, etc., required to back them) relative to the rates of return on those assets such as LA deposits, gilts, excess reserve assets, and net foreign currency assets, that they choose to hold and the quantities of those assets over which they have less discretion—retail deposits, bank lending, required reserve holdings, special deposits, etc.

Since CDs are included in the stock of £M3 these portfolio considerations imply an independent supply side influence on £M3. In addition, the institutional arrangements whereby the banks can increase their holdings of reserve assets independently of the outstanding stock of Treasury bills means that the supply of money cannot be characterised in terms of a simple quotient of the supply of reserve assets and the reserve ratio. For example, a special deposit call (equivalent to an increase in the legal minimum reserve ratio) could *increase* the supply of £M3 in the short term if the banks respond by financing the purchase of reserve assets from non-banks by issuing CDs. For this reason the Treasury model differs from the 'textbook' models of the money supply process used in the US and elsewhere.

In principle it should be possible to trace the consequences for £M3 of an external shock to the system, such as one which changes the PSBR, through separate demand and supply channels. It would then be possible to assess the relative importance of demand and supply side forces, and to investigate how the various terms in the conventional identity respond to demand side changes. However, the way in which the model is set up at the moment does not permit this. In particular, as noted above, bank lending is a mixture of demand and supply side factors.

The way that we proceed is to investigate what happens to the stock of £M3 when the PSBR changes and interest rates are fixed, and for simplicity we shall refer from now on to the observed changes in £M3 as being changes in the 'demand' for £M3. This is not strictly the demand for £M3, partly because of the treatment of bank lending, and partly because CDs are determined by banks' balance sheet considerations. This is not the only way to run the model. An alternative method would be to solve it with interest rates clearing the markets for financial assets, and with asset quantities such as £M3 or total gilts sales fixed. Where policy is defined by a monetary target it would be most realistic for many policy simulations to constrain the growth of £M3 to the target.

Some idea of the 'demand' function for £M3 that is implicit in the Treasury model can be obtained by simulating the financial sectors alone. Table 4.2 shows the effects on £M3 of changes in financial net wealth, real incomes, prices, and in interest rates, holding all the other variables constant, after 1,4,8 and 12 quarters. The net wealth change is assumed to result from an increase in the personal sector financial surplus in the first quarter and not from a change in the long rate. The various real income and price variables in the model are assumed to change by the same proportionate amounts in relevant simulations. The exchange rate is treated like any other price.

TABLE 4.2   THE IMPLICIT 'DEMAND' FOR £M3
(percentage changes in £M3 following 1 per cent changes in determinants)

Quarter	Financial net wealth	Real incomes	Prices	Long[a] rate	Treasury bill rate
1	0.76	−0.18	0.63	−0.4	+0.1
4	0.48	0.19	0.46	−1.0	−0.3
8	0.47	0.17	0.53	−1.3	−0.6
12	0.48	0.17	0.55	−1.5	−0.5

[a] Includes a wealth effect in so far as a rise in the long rate affects the market value of existing gilts.

Various points need to be noted about these figures. First, the effects of interest rate changes in the current version of the monetary sector of the model differ somewhat from those reported in the recent working paper. Various changes have been made since the working paper in the light of recent experience gained in using the model for forecasting and simulation, and although they are not described in detail here the nature of the more important changes is described in Appendix 1. The net effect of them is to reduce the interest rate elasticities somewhat, and also the net wealth elasticity (which was not reported in the working paper).

Secondly, care is needed in interpreting the size of the price, income and net wealth elasticities. Apart from a high initial net wealth elasticity, all are significantly less than unity, but this in itself does not mean that £M3 is in any sense an inferior asset in the model. Confusion can arise because, whereas in most empirical work the demand for money is typically related to income, prices and interest rates, our analysis separates the wealth and income/price effects. Net financial wealth is modelled explicitly in the Treasury model; this is important in the present context since the focus of our attention in this paper is the relationship between the PSBR and £M3. However, it is possible to gain some insight into the implied parameters of a 'standard' demand for money function by considering jointly pairs of elasticities in Table 4.2. Thus by adding the price and net wealth elasticities we can obtain a 'conventional' price elasticity, assuming a long-run unit elasticity between nominal wealth and prices, which after three years is unity. Adding the real income and net wealth elasticities and making the same type of assumption yields a 'conventional' real income elasticity of about two-thirds after three years.[8]

The 'conventional' price elasticity calculated in this way is consistent with most theoretical work on the demand for money and with much empirical work. The real income elasticity is, however, somewhat less than implied by some recent empirical studies of the demand for £M3, particularly those covering the period since the introduction of Competition and Credit Control in 1971.[9] But one would perhaps expect the structural approach to yield more reliable answers than simple reduced-form functions, particularly over this period.

Frequently studies of the demand for money include just one interest rate or, generally with wider aggregates, an interest rate differential, and it is thus difficult to compare the semi-elasticities in Table 4.2 with those in published work. But two relevant points should be made in this context. First, in order to compare the figures in Table 4.2 with those in studies which include only the long rate, such as the Hendry and Mizon study, it is important to remember that short rates have in the past fluctuated more widely than long rates, and therefore that it is probably necessary to add a multiple (say 2) of the short-rate effect to the long-rate effect to obtain comparable semi-elasticities. Secondly, it must be remembered that net *financial* wealth might be expected to be related to interest rates, but of course the *sign* of the effect, which most studies solve out, depends on the extent to which changes in interest rates accompany changes in the rates of return on real assets. The situation is further complicated by the fact that the long-rate effects quoted in Table 4.2 include a wealth

effect resulting from the effect of changes in the long rate on the market
value of existing gilts.

III. THE PSBR AND £M3

When interest rates are constant, the major determinants of the demand
for money are private financial net wealth, real income and prices. In this
section we consider the relationship between the PSBR and the demand
for £M3 operating through these variables.

Taking net wealth first, changes in the PSBR are likely to be
associated with changes in the private sector surplus, because of the *ex
post* identity which links them along with the current account surplus
and asset revaluation effects (which can be ignored in the present context
because we are assuming unchanged interest rates). It is very unlikely
that the current balance will change in the short term in such a way that
it exactly offsets the changes in the PSBR and there is no change in the
private sector surplus. In the very long run it might be argued that if the
rates of inflation and economic growth could be considered as given the
offset would be exactly one-for-one. But in the four-year period covered
by the simulations one would in practice expect changes in the PSBR to
be associated with changes in the private sector surplus.

It is one thing to say that there is an association, quite another that it is
systematic. Consider two cases, one where exports rise autonomously
and the other where private consumption rises. In both cases the PSBR
will fall because of the higher level of activity. But in the former case the
current balance will improve so that the fall in the private sector
financial surplus will be less than the fall in the PSBR—indeed the
private surplus would probably rise. In the latter case the current surplus
will fall, and the fall in the private sector financial surplus will be greater
than the fall in the PSBR. Thus the relationship between the PSBR and
private sector financial net wealth and hence the demand for money is
variable, and depends on the nature of the particular shock that is
applied to the system

A similar conclusion emerges from a consideration of the association
between the PSBR and £M3 through real incomes and prices, at least in
the short term. Thus an increase in indirect taxation causes a larger
increase in nominal income than an increase in income tax or public
expenditure cuts, because of the increase in prices which they bring
about. One would therefore expect a smaller reduction in the demand

for money, especially for M1, per unit of PSBR, when indirect taxes are increased.

In the remainder of this section we describe simulations on the Treasury model designed to quantify the relationship between changes in the PSBR and the money stock, primarily £M3 but to a lesser extent also M1. The determination of M1 in the model is, we believe, less reliable than that of £M3, but the results are still of some interest. Five different ways in which the PSBR might be reduced are examined, two autonomous changes in expenditure and three fiscal policy changes:

(1) an increase in consumers' expenditure;
(2) an increase in exports of goods and services;
(3) an increase in income tax;
(4) an increase in VAT;
(5) a reduction in general government expenditure on procurement of goods and services.

The simulations show that the size and even direction of the change in the money stock associated with a given change in the PSBR depend upon the source of the change in the PSBR. Not surprisingly, moreover, the results also depend on what is assumed about the behaviour of the exchange rate. Two alternative assumptions, a fixed exchange rate and a freely floating rate, were used for each change, making ten simulations in all. Under the floating rate assumption, the exchange rate moves so as to clear the foreign exchange market. It does this in the short term by changing the expected return on holding sterling and hence inducing short-term capital flows to offset the surplus or deficit on other balance of payments transactions. The expected return on holding sterling depends in part on expected changes in the exchange rate which are assumed to depend partly on changes in the money stock. Hence monetary growth influences the exchange rate through expectations. In the longer term the current account will respond to the change in the exchange rate, and offsetting short-term capital flows will diminish. Over a period as long as four years it is more realistic to assume that the rate will float rather than be fixed, and we would therefore put more emphasis on the results of the floating rate case.

The simulation results should be treated cautiously since the point estimates quoted are subject to large margins of error. They incorporate a certain amount of judgemental adjustment of the model because the objective was to use the model to obtain our best estimates of the relationships in which we were interested and not to explore the properties of the model itself.[10] Adjustments were only made, however, to correct known weaknesses of specification and not to obtain particular results. They were usually made at the input rather than the output stage, so that they interact in a fully consistent way with the rest of the model. All of the changes simulated were constrained to produce a reduction in the PSBR in the first year of £1000 millions. Consequently some of the changes are more realistic than others. The size of the two autonomous changes in expenditure is particularly unrealistic. The increase in consumers' expenditure is approximately 3 per cent *ex ante* and the increase in exports over 6 per cent *ex ante* in the fixed exchange rate case and about 5 per cent *ex ante* in the floating rate case. The two tax changes, on the other hand, are by no means unrealistic and every attempt has been made to model accurately such features as delays between payment of the tax by the income recipient or consumer and its receipt by the central government. The main element of unrealism attaching to the reduction in general government procurement expenditure is the assumption that it can take place with full effect from the beginning of year 1. In practice expenditure changes have to be planned well in advance. For present purposes, however, these problems are unimportant.

The simulations were carried out on a projection over four years. The underlying projection, which we shall refer to as the base, was specially constructed for this exercise. It is stylised, and is not intended to be a prediction of the future course of events. This probably does not greatly affect the results of the present exercise.

Any exercise involving a large economic model requires decisions about the assumptions on which the model is to be operated. The choice of assumptions can affect the results significantly. The nature of this choice is usually whether to specify certain variables as exogenous or endogenous and how to specify government policy. Often these two types of choice amount to the same thing. We have already mentioned two of the more important assumptions: for the exchange rate there are two alternative assumptions, of a fixed and a floating rate; and nominal interest rates are assumed to be unaffected by the change in the PSBR — they remain at the values they took in the base. A consequence of the second of these is that there are assumed to be no revaluations of holdings of gilts and no expectations of revaluations. Another consequence is that real interest rates change as a result of the initial change. This is not something which we would expect to obtain indefinitely: some reversal of real interest rates towards their base level seems a more sensible long-run property. The simulations should therefore be regarded as illustrating short- and medium-term behaviour, and inferences about the long term should not be drawn from them.

Average money earnings in the private sector are assumed to be freely determined by the equation in the model and not constrained by incomes policy. Average earnings in the public sector are assumed to move in line with those in the private sector. Two other assumptions which are particularly important for movements in the PSBR relate to the behaviour of local authority rates and nationalised industry prices. The former are assumed to respond freely to changes in local authority expenditure and non-rate income. Nationalised industry prices are assumed to react to changes in their costs but in the first year only half the change in costs is assumed to be passed into prices because of administrative lags and other constraints. Thereafter cost changes are fully reflected in prices. It is also assumed that all income tax allowances and bands, and specific indirect taxes, are indexed to the rate of retail price inflation. The volume of public expenditure on goods and services and capital investment is assumed to be exogenous.

The simulations are summarised in Tables 4.3 and 4.4 and reported in more detail in the tables in Appendix 2. The first simulation involves an exogenous increase in consumers' expenditure at unchanged levels of real income and wealth. Domestic output as measured by real GDP rises to meet this increase in demand, but a substantial proportion is satisfied by higher imports and so the current account of the balance of payments deteriorates. Prices rise because the higher level of activity induces an increase in average money earnings which are determined by an equation which is essentially an expectations-augmented Phillips curve. Effectively the simulation involves a switch by the private sector out of financial assets into consumer goods. We assume that it is a voluntary switch which is fully anticipated by financial markets, so that it does not affect inflationary expectations or desired real wages at any given pressure of demand. It is reflected in the large reduction in the private sector financial surplus and net financial wealth. The PSBR is reduced not only because increased consumption means higher indirect tax receipts but also because the second-round increase in incomes and activity generates higher tax receipts of all types, income and indirect, and lower social security payments, which more than offset the increase in value of public expenditure resulting from higher public sector earnings and procurement prices.

The effects described in the previous paragraph can be seen in Table 4.3, which also illustrates the significance of the exchange rate assumption. With a fixed exchange rate there is a sustained deterioration

TABLE 4.3   SUMMARY OF THE EFFECTS ON ACTIVITY, PRICES, AND SECTORAL FINANCIAL BALANCES DIFFERENCES FROM BASE

	Fixed exchange rate							Floating exchange rate							
	Real GDP % of base	GDP prices % of base	Nominal GDP % of base	Current balance (£m)	Private sector surplus (£m)	Public sector deficit (£m)	PSBR (£m)	Real GDP % of base	GDP prices % of base	Nominal GDP % of base	Current balance (£m)	Private sector surplus (£m)	Public sector deficit (£m)	PSBR (£m)	Exchange Rate % of base
Consumers' expenditure															
Year 1	1.7	-0.1	1.7	-1240	-2360	-1120	-1000	2.0	-0.3	1.9	-1550	-2700	-1160	-1000	-2.9
Year 2	1.5	0.4	2.0	-1830	-3690	-1860	-1820	2.3	1.0	3.4	-1350	-3420	-2110	-1980	-4.9
Year 3	1.0	0.9	2.1	-1720	-3820	-2110	-2070	2.1	2.3	4.6	-740	-3360	-2690	-2500	-5.7
Year 4	0.7	1.3	2.2	-1580	-4020	-2470	-2400	2.0	3.8	5.9	-110	-3140	-3150	-2860	-7.4
Exports															
Year 1	2.7	-0.4	2.2	2570	1470	-1100	-1000	1.4	-0.1	1.3	2140	1120	-1000	-1000	9.2
Year 2	3.1	0.2	3.2	3050	880	-2180	-2090	0.6	-1.4	-0.7	180	-1130	-1260	-1360	10.5
Year 3	2.8	1.1	3.9	4210	1750	-2500	-2390	-0.1	-2.3	-2.2	390	-380	-690	-890	13.1
Year 4	2.5	2.0	4.5	5350	2850	-2570	-2400	-0.3	-3.6	-3.8	-340	-1070	-610	-850	14.9
Income tax															
Year 1	-0.2	0.1	-0.2	250	-860	-1120	-1000	-0.3	0.1	-0.2	280	-830	-1110	-1000	0.7
Year 2	-0.5	0.6	0.1	490	-790	-1290	-1250	-0.6	0.4	-0.2	320	-920	-1240	-1220	1.2
Year 3	-0.6	1.0	0.3	510	-650	-1180	-1140	-0.8	0.6	-0.2	190	-850	-1050	-1040	1.6
Year 4	-0.7	1.1	0.4	370	-620	-1010	-990	-0.9	0.5	-0.4	-150	-950	-800	-830	1.8
VAT															
Year 1	-0.9	2.0	1.0	760	-930	-1710	-1000	-1.0	1.9	0.9	770	-860	-1650	-1000	1.5
Year 2	-1.4	3.1	1.7	1100	-270	-1410	-1250	-1.6	2.7	1.0	690	-580	-1300	-1180	1.9
Year 3	-1.6	3.8	2.2	940	—	-1000	-810	-1.9	3.0	1.1	400	-340	-780	-650	2.0
Year 4	-1.7	4.2	2.4	630	-230	-940	-750	-2.0	3.0	1.0	-100	-730	-670	-550	2.3
General government procurement															
Year 1	-0.8	-0.1	-0.8	410	-560	-960	-1000	-0.8	—	-0.8	460	-500	-960	-1000	1.3
Year 2	-0.8	-0.3	-1.1	700	-180	-880	-900	-1.0	-0.5	-1.5	360	-430	-770	-840	2.3
Year 3	-0.6	-0.6	-1.2	790	-370	-1140	-1180	-1.1	-1.1	-2.2	170	-730	-860	-960	3.0
Year 4	-0.5	-0.8	-1.3	910	-590	-1480	-1530	-1.0	-1.8	-2.8	90	-1180	-1030	-1170	3.9

in the current balance, while with a freely floating rate the exchange rate falls, moderating the deterioration towards the end of the simulation period. The fall in the exchange rate has other implications, especially larger increases in both real GDP and prices.

The effects of the increase in consumption on the components of the non-bank private sector balance sheet are shown in Table 4.4. As explained above, the change in money stock is largely the result of demand side influences. The first column in each panel shows the change from the base run in the level of non-bank private sector net financial wealth. It can be obtained by cumulating the changes in financial surplus shown in Table 4.3. Given the switch out of financial assets into consumer goods the simulation provides some indication of which financial asset holdings are reduced. The overall extent to which this has to occur is lessened by an increase in borrowing from banks. The increase in bank borrowing arises from the higher level of activity and prices. In the fixed exchange rate case holdings of public sector debt and £M3 fall by roughly equal amounts, except in the first two years, when £M3 falls more. As expected, M1, which is influenced more by transactions than by the level of wealth, falls to a lesser extent than £M3. In the floating rate case £M3 falls less than in the fixed rate case because the reduction in wealth is less and the increase in bank borrowing and capital inflows is greater.

In some ways the second simulation, an exogenous increase in exports, which may be visualised as a sudden improvement in the UK's non-price competitiveness, is very similar to the first. In the fixed exchange rate case an exogenous increase in expenditure increases domestic output and prices and reduces the PSBR. The crucial difference is that the current balance improves and private sector wealth rises rather than the current balance deteriorating and private sector wealth falling. Thus the counterpart to the fall in the public sector deficit and the PSBR is an increase in the deficit of the overseas sector and not a fall in the private sector surplus. Net finanical wealth rises and contributes to the large increase in gross financial wealth which also reflects large external capital inflows. The size of the inflows depends crucially on our assumption that speculators expect some increase in the exchange rate. For these reasons £M3 rises despite the reduction in the PSBR. Much of the increase in private sector wealth is held in the form of money. The demand for money also rises because of an increase in real incomes and prices.

The picture is very different with a floating exchange rate. A large appreciation of the exchange rate occurs which helps to reduce prices.

TABLE 4.4 SUMMARY OF THE EFFECTS ON THE NON-BANK

	Fixed exchange rate							
	Net financial wealth (£m)[b]	*Bank loans* (£m)	*Public sector debt* (£m)	*Overseas assets (net* (£m)	*Timing adj etc* (£m)	*£M3* (£m)	*£M3* % of base	*£M3 Velocity* % of base
Consumers' expenditure								
End Year 1	−2360(−3.9)	130	−960	−30	120	−1120	−2.0	3.6
End Year 2	−6050(−8.8)	610	−2400	0	150	−2890	−4.5	6.4
End Year 3	−9870(−13.0)	750	−4330	90	180	−4700	−6.6	8.9
End Year 4	−13890(−16.8)	870	−6540	200	220	−6460	−8.2	11.0
Exports								
End Year 1	1470(2.4)	40	830	−1560	100	2350	4.1	−0.8
End Year 2	2370(3.4)	850	2330	−2920	180	3990	6.3	−2.3
End Year 3	4120(5.4)	1330	3640	−3200	260	5270	7.4	−2.7
End Year 4	6970(8.4)	1780	5040	−2460	370	6530	8.3	−2.9
Income tax								
End Year 1	−860(−1.4)	60	−230	−30	120	−420	−0.7	0.6
End Year 2	−1660(−2.4)	180	−530	−50	150	−760	−1.2	1.5
End Year 3	−2310(−3.1)	270	−770	−60	180	−1040	−1.5	1.9
End Year 4	−2940(−3.6)	320	−1030	−120	170	−1290	−1.6	2.2
VAT								
End Year 1	−930(−1.5)	540	130	60	690	110	0.2	0.9
End Year 2	−1200(−1.7)	840	130	260	810	60	0.1	1.9
End Year 3	−1190(−1.6)	1100	240	490	930	110	0.2	2.2
End Year 4	−1430(−1.7)	1350	250	610	1040	110	0.1	2.4
General government procurement								
End Year 1	−560(−0.9)	−70	−160	−100	−30	−400	−0.7	−0.3
End Year 2	−740(−1.1)	−310	−340	−280	−60	−490	−0.8	−0.3
End Year 3	−1110(−1.5)	−430	−510	−460	−70	−650	−0.9	−0.3
End Year 4	−1710(−2.1)	−530	−790	−610	−100	−930	−1.2	−0.1

All columns show changes in stocks at end-period. The change in the stock of net financial wealth shown in the first column of each panel is obtained by cumulating the changes in the private sector financial surpluses shown in Table 4.3. All numbers are rounded and therefore components may not sum to totals.

[a] Net financial wealth = public sector debt + overseas assets (net) + £M3- bank loans − timing adjustments etc.
[b] As per cent of base in brackets.

PRIVATE SECTOR BALANCE SHEET^a: DIFFERENCES FROM BASE

M1	Net financial wealth ($£m$)^b	Bank loans ($£m$)	Public sector debt ($£m$)	Overseas assets (net) ($£m$)	Timing adj etc ($£m$)	$£M3$ ($£m$)	$£M3$	$£M3$ Velocity	M1
% of base							% of base	% of base	% of base
-0.4	-2700(-4.5)	410	-760	-970	150	-410	-0.7	3.0	0.6
-1.0	-6120(-8.9)	1440	-1470	-1800	240	-1170	-1.8	5.6	1.0
-1.7	-9480(-12.5)	2320	-2500	-2280	360	-2030	-2.8	7.9	1.4
-2.3	-12620(-15.3)	3410	-3500	-2390	530	-2800	-3.5	10.2	2.1
1.8	1120(1.9)	-730	-250	1330	20	-680	-1.2	1.8	-1.5
2.9	-10(-0.0)	-1060	-900	1450	-40	-1670	-2.6	1.2	-2.6
3.7	-390(-0.5)	-2130	-1700	1740	-170	-2740	-3.8	0.9	-3.9
4.5	-1460(-1.8)	-3180	-2720	1610	-290	-3820	-4.9	0.4	-5.0
-0.2	-830(-1.4)	–	-310	180	110	-590	-1.0	0.8	-0.4
-0.2	-1750(-2.5)	-10	-790	380	130	-1220	-1.9	1.8	-0.7
	-2600(-3.4)	-100	-1300	510	130	-1780	-2.5	2.2	-0.9
-0.2	-3550(-4.3)	-250	-1830	430	100	-2300	-2.9	2.5	-1.2
0.8	-860(-1.4)	370	-50	480	640	-290	-0.5	1.2	0.3
1.3	-1440(-2.1)	480	-390	910	720	-760	-1.2	2.3	0.3
1.6	-1780(-2.4)	490	-610	1160	810	-1020	-1.4	2.6	0.3
0.7	-2510(-3.0)	490	-900	1110	890	-1340	-1.7	2.7	0.1
-0.4	-500(-0.8)	-180	-280	300	-40	-740	-1.3	0.1	-0.8
-0.6	-930(-1.3)	-640	-830	530	-90	-1350	-2.1	0.3	-1.5
-0.7	-1660(-2.2)	-1090	-1460	660	-150	-2100	-2.9	0.4	-2.2
-0.9	-2840(-3.4)	-1620	-2320	640	-230	-3000	-3.8	0.7	-3.0

Nevertheless there is a significant loss of external competitiveness which ultimately offsets the effect on domestic output and the current balance of the exogenous increase in exports. In the final year output is lower than in the base and the current balance not significantly different. Private sector net financial wealth is initially higher than in the base as in the fixed exchange rate case but in the second half of the simulation period it is lower because of a fall in personal saving.

Thus in the floating exchange rate case both M1 and £M3 are lower than in the base run. M1 is lower primarily because nominal GDP falls. £M3 is lower initially because the increase in private sector wealth is offset by reduced bank borrowing and increased investment overseas. This response is consistent with the proposition that with a floating exchange rate balance of payments flows have a neutral impact on the money supply. A potential increase in the money stock arising from the improvement in the current account is largely offset by capital outflows from the private sector which are inevitable if the foreign exchange market is to clear in the absence of government intervention.[11] Throughout most of the period, however, the balance of payments as a whole is exerting an expansionary influence on £M3. The fall in £M3 is due mainly to the reduction in bank borrowing and a reduction in net wealth which is the counterpart of an improvement in the position of the public sector.

The three remaining simulations involve reductions in the PSBR brought about by changes in government policy. All three changes lead to a reduction in domestic output and an improvement in the current balance in the fixed exchange rate case and an appreciation of the exchange rate in the floating rate case. The main interest lies not in their similarites, however, but in their different effects on prices. Both the tax increases generate higher prices while the cut in public expenditure generates lower prices. It is mainly these differential price effects which are responsible for differences in the effects on the 'demand' for money.

The income tax simulation is fairly straightforward. The initial impact of the change is on consumers' expenditure through a reduction in personal disposable incomes. Consumers prevent the reduction in real incomes being fully reflected in spending by reducing their saving. Nevertheless consumption and real GDP fall. The reduction in activity generates downward pressure on prices through the Phillips curve mechanism but this is offset by an attempt by wage bargainers to maintain the ratio of their after-tax earnings to gross earnings (the 'retention ratio' effect). Prices are therefore higher than in the base. The reduction in domestic demand improves the current balance. The PSBR is reduced by increased income tax receipts, though these are partially offset by the effects of a lower level of activity and higher prices. The main difference between the fixed and floating exchange rate cases is that in the latter the exchange rate appreciates, thus increasing the fall in output, and moderating the rise in prices and the improvement in the current account.

The increase in income tax reduces net financial wealth which on its own reduces the demand for money. In the fixed rate case nominal GDP rises, however, because the effect of the increase in prices is greater than that of the fall in activity. To finance this higher nominal level of activity bank borrowing rises. The net effect of these two influences is to reduce the demand for money, though the fall in the demand for M1 is small because transactions demand effects are relatively more important. In the floating rate case the fall in financial wealth is larger and nominal GDP falls. With both these factors tending to reduce the demand for money, £M3 and M1 fall more than in the fixed rate case.

There are important differences between the way in which increases in income tax and VAT operate. An increase in income tax reduces real personal disposable income by reducing nominal disposable income. An increase in VAT directly raises consumer prices, thereby reducing real gross and disposable income with unchanged nominal incomes. Per pound of additional revenue, the impact of VAT on real personal disposable income is greater than that of income tax, mainly because it is concentrated on a smaller tax base (consumption rather than income). In addition to reducing real disposable income the increase in prices in the VAT case reduces the real value of the existing stock of wealth. This wealth effect exerts a powerful negative influence on consumers' expenditure which reinforces the real income effect. The existence of the wealth effect is another reason why, for the same revenue, an increase in VAT has a larger effect on output than an increase in income tax.

Scaling the changes to a given first-year effect on the PSBR also heightens the difference between changes in VAT and income tax. First the extent to which the higher tax receipts *ex ante* are offset *ex post* by the second-round public sector expenditure and revenue flows is much larger for VAT. Secondly, the lag between the payment of tax at its point of incidence and its receipt by the central government is longer for VAT than for income tax. This receipts lag also introduces differences between the effects of the tax changes on financial surpluses/deficits and the PSBR. The former are defined on an accruals basis and thus effectively ignore the payments/receipts lags. The PSBR is obviously a cash transactions concept and so a timing or accruals adjustment is necessary when moving to the PSBR from the public sector deficit. Such a timing adjustment is similarly necessary for the private sector accounts and is shown separately in Table 4.4, and in the quarterly tables. When looking at changes in private sector financial wealth for the light they throw on changes in the money stock it is preferable to use a transactions or payments basis. In other words the 'net financial wealth' and 'timing adjustments' columns should be taken together.

On a transactions basis the fall in private sector wealth following an increase in VAT is relatively small, particularly in the fixed exchange rate case. Moreover, there is a large increase in bank borrowing because of the direct effect on prices and the value of transactions. For these reasons £M3 is more or less unchanged, and M1 rises significantly in the fixed rate case. With a floating exchange rate the increase in prices is less and the fall in activity larger, as is the reduction in financial wealth. Consequently £M3 falls, but not by as much as in the income tax and procurement cases, and M1 rises to only a small degree.

A reduction in general government expenditure on procurement of goods and services reduces domestic output and prices, through the Phillips curve mechanisms and in the floating rate case also through an appreciation of the rate. The import content of procurement expenditure is lower than that of consumers' expenditure and therefore the improvement in the current account for the same reduction in demand is less for procurement. Private sector wealth, activity and prices all fall and consequently the demand for £M3 and M1 falls. This happens under both exchange rate assumptions.

The main points to emerge from these simulations are as follows:

(1) As expected, the relationship between the PSBR and the 'demand' for money in the short to medium term is not simple, nor always of the same sign. As the implicit 'demand' function set out in Table 4.2 suggests, the nature of the relationship with £M3 in any given case depends on the signs and relative sizes of the effects on real incomes, prices and financial net wealth.

(2) While a reduction in the PSBR is frequently associated with a reduction in the 'demand' for money, under a fixed exchange rate money 'demand' increases in the exports and VAT cases, and under a floating rate M1 (but not £M3) increases in the consumers' expenditure and VAT cases.

(3) Increases in the 'demand' for M1 are generally, although not always, associated with increases in nominal income. One excep-

tion is the consumers' expenditure increase under a fixed exchange rate, where the very large fall in wealth offsets the impact of higher nominal income, reflecting the existence of an asset demand for M1 as well as the need to hold it for precautionary and transactions purposes. Another exception, although smaller in scale, is the increase in income tax under a fixed rate.

(4) Since £M3 velocity is the ratio of nominal income to £M3, it rises most when financial net wealth falls most (or rises least) relative to nominal income. The largest increases therefore occur when consumers' expenditure rises and the largest fall when exports rise with a fixed exchange rate. The relative changes in velocity do not reflect relative changes in monetary tightness in any meaningful sense, since we are assuming that the changes in portfolio composition are demand-determined at given interest rates.

The implications of these results for fiscal policy in a world where the main intermediate objective of policy is to achieve a stated monetary target are interesting. Assuming that the target refers to £M3, how policy should react to an exogenous change which alters the 'demand' for £M3 and the PSBR depends on the source of the exogenous change and the exchange rate regime. Under a fixed rate, any given fiscal policy instrument should be used in the opposite direction when a given change in the PSBR is due to a change in consumers' expenditure rather than when it is due to a change in exports. Hence, the PSBR should sometimes be planned to fall and sometimes to rise to keep £M3 on course with a particular fiscal instrument in the face of an exogenous PSBR shock.[12] With a floating rate, the simulations suggest that a similar change in fiscal policy and the PSBR is needed to keep to the monetary target, although one cannot generalise this result to include other kinds of exogenous shocks (e.g. a change in world commodity prices or the growth of earnings).

The potency of the three fiscal instruments in terms of their impact in the first few years on the 'demand' for £M3 per unit of PSBR varies considerably, especially under a fixed rate. Indeed, when the rate is fixed, VAT has so little short-run effect because prices are working in the opposite direction from financial wealth and real incomes, and their effects roughly balance out, that it would not be sensible to use it to maintain monetary control. However, under a floating rate the sign of the effects of the three instruments on the 'demand' for £M3 is the same. And even the orders of magnitude per unit of PSBR are not all that different, especially if account is taken of the fact that the PSBR effect changes over time and Tables 4.3 and 4.4 are standardised on the first-year PSBR. But policy-makers should not only look at the monetary impact per unit of PSBR. Perhaps more important is the monetary impact per unit of real output or prices. Here the three instruments are less similar in the first few years. Reducing the 'demand' for £M3 below what it would otherwise be is less expensive in terms of higher prices if procurement expenditure is cut than if taxes are raised; in terms of output, increasing VAT is the least attractive course, and there is not much difference between the other two.

IV. ENVOI

This paper has explored the relationship between the PSBR and the growth of the money stock. The preceding three paragraphs summarise the findings. We make two final comments here.

First, the empirical results were derived from the Treasury macro-economic model, and they are subject to a wide margin of error. Some of the crucial relationships in the model, such as that which determines nominal earnings, have been difficult to establish empirically and it would not surprise us if the true relationships were somewhat different. Although at any one time the model that we have is the best available to us, it is being continuously improved by better specification and new estimation. Furthermore, the results are sensitive to the policy assumptions and to the various adjustments that we have made to allow for known deficiencies in the model. Work on the model should reduce the need for the latter, and we are continuously improving our simulation methods in an attempt to produce the most realistic set of policy and behavioural assumptions. The estimated relationship between the PSBR and £M3 will therefore change over time, and any conclusions based on it must also alter.

Secondly, the relationship between the PSBR and monetary growth has been discussed in this paper on the assumptions of fixed interest rates, no changes in other monetary policy instruments (e.g. the SSD scheme, open-market operations, calls for special deposits), and either a fixed or a freely floating exchange rate regime. In practice, of course, interest rates can alter, the authorities can use other monetary instruments, and they can intervene in the foreign exchange market to bring about an exchange rate which is neither fixed nor freely floating. Each of these would alter the relationship between the PSBR and £M3. Thus in setting fiscal policy in order to achieve a given monetary target it is not enough to take account of the relationships discussed in this paper. It is also necessary to estimate the effects of other policies, including exchange rate policies, on the money stock. In other words, fiscal, monetary and exchange rate policies must be simultaneously determined, in the light of their joint effects on the relevant intermediate and final objectives. The subject of this paper is only one, although an important one, of the relevant considerations.

NOTES

1. We gratefully acknowledge the assistance which we have received from colleagues in the Treasury, and especially from Steven Bell. Others who have helped include Stephen Powell, Gary Roberts, Peter Spencer and Ralph Wilkinson. We have made one or two revisions in the light of the discussion at the City University conference.
2. Various measures of constant employment budget balances have been estimated in an attempt to purge the PSBR of some of these endogenous factors. See, for example, Hartley, N. and Bean, C., *The Standardised Budget Balance*, Treasury Working Paper No 1, February 1978, and Ward, T. S. and Neild, R. R., *The Measurement and Reform of Budgetary Policy* (Heinemann Educational for the Institute for Fiscal Studies, 1978).
3. Tobin, J., 'Commercial Banks as Creators of Money', in Hester, D. and Tobin, J. (eds) *Financial Markets and Economic Activity* (Wiley, 1967).
4. The market clearing arrangements may be complicated by multiple rates or quantity restrictions. For example, separate rates are quoted for large transactions in wholesale deposits, and they are subject to a conventional minimum size of deposit, e.g. £10,000.
5. Attempts to model such disequilibrium have been made by Jonson, P.D., Moses, G. R. and Wymer, C. R., 'A Minimum Model of the Australian Economy' Research Discussion Paper 7601, Reserve Bank of Australia, and Coghlan, R., 'A Small Monetary Model of the UK Economy', paper prepared for the VIth International Conference of Applied Econometrics, Rome, February 1979.
6. *H. M. Treasury Macro-Economic Model Technical Manual*, 1979 (to be published).
7. *A Financial Sector for the Treasury Model: Part One, The Model of the Domestic Monetary System* by Peter Spencer and Colin Mowl; *Part Two, The Model of External Capital Flows* by Rachel Lomax and Michael Denham, Treasury Working Paper No 8, December 1978.
8. The assumption of a unit elasticity between real income and wealth in this case is a simplification used for illustrative purposes.
9. See, for example, Artis M. J. and Lewis M. K. 'The Demand for Money in the United Kingdom: 1963–1973', Manchester School (June 1976); Hendry D. F. and Mizon G. E., 'Serial Correlation as a Convenient Simplication, Not a Nuisance: a Comment on a Study of the Demand for Money by the Bank of England', *Economic Journal* (September 1978); Laumas, G. S. 'A

Test of the Stability of the Demand for Money', *Scottish Journal of Political Economy* (November 1978).

10. An exercise of the latter type using an earlier version of the Treasury model was described in the article by Laury, Lewis and Ormerod in the *National Institute Economic Review* (February 1978).

11. That the real world is rather more complex than suggested here is explained in 'Balance of Payments Flows and the Monetary Aggregates in the UK', HM Treasury Working Paper No 5, 1978.

12. We do not discuss here the appropriateness of maintaining an unchanged monetary target in the face of a shift in the demand for money associated, for example, with a shift in saving behaviour.

Appendix 1:
Changes to the
Monetary Sector
since the Working Paper

The version of the Monetary Sector of the Treasury Model which underlies the results presented in the present paper differs in some respects from that reported in the recently published working paper (Spencer and Mowl, 1978). It would be inappropriate to discuss in detail here all the changes that have been made, but the nature of the more important changes are discussed briefly below:

(1) The equation for the demand for gilts by the non-bank private sector (equation E1.5 in the working paper) has been changed so that total non-bank private sector asset holdings feed directly into the demand function and current price TFE does not appear explicitly. The long-run elasticity of total gilt holdings with respect to total assets is about 0.9 and total assets were included rather than, say, net worth because the former proved superior in estimation. The present treatment allows shifts in the relationship between total financial asset holdings and current price TFE to affect long-run gilt holdings directly in a plausible way.

(2) The equation for non-bank holdings of National Savings (equation E1.9) reported in the working paper has broken down since the policy of making them more attractive to investors was introduced in late 1976. The equation currently in use is an extremely simple one in which 10 per cent of any change in personal sector net acquisition of financial assets takes the form of a change in holdings of the various National Savings instruments.

(3) In the equation system for bank lending to the personal sector (E1.1 in the working paper) the interest rate elasticities have been reduced to take account of the recent apparently muted response of lending

163

to a higher level of rates. The equation being used for bank lending to other financial institutions (equation E1.3) now includes a real income effect and incorporates some other small amendments to the equation in the working paper.

(4) The effects of interest rate levels (as opposed to differentials) on non-bank private sector demands for interest-bearing reserve assets (equation E1.12), notes and coin (equation E1.11) and parallel money (E1.15) have been reduced. These changes reflect the recent performance of the equations.

Appendix 2

SIMULATION 1   EXOGENOUS INCREASE IN CONSUMERS' EXPENDITURE DIFFERENCES FROM BASE

	Consumers' expenditure % of base	Real GDP % of base	Average earnings % of base	Exchange rate % of base	GDP prices % of base	Current balance (£m)	PSBR (£m)
Fixed exchange rate							
Q1	3.1	1.4	0.1	–	−0.1	−170	−130
Q2	3.3	1.7	0.3	–	−0.2	−290	−210
Q3	3.4	1.8	0.5	–	−0.1	−350	−280
Q4	3.4	1.8	0.7	–	–	−420	−370
Q5	3.3	1.7	0.8	–	0.2	−450	−410
Q6	3.3	1.6	0.8	–	0.3	−460	−450
Q7	3.2	1.4	0.9	–	0.5	−460	−470
Q8	3.1	1.3	1.0	–	0.6	−460	−480
Q9	3.0	1.2	1.1	–	0.8	−460	−490
Q10	2.9	1.1	1.2	–	0.9	−440	−520
Q11	2.9	1.0	1.3	–	1.0	−420	−530
Q12	2.8	0.9	1.4	–	1.1	−410	−530
Q13	2.8	0.8	1.5	–	1.2	−400	−550
Q14	2.7	0.7	1.6	–	1.2	−400	−580
Q15	2.7	0.7	1.7	–	1.3	−390	−620
Q16	2.7	0.7	1.8	–	1.4	−390	−650
Floating exchange rate							
Q1	3.4	1.5	0.2	−0.9	0.2	−220	−140
Q2	3.5	1.9	0.4	−2.4	−0.6	−390	−220
Q3	3.5	2.2	0.6	−3.6	−0.3	−450	−280
Q4	3.5	2.3	0.9	−4.6	−0.1	−490	−350
Q5	3.3	2.3	1.1	−4.9	0.4	−440	−430
Q6	3.2	2.3	1.3	−4.8	0.8	−360	−480
Q7	3.1	2.3	1.6	−4.9	1.2	−300	−510
Q8	3.0	2.3	2.1	−4.9	1.6	−250	−550
Q9	3.0	2.2	2.5	−5.2	1.9	−220	−590
Q10	2.9	2.2	2.9	−5.4	2.2	−200	−630
Q11	2.8	2.1	3.2	−5.9	2.5	−170	−640
Q12	2.7	2.0	3.6	−6.4	2.8	−150	−650
Q13	2.6	2.0	4.1	−6.9	3.2	−110	−680
Q14	2.5	2.0	4.4	−7.4	3.6	− 60	−710
Q15	2.4	1.9	4.8	−7.7	4.0	10	−730
Q16	2.3	1.9	5.3	−7.8	4.4	50	−740

Net financial wealth	Non-bank private sector balance sheet (£m)					Timing adj	£M3	£M3 % of base	M1 % of base
	Bank loans	Gilts	National savings	Other govt debt	Overseas assets (net)				
− 360	− 180	− 30	− 70	− 70	− 20	50	− 280	−0.5	−
− 890	− 220	− 120	− 150	− 150	− 40	80	− 590	−1.1	−0.2
− 1550	− 90	− 250	− 220	− 210	− 30	100	− 820	−1.5	−0.2
− 2360	130	− 430	− 290	− 250	− 30	120	−1120	−2.0	−0.4
− 3240	360	− 630	− 360	− 290	− 20	130	−1450	−2.5	−0.5
− 4160	480	− 840	− 430	− 330	− 10	140	−1930	−3.2	−0.7
− 5100	550	−1080	− 510	− 420	− 10	140	−2400	−3.9	−0.9
− 6050	610	−1350	− 580	− 470	−	150	−2890	−4.5	−1.0
− 7000	660	−1640	− 660	− 590	20	150	−3310	−5.1	−1.2
− 7960	700	−1940	− 730	− 720	40	160	−3740	−5.6	−1.4
− 8920	730	−2250	− 810	− 880	70	170	−4160	−6.0	−1.6
− 9870	750	−2560	− 890	− 890	90	180	−4700	−6.6	−1.7
−10830	780	−2860	− 980	−1020	110	180	−5120	−7.0	−1.8
−11820	820	−3170	−1060	−1160	140	200	−5570	−7.4	−2.0
−12840	840	−3480	−1150	−1480	190	210	−5870	−7.6	−2.1
−13890	870	−3800	−1240	−1500	200	220	−6460	−8.2	−2.3
− 420	− 180	− 30	− 80	− 70	− 140	60	− 220	−0.4	0.1
− 1060	− 180	− 90	− 160	− 130	− 390	90	− 370	−0.7	0.1
− 1820	60	− 170	− 250	− 170	− 660	120	− 390	−0.7	0.4
− 2700	410	− 260	− 330	− 170	− 970	150	− 410	−0.7	0.6
− 3590	810	− 330	− 400	− 190	−1240	160	− 450	−0.8	0.8
− 4450	1060	− 390	− 480	− 210	−1450	180	− 670	−1.1	0.9
− 5280	1260	− 460	− 560	− 250	−1640	210	− 910	−1.5	1.0
− 6120	1440	− 570	− 630	− 280	−1800	240	−1170	−1.8	1.0
− 6940	1650	− 690	− 690	− 360	−1940	250	−1350	−2.1	1.1
− 8120	1860	− 830	− 760	− 430	−2060	280	−1570	−2.3	1.2
− 8640	2080	− 970	− 820	− 530	−2180	320	−1740	−2.5	1.3
− 9480	2320	−1100	− 890	− 490	−2280	360	−2030	−2.8	1.4
−10280	2590	−1230	− 950	− 550	−2360	380	−2210	−3.0	1.6
−11100	2870	−1350	−1010	− 630	−2400	430	−2430	−3.2	1.8
−11870	3130	−1460	−1070	− 760	−2410	470	−2570	−3.3	1.9
−12620	3410	−1570	−1130	− 800	−2390	530	−2800	−3.5	2.1

SIMULATION 2   EXOGENOUS INCREASE IN EXPORTS OF GOODS AND SERVICES DIFFERENCES FROM BASE

	Exports of goods and services % of base	Real GDP % of base	Average earnings % of base	Exchange rate % of base	GDP prices % of base	Current balance (£m)	PSBR (£m)
Fixed exchange rate							
Q1	6.6	2.0	0.2	–	−0.4	690	−100
Q2	7.0	2.6	0.6	–	−0.6	620	−200
Q3	7.3	3.0	0.8	–	−0.4	630	−280
Q4	7.6	3.1	1.1	–	−0.3	640	−410
Q5	7.8	3.1	1.2	–	−0.1	690	−470
Q6	7.9	3.1	1.3	–	0.1	730	−510
Q7	8.0	3.1	1.5	–	0.3	780	−540
Q8	8.1	3.0	1.7	–	0.5	850	−560
Q9	8.1	2.9	2.0	–	0.8	930	−580
Q10	8.1	2.8	2.2	–	1.0	1010	−610
Q11	8.1	2.8	2.5	–	1.3	1100	−610
Q12	8.0	2.7	2.8	–	1.5	1170	−590
Q13	8.0	2.6	3.0	–	1.7	1260	−590
Q14	7.9	2.5	3.3	–	1.9	1320	−600
Q15	7.8	2.5	3.5	–	2.0	1370	−610
Q16	7.7	2.4	3.8	–	2.3	1400	−600
Floating exchange rate							
Q1	4.3	1.4	0.2	4.3	0.2	610	−100
Q2	3.9	1.6	0.3	8.6	0.1	610	−190
Q3	3.2	1.5	0.4	11.1	−0.1	520	−290
Q4	2.5	1.3	0.3	12.9	−0.4	390	−420
Q5	2.0	1.0	0.1	11.1	−1.1	170	−360
Q6	1.7	0.8	−0.3	9.7	−1.5	–	−360
Q7	1.4	0.5	−0.7	10.5	−1.5	− 10	−370
Q8	1.1	0.3	−1.2	11.0	−1.6	20	−280
Q9	0.8	0.1	−1.6	12.1	−1.8	80	−240
Q10	0.6	–	−2.0	12.6	−2.1	100	−210
Q11	0.4	−0.1	−2.3	13.1	−2.4	100	−200
Q12	0.1	−0.1	−2.6	14.6	−2.7	110	−250
Q13	−0.2	−0.2	−2.9	15.2	−3.0	70	−240
Q14	−0.5	−0.2	−3.1	15.3	−3.4	− 30	−230
Q15	−0.8	−0.3	−3.5	15.0	−3.8	−150	−220
Q16	−0.8	−0.3	−3.8	14.1	−4.1	−230	−170

Net financial wealth	Bank loans	Gilts	National savings	Other govt debt	Overseas assets (net)	Timing adj	£M3	£M3 % of base	M1
			Non-bank private sector balance sheet (£m)						
570	− 330	30	–	10	− 160	20	370	0.7	0.4
960	− 440	110	10	80	− 520	40	890	1.6	0.7
1280	− 260	270	20	170	− 990	70	1610	2.9	1.3
1470	40	540	40	250	−1560	100	2350	4.1	1.8
1690	380	880	70	290	−1980	120	2920	5.0	2.2
1880	570	1220	100	310	−2350	140	3310	5.5	2.4
2110	720	1540	130	350	−2660	160	3620	5.8	2.7
2370	850	1810	170	360	−2920	180	3990	6.3	2.9
2710	980	2050	210	430	−3080	190	4280	6.5	3.1
3100	1110	2280	250	500	−3240	210	4640	6.9	3.3
3560	1220	2500	300	580	−3270	230	4900	7.1	3.5
4120	1330	2720	350	570	−3200	260	5270	7.4	3.7
4780	1440	2930	410	640	−3080	270	5580	7.6	3.9
5460	1550	3140	460	700	−2880	300	5880	7.8	4.1
6200	1650	3350	520	860	−2680	330	6110	7.9	4.3
6970	1780	3570	590	880	−2460	370	6530	8.3	4.5
500	− 300	− 20	–	− 30	410	10	− 150	−0.3	−0.2
920	− 570	− 70	10	− 40	780	20	− 320	−0.6	−0.6
1150	− 690	− 140	30	− 30	1100	20	− 470	−0.8	−1.0
1120	− 730	− 250	40	− 40	1330	20	− 680	−1.2	−1.5
920	− 760	390	50	− 50	1430	20	− 870	−1.5	−1.8
570	− 820	− 520	60	− 90	1420	10	−1110	−1.9	−2.1
210	− 900	− 670	60	−110	1430	− 10	−1410	−2.3	−2.3
− 10	−1060	− 830	60	−130	1450	− 40	−1670	−2.6	−2.6
150	−1290	−1000	50	−140	1520	− 60	−1930	−2.9	−2.9
− 220	−1550	−1170	30	−150	1590	−100	−2180	−3.2	−3.3
− 290	−1830	−1340	20	−160	1670	−140	−2440	−3.5	−3.6
− 390	−2130	−1520	–	−170	1740	−170	−2740	−3.8	−3.9
− 550	−2450	−1720	− 40	−180	1810	−180	−3050	−4.2	−4.3
− 770	−2730	−1920	− 70	−200	1800	−220	−3330	−4.4	−4.6
−1100	−2970	−2130	−110	−220	1730	−250	−3600	−4.7	−4.9
−1460	−3180	−2330	−150	−230	1610	−290	−3820	−4.9	−5.0

SIMULATION 3   INCREASE IN PERSONAL INCOME TAX
DIFFERENCES FROM BASE

	Real Personal disposable income % of base	Consumers expenditure	Real GDP % of base	Average earnings % of base	Exchange rate % of base	GDP prices % of base	Current balance (£m)	PSBR (£m)
Fixed exchange rate								
Q1	−1.0	−0.3	−0.1	−	−		30	−170
Q2	−0.9	−0.5	−0.2	0.1	−	−	60	−270
Q3	−0.9	−0.6	−0.3	0.3	−	0.1	80	−280
Q4	−0.9	−0.6	−0.3	0.6	−	0.2	90	−280
Q5	−1.0	−0.8	−0.4	0.8	−	0.4	110	−320
Q6	−1.0	−0.8	−0.4	0.9	−	0.6	120	−330
Q7	−1.1	−0.8	−0.5	1.0	−	0.6	130	−320
Q8	−1.0	−0.8	−0.5	1.2	−	0.7	130	−280
Q9	−1.1	−0.9	−0.6	1.3	−	0.9	140	−290
Q10	−1.1	−0.9	−0.6	1.3	−	1.0	130	−290
Q11	−1.1	−0.9	−0.6	1.4	−	1.0	130	−280
Q12	−1.1	−0.9	−0.6	1.5	−	1.0	120	−290
Q13	−1.0	−0.9	−0.6	1.5	−	1.1	110	−250
Q14	−1.0	−0.9	−0.7	1.5	−	1.1	90	−240
Q15	−1.0	−0.9	−0.7	1.5	−	1.1	90	−250
Q16	−1.1	−0.9	−0.7	1.5	−	1.2	80	−260
Floating exchange rate								
Q1	−1.0	−0.3	−0.1	−	0.3	−	40	−170
Q2	−0.9	−0.5	−0.2	0.1	0.7	0.1	70	−270
Q3	−0.9	−0.5	−0.3	0.2	0.9	0.2	90	−280
Q4	−0.8	−0.6	−0.4	0.5	1.0	0.2	90	−290
Q5	−0.9	−0.7	−0.5	0.7	1.1	0.3	90	−310
Q6	−0.9	−0.7	−0.6	0.8	1.2	0.4	80	−320
Q7	−1.0	−0.7	−0.6	0.9	1.3	0.5	80	−310
Q8	−1.0	−0.7	−0.7	0.9	1.4	0.6	70	−270
Q9	−1.0	−0.8	−0.8	0.9	1.4	0.6	70	−270
Q10	−1.1	−0.8	−0.8	0.9	1.5	0.6	60	−260
Q11	−1.1	−0.8	−0.9	0.9	1.6	0.7	40	−260
Q12	−1.1	−0.8	−0.9	0.9	1.7	0.6	20	−250
Q13	−1.0	−0.8	−0.9	0.9	1.8	0.6	−	−220
Q14	−1.0	−0.8	−0.9	0.9	1.8	0.6	− 30	−200
Q15	−1.1	−0.8	−0.9	0.8	1.8	0.5	− 50	−200
Q16	−1.1	−0.8	−1.0	0.6	1.9	0.4	− 70	−210

Net financial wealth	Bank loans	Gilts	National savings	Other govt debt	Overseas assets (net)	Timing adj	£M3	£M3 % of base	M1
− 250	10	− 10	− 20	− 10	− 10	110	− 80	−0.2	−0.1
− 460	30	− 30	− 40	− 20	− 20	100	−210	−0.4	−0.2
− 660	50	− 70	− 50	− 40	− 30	110	−320	−0.6	−0.2
− 860	60	−120	− 60	− 50	− 30	120	−420	−0.7	−0.2
−1090	90	−180	− 70	− 60	− 40	130	−510	−0.9	−0.2
−1300	120	−240	− 80	− 70	− 40	140	−610	−1.0	−0.2
−1500	150	−290	−100	− 80	− 50	150	−700	−1.1	−0.2
−1660	180	−330	−100	− 90	− 50	150	−760	−1.2	−0.2
−1820	210	−380	−110	−110	− 50	160	−800	−1.2	−0.1
−1980	240	−410	−120	−130	− 50	160	−860	−1.3	−0.1
−2140	260	−440	−130	−150	− 60	170	−930	−1.3	−0.1
−2310	270	−480	−140	−150	− 60	180	−1040	−1.4	−0.1
−2430	290	−520	−140	−170	− 70	150	−1090	−1.5	−0.1
−2580	310	−550	−140	−190	− 80	160	−1150	−1.5	−0.1
−2750	310	−590	−150	−220	−100	170	−1210	−1.6	−0.2
−2940	320	−630	−160	−250	−120	170	−1290	−1.6	−0.2
− 240	10	− 10	− 20	− 10	30	110	− 110	−0.2	−0.1
− 430	10	− 40	− 40	− 40	70	100	− 270	−0.5	−0.2
− 620	10	− 100	− 50	− 50	130	100	− 440	−0.8	−0.4
− 830	–	− 170	− 60	− 70	180	110	− 590	−1.0	−0.4
−1070	–	− 270	− 70	−100	230	120	− 750	−1.3	−0.5
−1310	–	− 360	− 80	−120	290	130	− 920	−1.5	−0.6
−1550	–	− 450	−100	−140	340	130	−1070	−1.7	−0.6
−1750	− 10	− 540	−110	−150	380	130	−1210	−1.9	−0.7
−1950	− 10	− 630	−120	−180	420	140	−1330	−2.0	−0.7
−2160	− 30	− 710	−130	−210	460	130	−1460	−2.2	−0.8
−2370	− 60	− 800	−140	−260	490	130	−1590	−2.3	−0.9
−2600	−100	− 880	−160	−260	510	130	−1780	−2.5	−0.9
−2790	−130	− 970	−170	−290	510	110	−1900	−2.6	−1.0
−3020	−170	−1060	−180	−320	500	110	−2020	−2.7	−1.1
−3280	−210	−1150	−200	−360	470	100	−2140	−2.8	−1.1
−3550	−250	−1230	−210	−390	430	100	−2300	−2.9	−1.2

Non-Bank private sector balance sheet (£m)

SIMULATION 4 INCREASE IN VALUE ADDED TAX
DIFFERENCES FROM BASE

	Real personal disposable income % of base	Consumers expenditure	Real GDP % of base	Average earnings % of base	Exchange rate % of base	GDP prices % of base	Current balance (£m)	P.S.B. (£m
Fixed Exchange rate								
Q1	−2.3	−1.4	−0.6	−0.1	−`	1.8	110	5
Q2	−2.5	−1.7	−0.9	0.1	−	1.9	180	−33
Q3	−2.2	−1.9	−1.1	0.4	−	2.1	220	−39
Q4	−2.1	−1.9	−1.1	1.0	−	2.3	240	−33
Q5	−2.1	−2.1	−1.3	1.4	−	2.7	270	−36
Q6	−2.2	−2.1	−1.3	1.8	−	3.0	280	−34
Q7	−2.3	−2.2	−1.4	2.0	−	3.3	280	−3
Q8	−2.2	−2.1	−1.4	2.2	−	3.4	270	−24
Q9	−2.3	−2.3	−1.5	2.4	−	3.7	260	−22
Q10	−2.4	−2.3	−1.6	2.5	−	3.8	250	−2
Q11	−2.4	−2.3	−1.6	2.6	−	3.9	230	−20
Q12	−2.3	−2.2	−1.6	2.7	−	4.0	200	−19
Q13	−2.4	−2.4	−1.7	2.9	−	4.1	180	−2
Q14	−2.4	−2.4	−1.7	3.0	−	4.2	170	−20
Q15	−2.4	−2.4	−1.7	3.0	−	4.2	150	−18
Q16	−2.4	−2.3	−1.8	3.0	−	4.2	130	−17
Floating exchange rate								
Q1	−2.2	−1.3	−0.6	−0.1	0.6	1.7	120	5
Q2	−2.2	−1.6	−0.9	0.1	1.4	1.9	210	−32
Q3	−2.0	−1.7	−1.1	0.4	1.9	2.0	230	−39
Q4	−1.8	−1.6	−1.2	0.9	2.0	2.1	220	−34
Q5	−1.9	−1.9	−1.4	1.2	2.0	2.4	200	−35
Q6	−2.0	−1.9	−1.5	1.5	1.8	2.6	180	−33
Q7	−2.1	−1.9	−1.6	1.6	2.0	2.7	170	−29
Q8	−2.1	−1.9	−1.7	1.6	1.9	2.8	140	−22
Q9	−2.2	−2.1	−1.8	1.7	1.9	3.0	130	−19
Q10	−2.3	−2.1	−1.8	1.7	1.9	3.0	110	−16
Q11	−2.3	−2.0	−1.9	1.7	2.0	3.1	90	−15
Q12	−2.3	−2.0	−1.9	1.8	2.2	3.1	60	−15
Q13	−2.3	−2.1	−1.9	1.8	2.3	3.1	30	−15
Q14	−2.3	−2.1	−2.0	1.8	2.3	3.1	− 10	−14
Q15	−2.3	−2.1	−2.0	1.7	2.3	3.0	− 50	−13
Q16	−2.3	−2.1	−2.0	1.7	2.2	3.0	− 80	−12

Non-Bank private sector balance sheet (£m)

Net financial wealth	Bank loans	Gilts	National savings	Other govt debt	Overseas assets (net)	Timing adj	£M3	£M3 % of base	M1
− 370	210	40	− 30	10	–	530	360	0.7	0.9
− 640	380	100	− 40	10	10	650	320	0.6	0.9
− 820	480	150	− 50	20	20	670	210	0.4	0.8
− 930	540	190	− 60	− 10	60	690	110	0.2	0.8
−1020	610	190	− 50	− 20	100	700	70	0.1	1.0
−1120	700	180	− 50	− 20	150	740	50	0.1	1.1
−1180	770	180	− 50	− 20	200	770	40	0.1	1.2
−1200	840	190	− 50	− 10	260	810	60	0.1	1.3
−1160	940	210	− 40	− 20	320	820	120	0.2	1.4
−1160	1010	240	− 30	− 30	390	860	150	0.2	1.5
−1160	1060	270	− 30	− 40	440	890	140	0.2	1.5
−1190	1100	290	− 20	− 40	490	930	110	0.2	1.6
−1230	1190	310	− 10	− 60	540	940	110	0.2	1.6
−1300	1260	320	–	− 70	580	980	110	0.2	1.7
−1370	1300	320	10	− 100	600	1010	110	0.1	1.7
−1430	1350	330	20	− 100	610	1040	110	0.1	1.7
− 350	190	30	− 20	–	80	500	280	0.5	0.8
− 560	320	70	− 40	− 10	210	610	140	0.3	0.6
− 730	360	90	− 50	− 40	350	620	− 90	−0.2	0.4
− 860	370	70	− 50	− 70	480	640	− 290	−0.5	0.3
−1010	390	–	− 50	− 90	610	640	− 440	−0.8	0.3
−1190	430	− 80	− 50	− 90	720	680	− 570	−1.0	0.3
−1340	460	−150	− 50	− 120	820	700	− 690	−1.1	0.3
−1440	480	−220	− 50	− 120	910	720	− 760	−1.2	0.3
−1510	520	−260	− 60	− 140	990	740	− 780	−1.2	0.4
−1580	530	−300	− 60	− 160	1060	760	− 830	−1.2	0.4
−1660	510	−330	− 60	− 190	1120	780	− 900	−1.3	0.3
−1780	490	−360	− 70	− 180	1160	810	−1020	−1.4	0.3
−1910	500	−410	− 70	− 210	1180	820	−1090	−1.5	0.3
−2080	510	−450	− 80	− 220	1180	840	−1170	−1.6	0.2
−2290	490	−500	− 80	− 260	1160	860	−1240	−1.6	0.2
−2510	490	−540	− 90	− 270	1110	890	−1340	−1.7	0.1

SIMULATION 5 REDUCTION IN GENERAL GOVERNMENT EXPENDITURE ON PROCUREMENT DIFFERENCES FROM BASE

	Real GDP % of base	Average earnings % of base	Exchange rate % of base	GDP prices % of base	Current balance (£m)	PSBR (£m)
Fixed exchange rate						
Q1	−0.7	−0.1	−	−	50	−270
Q2	−0.8	−0.2	−	−	100	−260
Q3	−0.9	−0.3	−	−	120	−250
Q4	−0.9	−0.4	−	−0.1	150	−220
Q5	−0.8	−0.4	−	−0.1	160	−220
Q6	−0.8	−0.4	−	−0.2	170	−220
Q7	−0.8	−0.5	−	−0.3	180	−230
Q8	−0.8	−0.6	−	−0.4	190	−250
Q9	−0.7	−0.6	−	−0.4	190	−260
Q10	−0.7	−0.7	−	−0.5	190	−280
Q11	−0.6	−0.8	−	−0.6	200	−300
Q12	−0.6	−0.8	−	−0.7	210	−330
Q13	−0.6	−0.9	−	−0.7	210	−350
Q14	−0.5	−1.0	−	−0.7	220	−370
Q15	−0.5	−1.0	−	−0.8	230	−390
Q16	−0.5	−1.1	−	−0.8	250	−430
Floating exchange rate						
Q1	−0.6	−0.1	0.4	−	60	−260
Q2	−0.8	−0.2	1.1	0.1	120	−250
Q3	−0.9	−0.3	1.6	0.1	140	−250
Q4	−1.0	−0.4	2.1	−0.1	150	−240
Q5	−1.0	−0.5	2.3	−0.3	120	−210
Q6	−1.0	−0.6	2.2	−0.4	100	−200
Q7	−1.1	−0.8	2.3	−0.6	80	−210
Q8	−1.1	−1.0	2.5	−0.7	70	−210
Q9	−1.1	−1.2	2.7	−0.9	60	−220
Q10	−1.1	−1.3	2.9	−1.0	50	−230
Q11	−1.1	−1.5	3.0	−1.2	40	−240
Q12	−1.1	−1.7	3.4	−1.4	30	−270
Q13	−1.1	−1.9	3.6	−1.6	10	−270
Q14	−1.0	−2.1	3.8	−1.7	− 10	−280
Q15	−1.0	−2.3	4.0	−1.9	− 40	−300
Q16	−1.0	−2.5	4.2	−2.1	− 50	−320

Non-Bank private sector balance sheet (£m)

Net financial wealth	Bank loans	Gilts	National savings	Other govt debt	Overseas assets (net)	Timing adj	£M3	£M3 % of base	M1
− 220	70	− 10	–	–	− 10	− 10	− 130	−0.2	−0.2
− 370	90	− 30	–	–	− 30	− 10	− 220	−0.4	−0.3
− 490	30	− 70	− 10	− 20	− 70	− 20	− 330	−0.6	−0.4
− 560	− 70	− 120	− 10	− 30	−100	− 30	− 400	−0.7	−0.4
− 610	− 180	− 170	− 20	− 30	−150	− 40	− 460	−0.8	−0.5
− 650	− 240	− 210	− 30	− 20	−190	− 40	− 480	−0.8	−0.5
− 690	− 280	− 240	− 40	− 30	⁻230	− 50	− 470	−0.8	−0.5
− 740	− 310	− 270	− 50	− 20	−280	− 50	− 490	−0.8	−0.6
− 810	− 350	− 290	− 60	− 30	−320	− 60	− 520	−0.8	−0.6
− 890	− 380	− 310	− 70	− 30	−370	− 60	− 550	−0.8	−0.6
− 900	− 410	− 330	− 90	− 30	−410	− 70	− 600	−0.9	−0.7
−1110	− 430	− 360	− 100	− 40	−460	− 70	− 650	−0.9	−0.7
−1250	− 460	− 400	− 120	− 60	−500	− 80	− 710	−1.0	−0.8
−1390	− 480	− 440	− 130	− 60	−540	− 80	− 780	−1.0	−0.8
−1540	− 500	− 490	− 150	− 80	−570	− 90	− 850	−1.1	−0.8
−1710	− 530	− 540	− 160	− 90	−610	−100	− 930	−1.2	−0.9
− 200	60	− 10	–	–	40	− 10	− 160	−0.3	−0.2
− 320	60	− 50	–	− 30	120	− 20	− 320	−0.6	−0.4
− 420	− 40	− 110	− 10	− 50	200	− 30	− 540	−1.0	−0.6
− 500	− 180	− 200	− 10	− 70	300	− 40	− 740	−1.3	−0.8
− 580	− 350	− 310	− 20	− 80	380	− 50	− 940	−1.6	−1.0
− 680	− 460	− 430	− 30	−100	430	− 60	−1070	−1.8	−1.2
− 800	− 550	− 540	− 40	−120	480	− 70	−1200	−1.9	−1.3
− 930	− 640	− 650	− 50	−130	530	− 90	−1350	−2.1	−1.5
−1090	− 740	− 760	− 70	−150	570	− 90	−1510	−2.3	−1.7
−1250	− 860	− 870	− 90	−170	600	−110	−1690	−2.5	−1.8
−1440	− 970	− 990	−110	−210	640	−130	−1860	−2.7	−2.0
−1660	−1090	−1110	−140	−210	660	−150	−2100	−2.9	−2.2
−1910	−1220	−1250	−160	−250	670	−150	−2300	−3.1	−2.4
−2180	−1360	−1390	−190	−270	670	−180	−2530	−3.4	−2.6
−2490	−1480	−1550	−230	−320	660	−200	−2390	−3.6	−2.8
−2840	−1620	−1710	−260	−350	640	−230	−3000	−3.8	−3.0

Comments on the Paper by
P. E. Middleton, C. J. Mowl,
J. C. Odling-Smee and C. J. Riley

David Laidler
University of Western Ontario

This paper is most welcome. If, shall we say five years ago, anyone who is now attending this conference had been asked about the probability in the foreseeable future of a paper on achieving monetary targets, originating in the Treasury, being discussed by a dyed-in-the-wool monetarist, with authors and discussant finding much to agree about, he would have set that probability low indeed. That such a state of affairs has come about is surely a sign of how much all sides have learned from one another in recent debates, and should not go unnoticed.

This does not mean that I agree with everything that is in this paper, but before I turn to my criticisms of it, let it be quite clear that I am in total agreement with its authors on the following important points. First, it is completely common ground that when it comes to matters of practical policy, it is impossible to discuss the ways and means whereby a target can be achieved for a monetary aggregate without also discussing the conduct of fiscal policy and exchange rate policy. Second, I am in complete agreement with the contention that the links between the Public Sector Borrowing Requirement and the rate of money creation are far from mechanical and automatic. They do indeed depend, not only upon the sources of variations in that borrowing requirement, but also and crucially upon the institutional framework of the financial system. Finally, there can surely be little doubt that an explicit econometric model, such as the Treasury model, is a useful tool to use in thinking about such matters, if only because it forces us to be consistent in our analysis. Having agreed with so much of this paper, the reader might wonder what there is left to disagree about. It seems to me that there are two matters that need more attention than they have been given here, and I will deal with them in turn.

As I have already remarked, it is common ground between the authors and myself that the way in which the money supply will respond to the Public Sector Borrowing Requirement depends very much upon institutional arrangements. However, though the authors do not neglect this matter they seem to me to take current institutional arrangements too much for granted. These arrangements are not immutable, and I would very much like to see further analysis of the type carried out in this paper devoted to exploring the consequences of a few alternative sets of rules and regulations. In particular, I have, from their very inception, been critical of that provision of the Competition and Credit Control rules that makes Treasury Bills (not to mention certain private sector Bills) a component of the reserve base.

Much monetarist analysis of the linkage between government deficts, money creation, and inflation has its origins in studies of Latin American experience; one of the key lessons of that experience is that, in the absence of a well-developed market for government debt, the link between fiscal deficits and inflation is close indeed. Thus, the existence of well-developed capital markets in Britain gives the policy-maker an extra and vitally important degree of freedom, because it makes it so much easier to insulate the quantity of money from the financial consequences of fiscal policy; and yet current arrangements do not permit maximum advantage to be taken of this state of affairs. So long as the market will absorb gilts, all is well and good, but the possibility of smoothing out the marketing of government debt without affecting the money supply by having resort when necessary to the Treasury Bill market at present is closed off.

Perhaps this does not matter much for the long-term pursuit of monetary targets—but over shorter periods I suspect it matters very much indeed. An important benefit of pursuing monetary targets is the extra degree of certainty about policy that this confers on the private sector, but the greater are the short-term deviations of actual from stated policy, the more is this advantage dissipated. Thus, and at the risk of appearing to ask the authors of this paper to ride the discussant's own hobby-horse, I would hope that if analysis of the kind presented in their paper is carried further, it will look into the consequences for the linkages between fiscal and monetary policy of altering the Competition and Credit Control rules by narrowing the range of assets that are eligible to be used as primary reserves by the banking system to see whether conjectures such as those I have just offered are indeed valid.

My second criticism of this paper is perhaps a more basic one. I have already said that I believe the use of an explicit model is helpful in analysing matters of the sort under discussion here because it forces us to think consistently about them. However, when using a model one must always remember that that is what it is—a model and not an actual economy. There are many enjoyable games that the econometrician can successfully play with the Treasury model which the Treasury had better not try to play with the British economy, and I would place the particular game played in this paper firmly in that category.

The basic question asked in the exercise under consideration is: What must be done to fiscal instruments in the face of a variety of shocks to keep the money supply on target and the rate of interest constant?' If one thinks about this question in terms of a simple IS–LM framework, its essential nature becomes clear. To keep the money supply on target means keeping the LM curve at a particular location, and to keep the interest rate constant then involves so manipulating the IS curve that it will intersect with the LM curve at a particular point. It *is* possible to carry out such an exercise with a model. We *do* know enough about its structure, and about the values of its exogenous variables, to perform the necessary calculations, and we *may* learn quite a bit about the model's internal logic by doing so. However, we certainly *do not* know enough about the British economy to be able to put any of the lessons that we might learn from the model to use in trying to achieve similar targets there.

The matter here goes deeper than simply saying that our knowledge of the real world is imperfect. The knowledge that it is assumed we have in carrying out the exercises presented in this paper would make the pursuit of targets for the money supply at best quite pointless, and at worst sub-optimal. If we did know enough about the world simultaneously to peg the interest rate and the money supply, we would also know enough to be able to ensure that the level of aggregate demand was always just where we wanted it; we would be able to carry out as finely tuned an optimal fiscal stabilisation policy as anyone could conceive. It is precisely because we do not have such knowledge that built-in stabilisers are attractive, and a money supply rule is after all a built-in stabiliser. The case for implementing it is that we *do not* know what shocks to aggregate demand might originate in the private and overseas sectors, or when they might do so; that it is *not* feasible to deploy fiscal policy rapidly and accurately enough to offset them; and that the interest rate and exchange rate fluctuation that they will automatically set in motion when a money supply rule is adhered to are the best weapon we have for insulating real income, employment and prices from their consequences.

And none of this is to mention that fiscal policy has other uses than stabilisation of the macroeconomy. Income and wealth distribution targets, and goals for the allocation of resources both between and within the public and private sectors, cannot be pursued coherently if tax and expenditure patterns are constantly being altered to achieve extraneous macro goals: recall for a moment the ludicrous situation in the late 60s when the school-leaving age was not raised because of the state of the balance of payments!

Thus, though the authors of this paper are to be complimented on bringing to the forefront the interconnectedness of fiscal and monetary policy, and although there is undoubtedly much to be learned about the structure of the Treasury model from their work, I would have found their analysis more interesting had they addressed a particular question about the pursuit of a monetary target that was more consistent with the view of the world that makes questions about the pursuit of such a target interesting in the first place. They do not seem to me to have thought as hard as they might about these matters before embarking upon their technical work.

That being said, they do have a framework in terms of which such more policy-relevant questions can be discussed and they have shown how it can be manipulated to deal with such questions. Without a doubt, then, they are to be complimented on what they have done so far and I hope that they will treat these comments as an incentive to carry their work further.

Comments on the Paper by
P. E. Middleton, C. J. Mowl,
J. C. Odling-Smee and C. J. Riley

James Trevithick
King's College, Cambridge

I would like to divide my comments on the Treasury paper into two parts. The first will deal with the structure of the argument presented in the Treasury paper. The second part will deal with some of the implications of the Treasury simulations. In particular I would like to discuss their findings in relation to the monetarist/non-monetarist controversy and to the desirability of pursuing monetary targets.

I. THE STRUCTURE OF THE TREASURY ARGUMENT

The inclusion of private sector net wealth in the Treasury demand for £M3 function is welcome. The connection between the desired stock of financial assets and the demand for money is all too often neglected in simple income-expenditure models. Unfortunately many controversial issues concerning the inclusion of net wealth in macroeconomic models were not touched upon, nor is the standard of exposition in this section as high as it is in the remainder of the paper.

There did not appear to be much of a theory of inflation. What there was seemed to be a curious blend of the expectations-augmented Phillips curve and real wage resistance. I would have liked to see a more explicit treatment of the underlying model of inflation and of how the model performs in explaining the recent inflation in Britain.

The Treasury paper quite rightly rejects the fractional reserve model of money supply determination. Dissatisfaction with such a mechanical approach to the determinants of the money stock in a British context has been widespread for a number of years. The Treasury argument is clearly at odds with the doctrine of monetarists—and I am thinking particularly of the writings of Jerome Stein—who maintain (a) that the reserve base of the monetary system is in the firm grip of the authorities; and (b) that there is a determinate arithmetical relationship between the reserve base and the total supply of money.

The Treasury simulations are based on the assumption that, in addition to there being a target for £M3, there is also a target for the money interest rate. Hence the money interest rate is constrained to being a constant in all of these simulations. This, in effect, makes the money supply endogenous. But what sense does it make to aim at a *money* interest rate target in times of varying inflation? Moreover, would not most monetarists object to this treatment of the money supply? They would argue that *if* the money supply were treated as a truly exogenous variable—in other words if the interest rate objective were abandoned—then very different results would be obtained. It is well known that Friedman advocates the abandonment of interest rate targets (real or nominal) on the grounds that it is impossible for the authorities to *know* what the 'natural' interest rate—or, in Keynesian parlance, the 'neutral' interest rate—actually is. (In fact I subscribe to the 'Keynesian' viewpoint that one of the objectives of monetary policy *should* be to iron out unwelcome fluctuations in the real rate of interest, but that is entirely another matter.) Monetarists would raise the methodological point that it is invalid to examine the relation between the money stock and the PSBR when the overriding objective of monetary policy is not the control of the money stock but the control of the money rate of interest. But it is not for me to defend the monetarist position—Milton Friedman could muster a legion of apologists to this end—so I shall move on to an examination of the simulation results.

II. THE SIMULATION RESULTS

The simulation results appear to refute the hypothesis proposed by Nicholas Kaldor that there is a close connection between changes in the money stock and the size of the PSBR. Kaldor's regressions covered the period 1954–68 which could explain the discrepant results. The Treasury paper puts forward a strong case for believing that the connection between £M3 and the PSBR is complex. The reasoning behind their argument strikes me as convincing.

The simulations show how a *given* change in £M3 is compatible with different levels of real aggregate demand and unemployment depending on which fiscal instruments are used to keep £M3 on its target course. For example, to achieve a given change in £M3, higher VAT produces a much larger decline in real income—and presumably a much larger rise in unemployment—than increases in income tax or cuts in government spending. In other words the level or rate of growth of £M3 does not bear a determinate relation to the level of real demand. If my interpretation of the Treasury results is correct, then it follows that £M3 is neither an important control variable nor a reliable monitoring variable. For example an autonomous rise in consumer expenditure *raises* real GDP but *reduces* the stock of £M3.

Now if one accepts, for the sake of argument at least, the theory of the vertical Phillips curve and the concept of the natural unemployment rate—and, in fact, I accept neither—it would appear that a *given* unemployment rate is compatible with different levels or rates of change of £M3 depending on which fiscal instruments are used to control £M3. Indeed, in view of the complex relation between £M3, the PSBR, real income and employment, what sense does it make to regard to control of £M3 as a primary objective of economic policy? This is the nub of the matter and, with the exception of Frank Blackaby, no-one has asked the most fundamental question: what respected empirical model of the British economy lends support to the view that monetary targets will be of any use in curing Britain's ills? If it is the monetarist model of inflation, with its short-run connection between the money supply and aggregate demand on the one hand, and a short-run connection between aggregate demand and inflation on the other, then surely the events of recent years have shown it to be woefully lacking.

5 General Comments on Monetary Policy

Lawrence K. Roos
Federal Reserve Bank of St. Louis

First of all, I want to thank the organisers of this conference for inviting me to participate in these very timely discussions. I can recall no period in recent history when economic issues have weighed as heavily on people's minds as they do now, and it is encouraging to know that so many of you, representing different nations and diverse points of view, are devoting your time and talents to search for a better way to assure the future growth and stability of the economies of the free world.

In my remarks, I shall concentrate on monetary policy-making as it is conducted in the United States with specific attention to monetary aggregate targeting. In so doing, I will first describe the process of monetary policy-making in my country, follow that with a discussion of some of the problems inherent in that process, and, finally, offer for your consideration some recommendations for changes that I believe would alleviate at least some of the present causes of economic instability.

From the outset, it is only fair to admit that my viewpoint is neither reflective of the prevailing opinion within the Federal Reserve System nor does it enjoy the enthusiastic support of all opinion-moulders within the United States. While this lack of widespread acceptance occasionally generates a degree of frustration for me and my colleagues at the Federal Reserve Bank of St Louis, it does not diminish our concern that current monetary policy-making practices are not achieving the goals for which they are intended. We are convinced that, in order to minimise the instability that has become characteristic of economic events over the past two decades, we must take a fresh approach to policy-making.

I also want to emphasise that I am fully aware that the recommendations I shall present will not, in themselves, assure the immediate or painless eradication of inflations and recessions. But, if they will at least enable us to eliminate *money-induced* economic fluctuations, we will have accomplished significant progress.

Let us first consider the process by which US monetary policy is currently conducted.

I am sure you are aware that since the development of the Federal funds market, the commercial banking system in the US in general does not maintain any substantial excess reserves. As a result, substantive increases in deposits—and thus in money stock—can occur only if the Federal Reserve supplies additional reserves to the banking system, either through its open-market operations or through a reduction in reserve requirements. Since reserve requirement changes are infrequently used to affect reserve availability, open-market operations are in reality our principal tool of money management.

As you know, the Federal Open Market Committee of the Federal Reserve meets ten times each year and at each meeting establishes two primary targets: a range for the Federal funds interest rate and a growth range for the monetary aggregates. These targets are set by a majority vote of the Federal Open Market Committee, and a directive is given to the open market trading desk at the Federal Reserve Bank of New York to implement the decisions of the Committee. If market forces threaten to move the Federal funds rate above the upper limit of the Committee's prescribed range, the trading desk, in order to resist the rise in the Federal funds rate, purchases securities in the open market, thereby supplying additional reserves to the banking system. Conversely, if the monetary aggregate growth rates reach the upper limits of their ranges, the desk withdraws reserves by selling securities, thereby limiting money expansion and causing upward pressure on the Federal funds rate.

A problem arises when *both* the Federal funds rate and the growth of monetary aggregates simultaneously reach the upper or lower limits of their prescribed ranges. When this happens, the Open Market Desk faces a dilemma of whether to let the Federal funds rate exceed its prescribed limits in order to keep money stock growth within established ranges, or whether to let money overshoot or undershoot *its* target range in order to meet the prescribed Federal funds target.

Let us examine the published history of the behaviour of interest rates and the monetary aggregates in the period since long-term monetary aggregate growth ranges were first announced in 1975. In the forty-seven months in which short-term policy ranges have been set, the Federal funds interest rate has fallen outside its target ranges only five times; in the same forty-seven months, M1 growth has fallen outside its ranges twenty-three times—essentially 50 per cent of the time.

The monetary aggregates (M1) have tended to exceed their targets during periods of *rising* Federal funds rates, to fall short of their targets during periods of *falling* Federal funds rates, and to usually remain within their targets during periods of *stable* Federal funds rates. For example, from June 1976 to December 1976, the Federal funds rate fell from 5.6 per cent to 4.5 per cent, and monetary aggregates fell short of their target ranges for three out of seven months. From April 1977 to October 1977, when the Federal funds rate rose from 4.7 per cent to 6.5 per cent, the monetary aggregates exceeded their targets for five out of seven months. From October 1977 to March 1978, the Federal funds rate remained fairly stable at approximately 6.6 per cent, and monetary aggregates remained within their ranges.

Two conclusions can be drawn from these observations. First, it is clear that in periods of incompatibility between the Federal funds ranges and the monetary aggregates targets, the Federal funds rate has reigned as the primary target in the conduct of monetary policy, and adherence to monetary aggregate ranges has played, at best, only a secondary role. Secondly, the principal thrust of monetary policy has been to stabilise the Federal funds rate and to resist both upward and downward market pressures on interest rates, even if it has meant permitting the growth of monetary aggregates to fall outside their ranges. Thus, monetary policy in the United States, either by design or by default, has been fashioned to stabilise interest rates, even if it has meant destabilising money growth.

The pro-cyclical effect of this bias towards interest rate stabilisation has contributed materially to the host of economic ills that have plagued our nations—accelerated inflation, deepened recessions, incompatible monetary growth among nations, exchange rate volatility, domestic and international trade restrictions, and, in all probability, lower economic growth than would otherwise have occurred. Because interest rate stabilisation has had these undesirable effects, it is only natural to question why, after all that has happened, we continue to use, defend, and protect interest rate targeting as a preferred method of policy-making? There are several contributing factors.

The first—and perhaps the most troublesome because it represents a crucial analytical error on the part of monetary policy-makers—is a failure to distinguish between the economic consequences arising from changes in people's demand for money and those created by changes in credit markets. Changes in money market conditions and changes in credit market conditions have substantially different economic effects and require fundamentally different monetary policy responses. Interest rate stabilisation is a justifiable monetary policy response to changes in money demand but leads to significant pro-cyclical consequences when used to resist changes in the credit market.

To illustrate what I mean, let us examine the effects of changes in the demand for money. People—households and businesses—tend to hold a certain amount of money in cash or similar liquid assets for their present spending needs and for protection against unforeseen future needs. The amount of such assets they desire to hold varies from time to time. A fundamental goal of monetary policy should be to provide enough money to satisfy people's money demand. If individuals and businesses want to hold more money, it is the responsibility of the central bank to supply the necessary amount of money to satisfy that desire. If they want to reduce their money holdings, the money supply should be reduced.

Consider how interest rate stabilisation fits into this money demand equation. If individuals and businesses decide for one reason or another to increase their holdings of cash balances, they can do so either by reducing their spending or by selling off other assets. In either case, the normal result is an increase in interest rates, a decline in demand for newly produced goods and services, a decline in output, and a decline in prices. Assuming that the legitimate goal of monetary policy is to achieve stability of output and prices, the correct policy response to *increases* in money demand is to supply more money to the economy. This, in turn, has the effect of exerting downward pressure on interest rates and preventing decreases in output and prices. Thus, interest rate stabilisation is justifiable when it is used as a response to changes in the demand for money.

Interest rate stabilisation, however, is *not* an appropriate response to increases in the demand for *credit*. If individuals or businesses resort to borrowing in order to expand their current spending, the results are significantly different from those I have previously discussed in connection with changes in money demand. Increased borrowing causes interest rates to rise. However, neither output nor the price level is necessarily affected by such increased borrowing, as any increased spending by borrowers is offset by reduced spending on the part of lenders. Since credit demand tends to rise in periods of economic expansion and fall in times of contraction, monetary policy geared toward increasing the money supply to resist increases in interest rates emanating from rising credit demand merely adds to the underlying growth of spending. Conversely, reducing the money supply to resist reductions in interest rates during periods of *decreasing* credit demand results inevitably in aggravating the downward movement of output and prices. Thus, efforts by monetary policy-makers to stabilise interest rates in the face of fluctuations in credit demand have the effect of accentuating rather than stabilising changes in output and prices.

Much of the inflation we are currently experiencing can be attributed to monetary policy directed towards the stabilisation of interest rates in times of rising credit demand. This, in turn, has reflected a failure on the part of policy-makers to differentiate between the economic consequences of money market disturbances and those created by changes in credit markets.

A second factor contributing to continued concentration on interest rate stabilisation is a fundamental misconception of exactly what monetary policy can and cannot accomplish. Regardless of its goals and purposes, monetary policy as practised in free market economies can directly affect only one variable—the rate of growth of the money stock. And it is the rate of growth of this variable that affects the economic activity and price levels throughout the economy.

Monetary policy-makers frequently go astray whenever they assume that their policy actions can affect only one specific market without affecting all markets. Interest rate stabilisation often carries with it the temptation to try to affect particular markets by manipulating interest rates. If, for example, policy-makers assume that certain markets such as housing, credit, or the international exchange market are bellwethers of economic activity, interest rate manipulation might seemingly offer a legitimate way to affect one or more of those markets. What they sometimes fail to take into consideration is that any attempt to use monetary policy to stabilise unemployment in a particular market will have the effect of destabilising other markets and lead to an increase in the general price level. Furthermore, policy aimed at stabilising financial markets in order to prevent interest rates from falling causes contraction in output and employment. Unfortunately, even after it becomes apparent that such manipulation causes detrimental results in other sectors of the economy, parochial pressures often persist.

If it were only understood that monetary policy is a powerful tool in the stabilisation of general economic activity and the price level, but is a weak and very costly tool for the stabilisation of individual economic sectors and markets, perhaps the bias towards interest rate control would abate. A great improvement in the effectiveness of monetary policy could be expected if policy-makers were to recognise that decisions to increase or decrease the growth of money stock can provide an environment in which free markets can function efficiently, but that their effect on particular transactions is minimal.

A third reason for interest rate stabilisation is the benefit it offers government. Whether we agree or disagree with the spending and revenue policies of our governments, interest rate stabilisation by a central bank removes an important budgetary constraint on government. As we know, expenditures by government must be financed either by raising taxes or by deficit spending. In a democracy, increases in taxes are ultimately subject to review by the citizenry at the polling booth. Budget deficits financed by the private sector necessarily entail an increase in interest rates as a result of an increase in the public's holding of government debt instruments and thus, are, open to public scrutiny. It is only when a central bank stabilises interest rates that government expenditures can be increased in a seemingly 'painless' and relatively hidden manner without a tax increase or a rise in interest rates. To be sure, transfer of wealth still occurs through subsequent inflation but only with a lag of a couple of years and without clear public recognition of what induced the inflation. Thus, interest rate stabilisation makes possible increased government spending *without* public awareness and *without* voter approval. While I am not suggesting that this practice is consciously being employed at present, it does represent a powerful incentive for government to encourage interest rate stabilisation.

In closing, let me summarise the points I have tried to make. I have described the mechanics of US monetary policy-making and implementation. I have shown how establishing multiple targets for the Federal funds interest rate and the monetary aggregates has frequently resulted in incompatibility, with the Federal funds rate usually emerging as the dominant target. I have suggested that, in recent years, monetary policy in the United States and elsewhere has been directed toward interest rate stabilisation. Whenever that has occurred, whether in the United States or in other nations, it has led to destabilisation of economic activity and accelerated inflation.

I have identified what I perceive to be some of the more important reasons for continued adherence to disproven policies: the confusion between money demand and the credit market; an unwillingness to admit that monetary policy is a very poor and very costly means of manipulating individual markets; and the fact that interest rate stabilisation relieves government of important budgetary constraints. All of these are powerful social and political factors and it is not surprising that changes in the manner of conducting monetary policy are difficult to enact.

I am convinced that there is a better way to accomplish the goals of monetary policy. That better way is to control the growth of the money stock so that it is consistent with the potential growth of output and with a pre-determined—preferably zero—rate of inflation. In order to achieve this goal, however, it will be necessary to abandon interest rate targeting and to announce publicly what our monetary policy goals are and what mechanism will be used to achieve them. Only if we are prepared to take these steps can we realistically hope that monetary policy will become a stabilising rather than a disruptive force.

I know that these proposals are not new and that contrary arguments persist against the feasibility of controlling the growth of money. Critics continue to assert that money stock growth cannot be measured with precision and thus cannot be controlled. My response to that argument is that a policy of explicitly controlling the growth of money has not been given a fair chance in the United States; in other economies that have made the effort, it has worked well. A second and more serious criticism is that, if money demand changes do indeed occur, a steady growth of money stock would lead to instability in economic activity. Empirical evidence clearly indicates that, over periods of a year or more, income velocity changes very slowly and predictably. In the very few instances when sudden changes in money demand have occurred, such as the one induced by the OPEC shock in 1973 and 1974 or those induced by institutional changes, they have been of temporary duration and were readily recognisable. Should exogenous changes occur, the rate of money growth can be temporarily changed to meet specific situations, and such changes should be announced publicly and the rationale behind them explained. A third argument frequently directed against a constant rate of money growth is that, if labour unions demand wage increases or businesses set prices in excess of the rate of growth of productivity, unemployment would result. This, I think, emphasises the critical importance of central bank credibility. If it becomes clear that monetary authorities are going to adhere to their announced money growth targets, I doubt that businesses or unions would risk the loss of sales or employment that would accompany exorbitant wage or price demands.

I would stress that we can no longer enjoy the luxury of pro-crastination. We cannot be content merely to debate and theorise as to the best methods of conducting monetary policy. The time has come to learn from our past policy errors.

Interest rate stabilisation as a means of seeking economic stability has had its day in court and its results have certainly been less than satisfactory. We are still experiencing persistent and accelerating inflation, and we again face the grim prospect of recession. If we respond as we have in the past—if we persist in repeating past errors—we will have failed in our responsibilities as monetary policy-makers. We must be prepared to try new methods which offer the potential for success. Targeting on interest rates at the expense of stabilising the growth of the money supply has resulted in the situation we face today. If we feel that there is a better way—and I firmly believe there is—I suggest that we move ahead without further delay.

6 A Central Banker's View of Targeting

G. E. Freeman
Bank of Canada

My comments on the subject of monetary growth targets are based primarily on my own personal reading of the particular monetary experience of my own country. I cannot claim that my colleagues at the Bank of Canada would necessarily subscribe without qualification to every word of what I have to say in this paper, let alone central bankers from other countries whose reading of their own particular monetary history and problems may well have led them to somewhat different conclusions.

I happen to work in a central bank that has been using explicit money growth targets as operating guides for the implementation of monetary policy since 1975. Thus, while we have acquired a certain amount of practical experience with targeting in Canada, our experience to date has not been long enough for any very strong conclusions to be drawn, and we ourselves are well aware that we still have much to learn. I should also point out that the particular approach that we have been following has evolved in response to economic and institutional circumstances peculiar to Canada. Thus it is only one of many possible approaches, and I hold no brief for its general applicability. The fact remains, however, that operating within a framework of monetary growth targets has gradually become an integral part of the way we think about and implement monetary policy at the Bank of Canada. We have come to feel more comfortable with this targeting approach as we have learned more about what to expect from it, how far we can safely rely upon it, and what its main problems and limitations are. We have, of course, encountered various problems along the way, but not—at least to date—problems so troublesome as to cause us to give serious considera-tion to abandoning the whole approach. On the whole we have been successful so far in keeping the trend rate of increase of the money stock broadly in line with our successive targets. While the near-term behaviour of the Canadian economy has continued to produce its share of surprises as it has in the past, and while the pace of improvement in Canada's underlying cost, price and balance of payments performance has not been either as rapid or as steady as might have been hoped, we are certainly not alone in our belief that Canada has made significant progress since 1975 in getting its inflation problem under better control, and that Canadian monetary policy has made an important contribution in this regard.

In short, the practice of monetary targeting is still very much alive and well in Canada. We have gained a certain amount of confidence in the approach we are following, we believe that it has helped to improve the performance record of Canadian monetary policy in controlling inflation, and we believe that we have been able to maintain an encouraging measure of public and political support for continuing to operate along these lines.

In arriving at our present operating approach in Canada we have had to work out our own pragmatic answers to many of the same questions that have troubled other central banks when they have taken a hard look at the possibilities and problems of working within a monetary targeting framework. I should like to offer a few comments on some of these issues, drawing on Canadian experience by way of illustration.

The first and broadest of these questions, I suppose, is what a central bank might hope to gain by adopting the practice of pursuing explicit monetary growth targets. Central bankers have never been in much doubt about the seriousness of the economic and social damage that is likely to result from a failure to preserve the value of money from rapid and unpredictable inflation. They have also long been aware that maintaining adequate control over the quantity of money supplied to the economy through the process of bank credit expansion is both a necessary condition for success in avoiding inflation and—in cases where inflation has nevertheless been allowed to develop—a sufficient condition for ensuring that inflation is eventually brought to an end. Nor have central bankers been ignorant of the mechanics of monetary control. As the only source of the basic cash that domestic banking institutions require in order to expand their loans and deposits, central bankers have long been familiar with how to use their technical powers to influence the pace of domestic monetary expansion, domestic interest rate levels and the external value of their currency on foreign exchange markets—and thus in turn the pressure of demand in markets for goods and services, the level of domestic capacity utilisation and net imports, and the trend of domestic prices and costs. How, then, is the patent inadequacy of monetary control in most countries during the late sixties and early seventies to be explained? And how might the pursuit of monetary growth targets be supposed to help improve matters?

As central bankers tend to see it, the main obstacle to the continuing exercise of adequate monetary control is that the central bank's freedom of action is inevitably constrained in practice by concern about a variety of often conflicting short-run objectives in such areas as unemployment, the exchange rate, debt management and so on. A related problem is the difficulty of predicting the economic consequences of central bank actions at all accurately in a complex economy whose inner workings are far from being perfectly understood but are obviously subject to a wide variety of unforeseen 'real' shocks, internal rigidities and response lags. Viewed in this light, tying a central bank's policy to anything as simple-minded as keeping the growth rate of some monetary aggregate within pre-determined limits would certainly seem on the face of it to be a rather foolhardy undertaking.

That was my own view of the matter until a few years ago. What changed my mind was both the growing empirical evidence for reasonably stable demand for money functions and a growing conviction that Canada, like many other western countries, was in for a very bleak future indeed unless some more effective policy approach could be devised for halting and reversing the accelerating decline in the value of money. The basic case for setting monetary growth targets, in my view, is that it puts the main emphasis in monetary policy squarely where it belongs—on the central bank trying to do what it alone can and must do if the value of money is to be preserved rather than on its giving equal weight to any number of competing short-run concerns that can only divert it from discharging its main responsibility. The steady pursuit of such targets provides some built-in assurance that short-run income disturbances in the economy will promptly evoke contra-cyclical feedback responses, thereby lessening the pressure on the central bank to attempt to predict in detail, and fine tune its operations in anticipation of, every turn and twist in the short-run behaviour of the economy that may happen to lie ahead. In this sense the pursuit of monetary targets is far from being an optimal strategy. But if following an optimal strategy is far beyond our reach in the present state of economic knowledge, surely there is something to be said for falling back on a fail-safe strategy that offers a realistic hope of sparing our countries further major episodes of pro-cyclical monetary policy of the stop-go variety and ever more severe inflation. Monetary targeting also gives the central bank much more solid ground on which to stand in its efforts to explain and defend the unpopular but necessary actions it must take on occasion. People can understand and accept intuitively the proposition that if inflation is ever to be contained, monetary growth must be kept firmly under control at all times.

I shall have a little more to say on this basic issue towards the end of this paper but in the meantime I should like to turn to some of the more important technical issues involved in the pursuit of monetary growth targets. It is one thing to understand how controlling the money supply might be supposed to work in theory, quite another to devise an operational approach for doing so in practice that is not only based on a reasonably well thought out and empirically-validated economic rationale, but that also fits the institutional realities of a particular country.

The first of these issues is whether the means of controlling the target monetary aggregate should be by using the central bank's control over the monetary base to exert direct control over the supply of money, or by indirect control over the demand for money through changes in the level of short-term interest rates. A second and closely related issue is which particular money aggregate the central bank should focus on as the target/indicator to be controlled.

In Canada these issues were resolved in favour of operating indirectly on the public's demand for money via interest rates, and by focusing on M1—a narrowly defined concept of money with a relatively high interest elasticity—as the target aggregate to be controlled. The first of a number of considerations that induced us to follow this route was that we preferred to continue to use operating procedures which were already well known to us—if we could—rather than venture into some radically different and unfamiliar operating approach that would probably require major changes in our existing system of statutory cash reserve requirements. This consideration pointed towards focusing on M1 as our target variable because of its ready controllability through interest rate changes. Broader monetary aggregates include interest-bearing savings and time deposits on which the Canadian banks can and do at times offer rates that are highly competitive with the rates obtainable on market instruments that are relatively close substitutes for such deposits. Thus it is difficult to see how the short-run growth rate of a broad aggregate could be effectively controlled in Canada through changes in short-term interest rates unless these changes were much larger and more frequent than in the past.

In Canada the econometric evidence indicates that there is in fact little to choose between M1 and broader aggregates either in terms of their usefulness as indicators of current nominal income or in terms of their having displayed a reasonably stable relationship to income and interest rates in the past. The demand function for broad money is, however, significantly more complex than that for M1, so that changes in the demand for broad aggregates are more likely to occur for reasons unconnected with changes in the growth rate of nominal income. The growth over time of narrowly defined money often follows a sub-stantially different path from that of more broadly defined monetary aggregates, especially over periods as short as a year or so. Thus in Canada the use of a broad money target would seem to involve a significantly higher risk of imposing unwarranted changes in interest rates on the economy and generating undesired movements in nominal national income.

It is conceivable that a way could be found of controlling the supply of money directly via the monetary base that would lead to greater short-run precision of control and more prompt and vigorous feedback responses to income disturbances. But provided that undesired move-ments in the trend of M1 do not persist for more than a few months before they can be corrected—as they generally can be using control via interest rates—I doubt whether such temporary deviations are likely to be very damaging in economic terms. And although reliance on the relatively high interest sensitivity of M1 for control purposes may indeed imply a significantly less prompt and vigorous feedback response to undesired deviations in income than one might expect with a broad money target, this could well be an advantage when—as is bound to happen from time to time—the deviation in monetary growth merely reflects some disturbance of financial origin and is thus giving a misleading signal.

I do not know how much weight these considerations would carry in the institutional circumstances of countries other than Canada in choosing their own target aggregate and method of controlling it. Although the issues involved are quite important in terms of the central bank's shorter run objective of minimising deviations of nominal national income from some desired trend rate of growth, they would seem to be much less important in terms of its longer run objective of achieving a greater degree of price stability. Regardless of which aggregate it chooses to control or how it chooses to control it, over the longer run the central bank should in theory be able to bring the trend rate of inflation broadly into line with its objectives, provided either that the demand function for the aggregate in question is reasonably stable over time or that the central bank is willing to adjust its monetary targets whenever a shift in the demand function is identified.

In any event, it is our belief at the Bank of Canada that we do have a monetary targeting approach that is both operational and makes a certain amount of sense in economic terms. Let me summarise it briefly. The Bank of Canada has long been accustomed to using its ability to determine the supply of cash reserves to the banking system in a way that works roughly as follows. During any given reserve-averaging period, the aggregate demand for cash reserves on the part of the banking system is largely pre-determined by a lagged differential reserve requirement based on the system's recent levels of demand deposits on the one hand and notice or time deposits on the other. The system's demand for excess reserves, though not entirely predictable, is normally quite small. Depending on how readily or otherwise the central bank satisfies the banking system's demand for excess cash reserves, it can induce short-run portfolio responses on the part of the system banks strong enough to give it a dominant influence over the short-run behaviour of Canadian short-term interest rates. Cash stringency induces the banks to liquidate money market assets and become more aggressive in bidding for term deposits, with consequent upward pressure on the whole interest rate structure radiating out from the money market. As Canadian interest rates are forced higher in relation to foreign interest rates, the spot value of the Canadian dollar normally strengthens in the foreign exchange market both in relation to its forward value in absolute terms. Providing cash reserves more readily, on the other hand, induces responses similar in kind but in the opposite direction.

The way in which the Bank of Canada attempts to keep the growth trajectory of M1 within the limits of the current target range requires little change in its normal operating techniques. If M1 begins to grow more rapidly than is desired—presumably because of a correspondingly rapid expansion of money incomes in the economy—the Bank can rein in the supply of cash reserves to the banking system and let short-term interest rates rise. Higher short-term interest rates raise the opportunity cost to the public of holding non-interest-bearing transactions balances, and this will soon induce the public to adjust downwards the quantity of such balances it will readily hold per dollar of income. Supplying cash reserves more readily and letting short-term interest rates fall works in the opposite direction: it raises the public's demand for M1 balances per dollar of income and can thus be used to correct an undesired slackening of the growth rate of the money stock. Econometric estimation techniques can be of help to the central bank in judging the approximate timing and magnitude of the changes in short-term interest rates required to put M1 growth back on track, provided that the near-term growth rate of nominal national income can be predicted with a fair degree of reliability.

Given a reasonably stable M1 demand function, for any particular trend rate of increase of the money stock there will be a corresponding trend rate of increase of nominal national income at which the growth in money demand and money supply should remain in approximate balance. So long as—for whatever reason—nominal income growth exceeds this rate, rising interest rates will be required to prevent the rapid growth in the demand for money from out-running the rate of growth in the money supply at which the central bank is aiming. In an open economy, rising domestic interest rates will also put upward pressure on the exchange rate, and through these related market channels the influence of central bank resistance to an acceleration of monetary growth will feed back on spending decisions with a weight that increases over time. In due course, therefore, the growth rate of nominal demand can be expected to slacken off again in response to rising interest rate and exchange rate pressures. If nominal income growth should slow down excessively, this chain of events would be reversed: the interest rate and exchange rate pressures called into play would be of the opposite sign, and would work in the opposite direction.

There are a few subsidiary issues of a technical nature that I propose to touch upon only briefly. How does the central bank decide at what levels to set its interim monetary growth rate targets, when to change these target levels and by how much? Should an attempt be made to maintain as much continuity as possible between these successive target ranges, or should a certain amount of 'base drift' be regarded as acceptable? How should the target range be defined and how much latitude should it provide? How rigidly should the central bank feel obliged to adhere to its current target range and under what circumstances, if any, should it contemplate raising its targets (at least temporarily) rather than holding them steady or lowering them?

Here again the answers we came to in Canada may not strike other central banks as the right ones for their particular circumstances. In our own case we started from a situation where both the rate of inflation and the rate of monetary expansion were generally viewed as having been much too high for several years. Thus at the same time as we announced our initial target range for the growth rate of M1, we indicated that this

range would have to be lowered gradually over time for monetary policy
to be consistent with the objective of ensuring a continuing gradual
decline in Canada's inflation rate over the medium term. The upper and
lower limits of our initial target range were set respectively at annual
growth rates of 'well below 15 per cent' but not less than 10 per cent.
These limits were chosen rather eclectically, the objective being to ensure
at least some deceleration from the current trend rate of increase of M1
but not so sharp a deceleration as to risk unacceptably disruptive
effects on economic activity levels in Canada. Given an income elasticity
of demand for M1 in Canada of close to unity, the limits of this initial
target range implied that the Bank was prepared to accommodate a
trend rate of increase of nominal national income of the order of (say) 11
to 15 per cent a year, but that it would feel compelled to raise or lower
interest rates to the extent required to prevent income growth from
moving outside the limits of this range or at least from doing so for any
extended period of time.

We have subsequently lowered these target range limits at approximately annual intervals in successive gradual steps, generally by 1 per
cent a year, to their current level of from 6–10 per cent a year. In doing
so we have tried to update the new base level from which these growth
rates are measured in such a way as to minimise 'base drift' and thereby
maintain the credibility of our targeting approach. Although of course
neither the short-run path of income growth nor that of the GNE price
deflator have shown the same steady deceleration since 1975, their trend
rates of increase have indeed moved downward sufficiently over the
period to permit real economic growth to continue, albeit at a rather
subdued rate. For precautionary reasons, however, we have been careful
not to tie our hands in advance by announcing the duration of the period
to which any given target range will apply, and before moving to a new
target range we try to examine its possible implications as best we can in
the context of current forecasts of the near-term behaviour of the
economy. The projected growth rates of output and prices derived from
these forecasts are helpful to us in judging the possible direction and
magnitude of the interest rate changes that may be required to keep M1
on track over the next several months. We have not so far found it
necessary to contemplate raising our targets, and while one can imagine
circumstances arising in which there seemed to be little option but to do
so, we could be extremely loth to take such a step unless we felt we could
make a convincing case in public that it had to be done for very
compelling reasons and that it was clearly temporary.

One Canadian innovation that may be of interest to other central banks is that our target ranges are defined for practical purposes not as the gradually widening area between two diverging growth rates but as a band of uniform width with limits 2 per cent above and 2 per cent below the midpoints of the range. This way of defining our target range gives us the same degree of latitude in trying to stay on track at the beginning of a new targeting period as we have towards the end of it. Even with this substantial degree of latitude, we have on occasion permitted M1 growth to rise somewhat above or fall somewhat below the limits of the band for a time. There have been times, for example, when the level of M1 has been greatly inflated temporarily because of postal strikes and similar disruptions in financial markets which we felt we should ignore rather than resist by pushing up interest rates. In late 1976 and early 1977, on the other hand, we had reason to believe that the introduction of new banking practices to enable bank customers to economise on the amount of their balances held in non-interest-bearing demand accounts was a special factor serving to depress M1 below its forecast levels, and thus for some months we permitted M1 to run somewhat below our target range. Since this behavioural shift was apparently a once-and-for-all phenomenon that has not so far reappeared, the Bank was also able to allow for it to some extent when up-dating the base for the subsequent target range. Judging by US experience, however, we are well aware of the possibility that further shifts of this character could occur in Canada which might seriously impair the usefulness of M1 as a target/indicator at least for a time, and which would imply the need for appropriate revision of the M1 demand function—perhaps by adjusting the constant term in the equation—or resort to some other aggregate for targeting purposes.

One interesting question about using interest rates to control the demand for M1 is how this can be squared with the need to respond at times to urgent debt management or exchange rate concerns, given that the focus of the approach is essentially on influencing the growth path of nominal national income. To date, I am not aware that debt management concerns have created any major instances of conflict with the targeting approach that we have been following, presumably because the Government accepts the need to pay going market rates of interest on its borrowings even though these borrowings have recently been very large. The situation is less clear with respect to possible conflicts between monetary targeting and exchange rate concerns. I think it is fairly obvious that the pursuit of domestic monetary growth targets requires a floating exchange rate regime, and that in a sense such targets serve as an alternative policy guide for central bank operations to that provided under a pegged exchange rate regime by the need to maintain the external value of the currency within narrow specified limits. The differences are far from being absolute, however: even under a floating exchange rate regime the authorities are unlikely to be totally indifferent to what is happening to the external value of the currency, especially in periods of marked instability in foreign exchange markets.

During the course of 1978, for example, the Bank of Canada became increasingly concerned about the problem of maintaining confidence in the foreign exchange market in the face of persistent downward pressure on the value of the Canadian dollar arising in part from the rapid upward movement of interest rates in the United States. A substantial downward adjustment of the foreign exchange value of the Canadian dollar had already occurred for reasons that were well understood and accepted as necessary, but it was feared that the direct impact on Canada's price level of further substantial exchange depreciation could, by reinforcing already existing price pressures from other sources, set off a renewed outbreak of serious wage inflation. For this reason the Bank decided that it ought for the time being to give special weight in its interest rate policy to the exchange market situation, raising domestic interest rates repeatedly to keep them more or less in line with US rates, even though it was aware that this course of action involved a risk of depressing monetary growth somewhat below its current target range for a time. As things have turned out so far, this risk has not in fact materialised: M1 growth has fallen close to the lower limit of the target range but not significantly below it, and a strong rebound has occurred recently in the value of the Canadian dollar on foreign exchange markets. Nevertheless, the possibility remains that on occasion exchange rate concerns may suggest the need for interest rate responses rather greater in magnitude than the central bank's current monetary targets would seem to require.

There are, of course, many other reasons why a central bank cannot regard the pursuit of monetary growth targets as a purely mechanical exercise. Targeting certainly does not obviate the need for analysing a much broader range of economic and financial information and making judgements about the action the central bank should take within a much wider frame of reference. Broad economic judgements obviously have to be made, for example, in deciding what upper and lower limits should define the target range for monetary growth during any particular period, when they should be adjusted and by how much. If a central bank is to make a serious effort to adhere to monetary targets, it will want to feel reasonably sure that pursuing them will prove a sensible way of attempting to realise its ultimate economic objectives.

Seen in this perspective, the pursuit of publicly announced monetary growth targets is certainly no substitute for the difficult judgements central banks are inevitably called upon to make. The practice can, however, serve as a useful and important adjunct to the technical approach customarily followed by central banks in the exercise of their monetary control responsibilities, by providing a disciplined framework within which to appraise the longer run risks of the policy being followed in the short run. In addition, it offers the possibility of exerting a constructive influence on the public's expectations with respect to future inflation by expressing the intermediate goals of monetary policy in a direct and simple manner. With the passage of each successive year in which the central bank manages to hold to its announced targets, the chances will increase, it seems to me, of gaining widespread public acceptance of the need for a continuing degree of monetary discipline that has been lacking in many western countries for some time.

Comments on Dr Freeman's Paper

J. R. Gaster
Williams & Glyn's Bank Limited

As a supporter of monetary targets and as someone who works in an institution on the receiving end of monetary policy, I was much heartened by Dr Freeman's paper. Monetary policy has been conducted in a pragmatic way, tailored to Canada's particular circumstances, and has been remarkably successful. Moreover, there has been no resort to devices like the 'corset'.

Monetary targeting in the UK has not so far found favour to the same extent, and there are indeed some who claim that it has already been discredited. This is partly the fault of some advocates of targeting, who made predictions as though the implications of such an approach had been almost instantly absorbed and its rationale largely accepted. But there are of course many reasons why this should not be so. It obviously takes time for people to adjust to a change of this sort and for their expectations to be influenced in the way desired. Moreover, those of us who were actually involved in the forecasting business in the early stages could surely be forgiven for our reservations about the government's ability to stick to the announced targets. Until the government has proved its ability to achieve prudent targets over a number of years, it would be premature to pass judgement on the success or failure of targeting in this country.

Comments on Dr Freeman's Paper

Monetary Targeting in Canada and the United States

Michael J. Hamburger
Federal Reserve Bank of New York

It is a pleasure to discuss George Freeman's account of Canadian experience in using monetary growth targets as operating guides for the implementation of monetary policy. Among the increasing number of monetary authorities that have adopted such guides, the Bank of Canada has clearly been one of the most successful in achieving its announced targets. This discussion seeks to put Canada's performance through 1978 in perspective by comparing it to that of the United States. On the basis of Freeman's remarks it would appear that the former has been far superior to the latter. The paper begins with a look at the historical record: the types of monetary growth objectives that have been set in the two countries and the actual behaviour of the aggregates relative to those objectives. To anticipate the conclusions, the evidence suggests that while the Bank of Canada's record is better than the Federal Reserve's, it does not seem to warrant Freeman's glowing appraisal.

The latter part of the paper considers two explanations for the greater success of the Canadian authorities. One focuses on the operating techniques used to control monetary growth, while the other stresses the importance that the two central banks attach to the aggregate targets. The evidence presented below does not make a definitive case for either explanation. Nevertheless, it raises questions as to the importance that the Federal Reserve gives to achieving the monetary aggregate targets.

I. THE HISTORICAL RECORD

The Formulation of Monetary Aggregate Objectives

In the fall of 1975 the Bank of Canada made its first public announcement of a target range for monetary expansion. This followed a similar
move by the Federal Reserve System by approximately one-half of a
year. For both institutions, the announcement of a specific longer term
policy objective represented a fundamental change from the past.
However, an examination of the targeting mechanics indicates that the
two central banks chose to retain a considerable amount of policy-
making discretion, albeit in different ways.

The Federal Reserve chose to specify one-year growth ranges for
three measures of the money supply (M1, M2 and M3) and until
1978 it rolled the target periods forward every three months.[1] In
contrast, the Bank of Canada concentrates solely on the narrow money
stock (M1) and thus far has generally not set targets for overlapping
time periods, i.e. it moves the target intervals ahead approximately once
a year. In both respects the latter approach is more straightforward and
represents a more specific policy commitment. Having targets for a
number of variables gives a central bank some degree of flexibility, that
may be appropriate in an uncertain world, but may also impair the
underlying purpose of the procedure. Unless all the targets are hit or
missed together, it will be more difficult for the public to determine the
thrust of policy and to assess the quality of the central bank's
performance. Moreover, frequent updating of the target intervals, and
more importantly the base levels from which growth of the aggregates is
calculated, could introduce the so-called 'base drift' problem and cause
monetary targeting to lose most of its meaning.

The aspects of the target setting procedure discussed above provided
the Federal Reserve with more flexibility than the Bank of Canada and
hence a greater opportunity to avoid the discipline intended. For their
part, the Canadian authorities sought to retain some freedom of action
by setting relatively wide growth ranges and, as Freeman states, being
'careful not to tie our hands in advance by announcing the duration of
the period to which any given target range [would] apply'. In practice,
the Canadians have set target ranges with widths of 4 to 5 percentage
points that have been maintained in effect for periods of from ten to
fifteen months. This differs from the American custom of setting one-
year ranges with widths of 2 to 3 percentage points.

The Results

The results obtained by the United States and Canada in achieving their monetary aggregate objectives through 1978 are summarised in Figures 6.1 and 6.2. Since the US objectives have been specified for uniform time intervals—annual growth rates over successive four-quarter periods— they are easy to illustrate and compare to the actual movements of the aggregates, see Figure 6.1. Each panel deals with a different measure of the money supply—M1, M2 and M3. The dashed line shows the growth of the aggregate over the four quarters ending in the indicated quarter, while the solid horizontal lines denote the growth range that had been set for the period ending that quarter. In the Canadian case (Figure 6.2) the dashed line in the upper panel again shows the growth of the targeted aggregate (M1) over four-quarter periods but the solid horizontal lines provide only approximations of the target ranges. Because of the irregular time intervals used by the Canadian authorities, it is difficult to compare the targets to any single measure of monetary growth. The lower part of the exhibit records the precise targets that have been specified together with the actual growth of M1 over those periods.

Two features of the published record are clear: (i) the Bank of Canada has been more successful than the Federal Reserve in meeting its announced objectives and (ii) both central banks have fulfilled their stated intentions of gradually lowering the levels of the target ranges over time.[2] However, neither monetary authority has succeeded in reducing the *actual* longer term growth rates of the aggregates. This discrepancy is particularly evident for the United States where the one-year growth rates of the aggregates rose from their 1975 lows to levels approaching the record growth rates of the early 1970s. (In 1971, M2 and M3 increased by $11\frac{1}{2}$ and $13\frac{1}{2}$ per cent, respectively, while in 1972, M1 rose at a record $8\frac{1}{2}$ per cent rate.) Subsequently, there was some deceleration in M2 and M3, but their rates of advance remained above the levels that preceded the targeting era.

For Canada, there has been no increase in monetary growth since the start of the first target period in early 1975, but neither has there been a decline. Instead, the advance in M1 has fluctuated around a 10 per cent rate. This difference between actual and targeted growth is capable of explaining Freeman's quandary as to why the rate of inflation in Canada has not 'shown the same steady deceleration [as the target range] since 1975'. It would not seem necessary to be a strict adherent of rational expectations to believe that the behaviour of the economy (and the public's expectations of that behaviour) ultimately depends on the

FIG. 6.1 Targeted and actual United States monetary growth from four quarters earlier

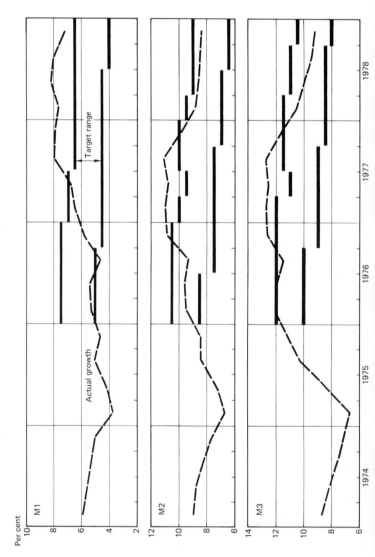

FIG. 6.2 Actual M1 growth in Canada from four quarters earlier and approximate target ranges

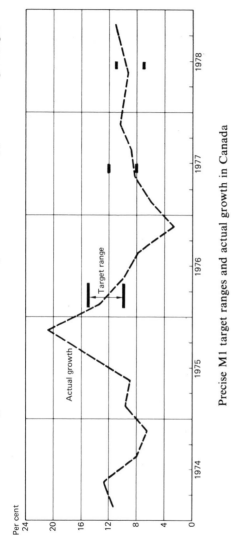

Precise M1 target ranges and actual growth in Canada

Target period:	Target range *	Actual M1 growth *
April/May/June 1975 – Feb/Mar/Apr 1976	10–15	10.9
Feb/Mar/Apr 1976 – June 1977	8–12	8.1
June 1977 – June 1978	7–11	9.1
June 1978 –	6–10	8.2[†]

* Annual percentage rate   † Growth from June 1978 to May 1979

policy pursued by the authorities rather than their announced intentions.

On the basis of these findings, it is difficult to share Freeman's highly favourable appraisal of the Bank of Canada's experience with monetary aggregate targets. By choosing relatively wide ranges (4 to 5 percentage points) the Canadian authorities have been able to meet a succession of lower targets, but have not reduced the underlying rate of monetary expansion. Nevertheless, in contrast to the Federal Reserve, they did not permit aggregate growth to return to the very high rates of the early 1970s.[3]

II. TWO POSSIBLE EXPLANATIONS

This section takes another look at the recent behaviour of the monetary aggregates. Its purpose is quite limited: to evaluate two possible explanations of the superior performance of the Canadian authorities. One is that their operating techniques are better suited to controlling monetary growth, while the second is that the Canadians attach greater importance to achieving the targets.

In considering the suitability of the operating techniques it should be noted that there are important similarities in the general methodology employed by the two central banks. They both rely largely on open-market operations to exert indirect control over the money supply by changing the level of short-term interest rates and thereby influencing the demand for money. Consequently, any comprehensive analysis of the specific procedures used to accomplish these objectives would need to determine how appropriate they are for the institutional settings involved.

The present investigation focuses solely on the data in Table 6.1. These are one-quarter growth rates of M1 for the United States and Canada, expressed as compounded annual rates of change.[4] The difference in the variability of the two series is striking. For the United States the largest of the twenty one-quarter growth rates in M1 (9.6 per cent in 1978:3) exceeds the smallest (2.0 per cent in 1975:1) by 7.6 percentage points. For Canada the comparable difference between the largest and smallest M1 growth rates is more than 4 times as large (26.9 per cent in 1975:4 as opposed to −5.5 per cent in 1974:3) and the 7.6 percentage point gap is exceeded in every year but one, 1977.

In the face of such evidence it is difficult to attribute Canada's greater success in monetary targeting to tighter short-run control of the

TABLE 6.1 ONE-QUARTER GROWTH RATES FOR M1 IN
THE UNITED STATES AND CANADA (expressed as compounded
annual rate of change)

	US M1	CANADIAN M1
1974: 1		10·6
2	4·2	20·1
3	4·1	5·5
4	4·7	2·3
1975: 1	2·0	24·3
2	5·9	17·0
3	7.4	16.2
4	3·0	26·9
1976: 1	4·7	− 4·7
2	6·6	3·3
3	4·2	7·6
4	7·7	4·2
1977: 1	7·6	8·7
2	7·6	12·0
3	8·9	10·1
4	7·6	11·2
1978: 1	6·8	5·8
2	9·6	9·8
3	8·4	14·4
4	4·4	14·7

aggregates. Indeed, it is hard not to reach the opposite conclusion, namely that Canada has succeeded despite a lack of close monetary control. From this point, some might argue that a portion of the Federal Reserve's target misses are due to a lack of strong policy commitment. This is the view expressed by Lawrence Roos, who has regularly attended Federal Open Market Committee meetings since early 1976.[5]

The pattern of M1 growth rates for the United States in Table 6.1 supports this hypothesis. Over the six quarters from 1975:2 to 1976:3 these rates hovered just above 5 per cent, which was at or near the lower end of the target ranges during that period. In the eight subsequent quarters, the expansion in M1 shifted to a higher plateau, with each of the annual rates of change holding close to 8 per cent, well above the upper end of the ranges.[6] It seems highly unlikely that the Federal Reserve intentionally sought to achieve these particular growth rates. Nevertheless, the consistency with which monetary growth was first below and then above the announced targets raises questions as to the importance attached to the targets in implementing Federal Reserve policy.

NOTES

1. The Full Employment and Balanced Growth Act of 1978 (the 'Humphrey–Hawkins' Act) requires the Federal Reserve to specify targets on a calendar year basis.
2. The Bank of Canada indicated its intention gradually to lower the target ranges when the first range was announced and has repeated it in each subsequent issue of the Bank's Annual Report. The Federal Reserve's commitment to reducing the aggregate growth ranges over time was spelled out in Chairman Burns' first presentation to Congress and it has been restated frequently since then.
3. Discounting the latter part of 1975 when the monetary statistics were distorted by a nationwide postal strike, Canadian M1 reached its highest longer term growth rate during the 1971–72 period when it averaged about 15 per cent.
4. This analysis deals solely with the narrow measure of the US money stock because it corresponds to the aggregate targeted in Canada and because it was generally given the most weight by the US authorities.
5. Lawrence K. Roos, President, Federal Reserve Bank of St Louis, pp. 184–5 this volume. Roos' statistical analysis is based primarily on the Federal Reserve's shorter, two-month, targets for the monetary aggregates, but his conclusions are more general.
6. The return to a slower pace in late 1978 is generally believed to be, at least, partially due to problems with the official money supply data. For discussions of these problems see 'A Proposal for Redefining the Monetary Aggregates', *Federal Reserve Bulletin*, January 1979, and John Wenninger and Charles M. Sivesind, 'Defining Money for a Changing Financial System', *Quarterly Review*, Federal Reserve Bank of New York, Spring 1979.

7 Targeting the Base – the Swiss Experience[1]

Kurt Schiltknecht
Swiss National Bank

I. INTRODUCTION

At the beginning of 1975, the Swiss National Bank decided to adopt a money stock target. The adjusted monetary base was chosen as an instrument for controlling the growth in the money stock. The aim of this policy was to maintain a stable price level. When the decision for targeting the money stock was taken, the Swiss National Bank realised that a revaluation of the Swiss franc would be inevitable. However, the size of the revaluation came as a surprise. The exchange rate difficulties emerging in the autumn of 1978, in particular, have raised the question whether money stock targeting under a system of flexible exchange rates is the appropriate way of conducting monetary policy in a small open economy.

In response to the exchange rate problems, the Swiss National Bank, last autumn, decided to modify its approach to monetary policy. The practice of specifying a target growth for the money stock was temporarily abandoned in favour of a target for the franc/Deutsche mark exchange rate. Moreover, for the current year, the Bank has declined to announce a target for the money stock, indicating that the exchange rate still serves as the focal point of monetary policy.

In the following sections, it will be shown that the recent change in the policy stance does not mean that the Swiss National Bank has abandoned the principles of monetary policy adopted in 1975. The point of departure will be a brief description of the basic ideas behind our monetary policy. Next, I shall deal with the operational methods for controlling the money stock. This is followed by a section attempting to assess the implementation of monetary policy, in particular the use of

211

the monetary base as an instrument for controlling the money stock in the presence of strong exchange rate fluctuations. Finally, the last section draws a number of tentative conclusions from the Swiss experience.

II. MONEY STOCK TARGET AND METHODS OF CONTROL

With the adoption of a monetary target in 1975, the Swiss National Bank stipulated a growth rate of 6 per cent for the narrowly defined money stock M1 for that year. This decision was not the outcome of sophisticated research work; it simply reflected the following three casual observations:[2]

(1) A sharp acceleration in the growth rate of M1 has always been followed by an acceleration in the inflation rate.
(2) A growth rate of M1 which has been persistently greater than the growth rate of real GDP has been accompanied by inflation.
(3) The growth rates of M1 have fluctuated during periods of stable prices around 3 to 4 per cent.

From the beginning, the policy of well-controlled, stable monetary growth was viewed as a medium- or long-term policy. In the short run, the National Bank was prepared to depart from the target in order to dampen excessive fluctuations in exchange rates as well as to accommodate increases in the prices of primary commodities such as oil and to absorb exogenous disturbances in the demand for Swiss exports. Therefore, it appeared that a band of 3 to 7 per cent for the annual money stock growth was needed in order to achieve stable growth of the Swiss economy at a zero inflation rate.

In subsequent years, more research work in the area of monetary policy was undertaken.[3] However, these studies did not cast doubt on our approach to fixing a money stock target until the end of 1978.

As a result of the changeover to a monetary target, it became necessary to develop a method for controlling the growth of the money stock. Given the fact that the adjusted monetary base is the only monetary aggregate which is under the full control of the monetary authorities, this aggregate is used for control purposes. The question then arises how much the monetary base has to be altered in order to achieve the desired growth in the money stock. From 1975 onwards, this calculation was mainly undertaken on the basis of a money multiplier forecast. While the longer term forecast was largely based on an analysis of the cyclical pattern of the money multiplier and its components, the short-term forecast of the money multiplier was based on a simple mechanistic procedure. Starting point was the following naïve model:[4]

$$m_t = m_{t-1} + m_{t-12} - m_{t-13} + E_t$$

where $m_t = M_t/B_t$

m_t: money multiplier in month t

M_t: money stock M1 in month t

B_t: adjusted monetary base in month t

E_t: disturbances in month t

Inspection of the error term E_t has shown that this term is negatively correlated with the difference between the change in the monetary base compared to the previous month and the change compared to the corresponding month of the previous year. Exploiting this naïve model, it was possible to forecast the money multiplier for the next three months rather accurately.

This approach was used from the beginning of 1975 to the autumn of 1976. Since then, an econometric model has been applied to predict the money multiplier. This money multiplier model is based on the following main assumption:[5] since, as a result of short-term capital movements triggered by currency speculation and political uncertainties, the monetary base has proved extremely volatile, banks do not instantaneously adjust their earning assets in response to changes in the base. Banks would only react instantaneously if they knew that the change in the base was permanent. Given the huge fluctuations in the monetary base, banks therefore face a very difficult decision problem. They have to evaluate the extent to which a change in the monetary base is due to permanent or transitory shifts in central bank policy. In the money multiplier model it is assumed that the money stock only adjusts to a change in the monetary base that is judged as being deterministic or permanent. On the other hand, a change which is considered as transitory is absorbed by a variation in the reserves of the banking system. This hypothesis is formalised in the following way.[6]

Let the growth rate of the monetary base be defined as

$$\frac{\dot{B}}{B} = \frac{\dot{B}^p}{B^p} + \varepsilon, \; E(\varepsilon) = 0, \tag{1}$$

where $\dfrac{\dot{B}}{B}$: actual growth rate of the monetary base

$\dfrac{\dot{B}^p}{B^p}$: growth in the permanent component of the monetary base

ε : transitory term

Similarly the growth rate of the money stock is defined as

$$\frac{\dot{M}}{M} = \frac{\dot{M}^p}{M^p} + \mu \quad E(\mu) = 0 \tag{2}$$

where $\dfrac{\dot{M}}{M}$: growth rate of the money stock

$\dfrac{\dot{M}^p}{M^p}$: permanent component of the growth rate

μ : stochastic component

The actual growth rate of the money stock can be approximated by

$$\frac{\dot{M}}{M} = \frac{\dot{m}}{m} + \frac{\dot{B}}{B} \tag{3}$$

where $\dfrac{\dot{m}}{m}$ = growth rate of the money multiplier,

and similarly the relationship for the permanent parts is given by

$$\frac{\dot{M}^p}{M^p} = \frac{\dot{m}^p}{m^p} + \frac{\dot{B}^p}{B^p} \tag{4}$$

Combining equations (1) to (4), the actual growth rate of the money multiplier is obtained:

$$\frac{\dot{m}}{m} = \frac{\dot{m}^p}{m^p} + \frac{\dot{B}^p}{B^p} - \frac{\dot{B}}{B} + \mu \tag{5}$$

With regard to bank behaviour, it is assumed that banks form their expectations about the permanent parts of B on the basis of past and current information. The rate of growth in B_t^p is determined by a linear combination with variable coefficients.

$$\left(\frac{\dot{B}^p}{B^p}\right)_t = \sum_{j=0}^{l} \beta_j \left(\frac{\dot{B}}{B}\right)_{t-j} \tag{6}$$

If equation (6) is a minimum-variance estimator, it can be shown that the weights and, therefore, the speed of adjustment, depend on the relative variance of the permanent and transitory increments of the monetary base.[7] Since the fluctuations of the monetary base were large, long adjustment periods were expected and found.

Using an analogous combination for the change in the permanent money multiplier (with α_i standing for the respective weights), substituting equation (6) into equation (5) and rearranging terms, an equation is obtained which can be estimated using a generalised form of a Box–Jenkins transfer function model.

$$\frac{\dot{m}_t}{m_t} = \sum_{i=1}^{k} \frac{\alpha_i}{1-\alpha_0} \frac{\dot{m}_{t-i}}{m_{t-i}} + \sum_{j=1}^{l} \frac{\beta_j}{1-\alpha_0} \frac{\dot{B}_{t-j}}{B_{t-j}} - \frac{1-\beta_0}{1-\alpha_0} \frac{\dot{B}_t}{B_t} + \frac{\mu_t}{1-\alpha_0} \quad (7)$$

The best forecasting properties were obtained[8] by using $i = 1$, 6 and 12 months and $j = 0$, 3, 6, 9 and 12 months. The analysis of the estimated model has shown that the prediction process is stable and that the confidence region is quite narrow. The model further seems to indicate that the changeover from a fixed to a flexible exchange rate system has not affected the money supply process. As can be seen from Table 7.1, the application of this money multiplier model to monetary policy has shown that the money multiplier can be reliably predicted.

In order to test the forecasting properties of the model, the forecasts made on 22 October 1976 and 7 January 1977, are presented as examples. The forecasts made on the first date are very accurate. The biggest error of 1.8 per cent in the predicted growth rate for December 1976 is likely to be explained by the rather large deviation of the observed from the assumed adjusted monetary base. At a first glance, the forecasts of 7 January, for the whole year, also perform rather well. But a more careful look at the results indicates that the monetary growth was significantly underestimated during the period June to September. During this period, the level of the observed adjusted monetary base was much higher than the level of the base used to carry out the forecasts. Taking this into consideration, one might conclude that, contrary to the statistical results of the money multiplier model, the predictions of the multiplier start to deteriorate after three or four months. However, this conclusion is misleading. The reasons for these rather big prediction errors mainly stem from the so-called Chiasso fiasco of the Swiss Credit Bank which occurred in May 1977. This event prompted the banks to increase their demand for precautionary reserves. Although the rate of growth in the monetary base was increased, the expansion in bank reserves was not sufficient to accommodate the shift in the demand. As a

TABLE 7.1 FORECASTS OF THE GROWTH RATES OF THE MONEY STOCK

| Month | Actual annual growth rates of M1 | Forecast of 22 October 1976 | | Forecast of 7 January 1977 | | Adjusted monetary base in billion SFr | | |
		predicted	error	predicted	error	actual	assumed 22/10/1976	assumed 7/1/1977
July 1976	9.5	9.6[a]	+0.1			24.7		
August	9.7	9.0[a]	−0.7			24.5		
September	9.1	9.4[a]	+0.3			24.6		
October	8.6	8.1	−0.5			24.1	24.6	
November	6.9	7.1	+0.2			24.5	24.6	
December	8.1	6.3	−1.8			26.0	24.6	
January 1977	7.1			6.2	−0.6	25.9		24.2
February	9.6			7.8	−1.8	24.8		24.2
March	7.1			7.3	0.2	24.1		24.2
April	6.3			6.4	0.1	24.0		24.2
May	4.7			6.5	−1.8	24.2		24.2
June	3.7			6.2	−2.5	24.4		24.2
July	3.1			6.7	−3.6	25.2		24.2
August	3.6			7.2	−3.6	25.1		24.2
September	4.5			6.2	−1.7	25.2		24.2
October	6.0			4.7	1.3	25.6		24.2
November	5.5			4.9	0.6	25.3		24.2
December	4.1			2.5	1.6	26.9		24.2

[a] Forecast, using actual figures for the adjusted monetary base.

result, short-and even medium-term interest rates started to rise. This induced a shift from demand to time deposits and, therefore, a reduction in the growth rate of the money stock M1. Later in the year, commercial banks restored their normal levels of reserves and the growth rates of the money stock M1 began to accelerate again.

III. IMPLEMENTATION OF MONETARY POLICY

To date, the decision about fixing an annual money stock target has always been made at the end of a calendar year. The size of the target is based on the expected and desired economic growth for the year to come and on the assumption of the next year's income velocity. The quantitative setting of the target is always a compromise among empirical findings in demand for money equations, theoretical ideas and, last but not least, political considerations. Before the board of management of the Bank makes its final decision on the money stock target, the government is informed about the intentions of the board. However, it must be emphasised that the responsibility for establishing a money stock target rests solely with the board of management.

The following schematic procedure was applied to control the growth in the money stock when the Bank began to set monetary targets:

(1) Targeting the growth rate of the adjusted monetary base that is necessary to reach the money target.
(2) Drawing up guidelines for the size and mode of the increase of the adjusted monetary base for the first quarter of the year.
(3) Monthly control of the outcome and, if necessary, revising the targeted growth rate of the adjusted monetary base.
(4) Targeting the increase in the adjusted monetary base for the second quarter and so forth.

This procedure was modified at the end of 1976 when a weekly meeting for the control of the monetary base was instituted. This meeting is chaired by a member of the board of management and is attended by the head of the foreign exchange department, who is also concerned about money market conditions, the head of the economics department and by one or two other members of the two departments. The main purpose of the meeting is to reconcile short-run money market and exchange rate considerations with the money stock target. For each meeting, all available information on factors affecting the monetary base in the near future is collected. Furthermore, forecasts are made for the next week's currency in circulation, advances to commercial banks and government deposits at the Bank. These forecasts are used to predict the reserve situation of the commercial banks in the week ahead.

At these weekly meetings, decisions as to deviations from the target for the adjusted monetary base that are required for various reasons are taken. Furthermore, the measures necessary to attain the next week's target for the adjusted monetary base are discussed. Naturally, under a system of flexible exchange rates it would be easy to expand the adjusted monetary base at a constant rate. However, it was never the aim of the Bank to achieve smooth monetary growth over short periods of time. On the contrary, it was always felt that short-run flexibility in the money stock policy was needed to soften the impact of all kinds of transitory shocks on the money and foreign exchange markets.

Except for the period of the so-called Chiasso fiasco and for periods with seasonal liquidity problems (e.g. at the end of the year), the adjusted monetary base has seldom deviated from the medium-term target because of money market problems. This is due to the fact that, in general, there is a belief at the Bank that short-run fluctuations in money market interest rates do not affect the economy as long as the level of the interest rates is not altered systematically.

On the other hand, the extensive fluctuation in the exchange rate of the Swiss franc has been of considerable concern to the Swiss National Bank. The Bank has exploited the sluggish adjustment of the money stock to a change in the adjusted monetary base in order to dampen exchange rate fluctuations. Intervention purchases in the foreign exchange market have little impact on the money stock as long as these interventions are reversed within the next two to three months. Therefore, short-run operations in the foreign exchange market can be conducted without jeopardising the money stock target. It can be seen from Table 7.2 that this short-run flexibility in the control of the monetary base has been widely used. Monthly changes of 2 to 6 per cent in the adjusted monetary base have been quite normal. Despite the unstable pattern of the adjusted monetary base, it has been possible to keep the growth of the money stock M1 close to the desired level. While in 1975 the actual growth rate of M1 was only 1.6 per cent below the target of 6 per cent, in 1976 the target of 6 per cent was overshot by 1.7 per cent. In 1977, the actual growth rate came quite close to the target rate. Instead of 5 per cent, the money stock grew by 5.5 per cent. Only in 1978 was the target rate of monetary growth overshot by a wide margin (17.3 per cent instead of 5 per cent). This was not the result of an erroneous control

TABLE 7.2   PERCENTAGE   CHANGE   IN   THE   ADJUSTED
MONETARY BASE COMPARED TO THE LEVEL IN THE
PREVIOUS MONTH

Month	Year			
	1975	1976	1977	1978
January	2.0	5.0	0	6.0
February	2.3	−5.8	−4.5	1.3
March	−1.6	−0.6	−2.8	1.2
April	−1.0	1.1	−0.4	1.9
May	2.8	0.8	0.8	−4.8
June	1.9	5.9	0.7	−3.1
July	−1.2	−6.0	3.1	5.0
August	2.2	−6.2	−0.4	0.4
September	0.4	7.9	0.4	5.8
October	0.4	−2.1	1.9	18.3
November	−0.6	1.7	−1.5	5.6
December	1.9	6.0	6.3	3.2
Average	1.5	4.1	1.9	4.7

procedure, however, but rather represented, as will be explained later on, a shift in monetary policy in response to the strong appreciation of the Swiss franc.

Before turning to the dilemma faced by the policy-makers in trying to set simultaneously money stock and exchange rate targets, a few remarks will be made about the operational techniques of controlling the monetary base.

Domestic Swiss money markets are – probably as a result of the small indebtedness of the public sector and the usually rather high liquidity of the private sector – not very well developed. Therefore, domestic money market conditions are mainly influenced by the Swiss National Bank via operations in the foreign exchange market. In the post-war period the increase in the monetary base was almost exclusively the result of intervention purchases in the foreign exchange market. Up to now, the creation of base money through purchasing of domestic assets or through advances to commercial banks has been negligible. This is not the outcome of a specific strategy; it is simply the result of the balance of payments situation under the system of fixed exchange rates. Although the discussion on the optimal way of changing the monetary base in a small open economy[9] is still going on, the Swiss National Bank has adopted the following strategy. The Bank intervenes in the foreign exchange market if the secondary objective of the change in the monetary base is to exert a short-run effect on the exchange rate. If interest rates are the objective, the Bank will operate in the domestic money market. This strategy is based on the assumption that, at least in the short run, domestic and foreign assets are not complete substitutes.

Until this year, excess liquidity was almost never reduced through direct selling of foreign currency in the foreign exchange market. Excess liquidity was mopped up mainly by selling sterilisation rescriptions issued by the government or by imposing minimum reserve requirements on the banks. Furthermore, excess liquidity could also be removed by means of requirement compelling commercial banks that raise Swiss-franc loans on behalf of non-residents to convert a certain percentage of the loan into dollars (up to 100 per cent) directly at the Swiss National Bank. While until recently swaps of foreign currency between the Swiss National Bank and commercial banks were undertaken only to ease seasonal stringencies in the money market, the Bank is now occasionally varying the monetary base through swap operations.

Although I do not deny that the operational aspects of controlling the monetary base are important, I am of the opinion that the mode of changing the base in the medium term is much less important than the size of the change. We do not have much evidence on this point, but it seems that the money stock growth is not affected significantly by the composition of the monetary base. The money multiplier model, which does not take into account the explicit structure of the monetary base, would appear to lend itself to this view.

More interesting is the question to what extent exchange rate fluctuations can be dampened by short-run variation of the base within the context of a monetary target.

It is probably fair to state that the extent of exchange rate variability observed in the past six years has been much larger than was anticipated before the transition to a floating exchange rate system. Highly volatile exchange rates cause difficulties for importers and exporters. Therefore, these fluctuations cannot be completely neglected in the conduct of monetary policy.

A possible explanation for the overshooting of the exchange rates is based on the assumption that the prices of goods and services adjust much more slowly to new monetary conditions than do the prices of financial assets. To counteract this kind of overshooting of the exchange rate and to reduce the competitive disadvantages of the foreign sector, the Swiss National Bank has from the beginning handled the monetary target in a flexible manner. During periods of strong appreciation of the

Swiss franc, the Swiss money supply was expanded at a higher rate than initially targeted and vice versa. Initially, it was believed that official intervention in the foreign exchange market coupled with a temporary increase in the monetary base would be sufficient to weaken the upward pressure on the Swiss franc. It took some time to realise that this belief was not consistent with our view of how the money supply was determined. As mentioned before, we are of the opinion that banks do not instantaneously adjust their earning assets in response to changes in the monetary base. Since this view of the money supply process is supported by the empirical evidence, it is difficult to understand why a change in the base should almost immediately alter the distribution of foreign and domestic assets holdings in the private sector. The results of cross-correlation analysis seem to indicate that the exchange rate also adjusts slowly to a change in the monetary conditions. These results are in line with the observation that official intervention in the foreign exchange market has had almost no effect on the Swiss franc in the short run. Longer lasting deviations from the monetary-base target are necessary in order to influence the exchange rate.

The way economic agents form their price expectations is sometimes put forward as an explanation for the huge exchange rate fluctuations. Today it has become fashionable to relate the expected inflation rate to the actual growth rate in the money stock. Although I am an advocate of the quantity theory of money, I believe that the relationship between the actual growth rate in the money stock and the expected inflation rate is not straightforward. Market participants face, in my view, a very difficult forecasting problem. In a world characterised by different monetary policy strategies, different definitions of the monetary aggregates and high variability of the growth rates in the money stock, it is very difficult to know whether a change in the observed growth rate of a monetary aggregate is permanent or transitory and whether any particular inflation rate will be the outcome of the specific growth rate. Considering these uncertainties, market participants are likely to make use of other information as well. Specifically, the performance of a central bank over the past years will be of some relevance for forming expectations about future inflation. If—as was the case in Switzerland—the growth in the money stock during three consecutive years was more or less on target, if the inflation rate were down to 1–2 per cent and if every deviation from the money stock target tended to be corrected after a few months, then a deviation from the money stock target would at first be judged as temporary. By contrast, if a central bank has a bad record, then a change in the growth rate of the money stock is likely to be judged as permanent. This asymmetry in respect to the evaluation of an observed change in the growth rate of the money stock might be one of the reasons for the overshooting of the exchange rate. In any case, the asymmetry complicates the correction of the overshooting. If, for example, the Swiss National Bank, in an effort to reduce the appreciation of the Swiss franc, increases the money supply, market participants will not adjust their portfolios in the short run. It will be quite a long time before the change or, at least a part of the change, in the monetary policy will be considered as a permanent change. Therefore, the effect of a flexible money stock policy on the exchange rate will be the smaller the more often this kind of policy is applied. In other words, to influence the exchange rate not only bigger and bigger deviations from the money stock target, but also deviations of longer duration, are necessary. The difficulties of such a policy are obvious. In particular, there is always the danger of achieving too much or too little.

These ideas about the feasibility of dampening the exchange rate fluctuations by varying the money supply have influenced last year's decision to give the market a signal in the form of an exchange rate target, thereby pushing the policy of money stock targets temporarily into the background. The immediate cause of the change in the policy stance, however, was the particularly pronounced upsurge in the value of the Swiss franc. The peak was reached on September 26 when the trade-weighted appreciation of the Swiss franc had reached well over 40 per cent in nominal and close to 30 per cent in real terms over the previous year.

The enormous appreciation of the Swiss franc in 1978 was likely to be the result of a shift in the demand for that currency. It is not clear which factors were causing the shift, and it is even less obvious whether the shift in the demand for the Swiss franc was a permanent or transitory affair. It seems that part of the shift in the demand is due to changes in the pattern of holdings of reserve currencies. While the dollar still serves as the principal means of international payments, recent experience indicates that liquid assets, to an increasing extent, are held in the form of Deutsche marks, Swiss francs and other European currencies. The desire to build up liquid balances in these currencies tends to put upward pressure on the respective exchange rates. The increase in the demand for liquid assets, in turn, exerts a deflationary impact on countries whose currencies tend to be revalued. To protect the economy against these deflationary effects, the additional foreign demand should be satisfied through an expansion in the domestic money supply. The difficulty of such a policy is knowing by how much the money supply has to be increased. If the size of the shift in the demand for money is known, a meaningful money stock target can be formulated. The evidence drawn from the econometric work on the demand for money in Switzerland lends rather weak support to the shift hypothesis. This might be due to the fact that few equations for the demand for money have been estimated covering the observations for the flexible exchange rate period. The econometric work is further complicated by the lack of quarterly figures on Swiss GNP. Also, the choice of the functional form of the demand-for-money equation becomes very crucial when short-term interest rates drop to levels as low as $0 - \frac{1}{4}$ per cent, as was the case during the past six months. Under such conditions, it is rather difficult to find out whether the prediction errors of a demand-for-money equation are due to a systematic shift in the demand for money or to erroneous specification of the equation. Another unresolved problem is the role of exchange rate expectations in a demand-for-money function.

Given all the uncertainties about the short-run stability of the demand-for-money function and exchange rate fluctuations of the kind that occurred in 1978, it is clear that the pursuit of a policy aimed at price stability does not always imply a simple policy of constant and rigidly adhered to rates of monetary growth, but rather should be based on a policy which attempts to take into account monetary developments in the rest of the world and their effects on international portfolio compositions and exchange rates. The decision temporarily to abandon the money stock target in favour of an exchange rate target should be interpreted in this sense.

At present, both the growth in the money stock and the exchange rate serve as reference points for monetary policy. In the short run, priority—as is actually the case—might be given to exchange rate objectives. In the medium run, however, the Bank will expand the money stock along a path designed to keep prices stable. The stability in the foreign exchange market during the past weeks has allowed the Swiss National Bank to reduce the monetary base by almost 20 per cent and to move back in the direction of this medium-term path.

IV. CONCLUSIONS

I am of the opinion that, in principle, the money stock policy, in general, and targeting the monetary base to control the growth in the money stock, in particular, have been very successful. The aim of the money stock policy, namely stable prices, has practically been achieved. The annual increase in the price index over the past years has fluctuated mostly between 1–2 per cent. The economy has adjusted to an inflation-free environment and the inflationary distortions in the production sector are disappearing. Innovation and productivity gains which can be attributed to a certain extent to the tough competition on world markets resulting from the appreciation of the Swiss franc have had a beneficial effect on Swiss industries.

Despite last year's decision of the Swiss National Bank to abstain from fixing a money stock target for 1979, it would be wrong to argue that for a small open economy a money stock target would be an inappropriate approach. The decision only indicates that a policy aimed at price stability is made more difficult if the rest of the world does not pursue a similar policy. The conclusions drawn from the foreign exchange market developments last autumn, therefore, would be not to abandon a money stock target, but to recommend countries with high inflation rates to adopt a similar target and to opt for an efficient control procedure. From the Swiss experience, I would conclude that the monetary base can serve as a very effective control instrument.

NOTES

1. For helpful comments and criticism I am especially indebted to George Rich. I have also benefited from discussions with members of the Research Division at the Swiss National Bank.
2. For a more detailed discussion see Schiltknecht (1979) pp. 325–28.
3. See for example Buomberger and Müller (1978).
4. See for this point Schiltknecht (1979) p. 329
5. A full account of the model is given in Büttler et al. (1979)
6. This formal part follows almost exactly the deduction of the model in Büttler et al. (1979)
7. See Lucas (1976).
8. For the detailed result see Büttler et al (1979).
9. On this point see Niehans (1978).

REFERENCES

Buomberger, P. and Müller, B. (1978), 'Geldmengenaggregate und Bruttosozialprodukt—Empirische Untersuchungen für die Schweiz', Beilage zum Monatsbericht der Schweizerischen Nationalbank, January.
Büttler, H.-J. et al. (1979), 'A Multiplier Model for Controlling the Money Stock', forthcoming in *Journal of Monetary Economics*.

Lucas, R. E. (1976), 'Econometric Policy Evaluation: A Critique', in *The Phillips Curve and Labor Markets*, ed. Brunner, K. and Meltzer, A. H., Vol. 1 of the Carnegie–Rochester Conference on Public Policy (North-Holland).

Niehans, J.(1978), 'Beurteilung der Zins- und Wechselkurswirkungen alternativer Instrumente zur Beeinflussung der monetären Basis', mimeo.

Schiltknecht, K. (1979), 'Monetary Policy under Flexible Exchange Rates, the Swiss Case', in *Inflation, Unemployment and Monetary Control*, ed. Brunner, K. and Neumann, J. M. (Berlin).

Comments on Dr Schiltknecht's Paper

Richard G. Lipsey
Queen's University, Ontario

This is an excellent paper that I both enjoyed and profited from reading. Since I have neither technical nor conceptual criticisms to make of it, I shall confine myself to a few general observations suggested by the paper.

When it comes to inflation, I am neither a monetarist nor an anti-monetarist. I am merely a potential consumer waiting to use an anti-inflationary package once an effective one is produced. As an onlooker I became convinced around 1970 that there was a strong *prima facie* case for at least a weak version of monetarism: the money supply has something to do with inflation. I thus welcomed the experimentation with monetarist cures undertaken by many central banks in the 1970s. The first results of such experimentation are now being assessed at conferences such as this one. Some of the issues now before the profession are illustrated by the present paper.

First, should monetarist central banks follow rigid rules for monetary expansion or should they be allowed some discretion? The outcome of the theoretical debate concerning Friedman's rigid rule of monetary expansion was that a flexible policy based (in theory at least) on some form of optimal control can almost always do better than can a rigid rule. This result transferred the debate to the practical level: would central banks in fact do better than rigid rules if they were left a measure of discretion? Friedman makes a strong case that the Federal Reserve did worse by exercising discretion in the 1950s and 1960s than it would have done if it had been constrained by a rigid rule. For all I know, the institutional set-up of the Federal Reserve may make this a likely outcome into the foreseeable future. Also a central bank whose monetary control has been lax in the past may have to stick to a rule through thick and thin, at least until it has narrowed the credibility gap between its past performance and its current monetarist pretentions.

Be that as it may, we now have evidence (from George Freeman and Kurt Schiltknecht) that an enlightened central bank, free from short-term political influence, can sometimes do better by exercising a degree of discretion than by operating a rigid rule. Discretion seems particularly important when unexpected circumstances arise. I take it then that the proposition 'it is *always* better to operate monetary targets as rigid rules rather than as goals subject to discretionary variation' has been pretty conclusively refuted as a matter of direct experience. (Of course it is always possible to construct an unreal model in which discretion buys you nothing, or even a reduction in performance.)

Second, a critical part of the monetarist theory is a stable demand for money. Anti-monetarists were quick to point out (as we have heard at this conference) that a close correlation between money income and interest rates on the one hand and any one of a number of monetary aggregates on the other was quite likely as long as the latter were endogenous (in a behavioural sense). They argued, however, that if you sought to reverse the causality by influencing money income through controlling a monetary aggregate, the relation would quickly break down. A final conclusion on this debate is not yet possible, but evidence presented here in the last two days (and elsewhere) suggests to me that demand functions have not proved as stable as many monetarists expected, but neither have they been so unstable as to render monetary policy impotent. In the present paper we see an added complication understandably not stressed by American monetarists in the fifties and sixties: the role of exchange fluctuations, exchange speculations, and reserve holdings in the demand functions for domestic money. This, as we have just heard, can be an important issue for any open economy.

Third, another issue long debated between monetarists and their opponents concerned the central bank's ability to control any chosen monetary aggregate: could it and would it? Some said central banks did not have the power, others said they would not have the will (particularly when monetary targets came into conflict with full employment targets). Much ink has been spilled over these issues. It seems to me, however, that the present paper (and Freeman's) provides strong evidence that, at least for several years, some central banks have both the ability and the determination to control a chosen monetary aggregate. (What remains at issue is how long this control can and will be exerted and the influence it will have on the real behaviour of the economy.)

Fourth, one important issue raised by this and other papers at the conference is 'Which aggregate should be controlled?'. I confess to being confused on this issue and, as an outside observer, I must say to monetarists in the audience that I perceive no small amount of confusion within your own ranks. Some monetarists hold that it really does not matter which aggregate is controlled. (Nicky Kaldor likes to tell the story of the visiting IMF team being asked 'which aggregate should be controlled' and replying 'we don't care which you control, all we know is there's too much of it'.) Others take the view that if you control aggregate X that is highly substitutable with aggregate Y you may have little effect on $X + Y$ (which is really a 'composite good') and hence have little effect on anything else. On a more specific level, George Freeman, one of the most academically inclined of the world's central bankers, told us at this conference that M1 is the right magnitude to control; while Tom Courchene, who is one of the best of the Canadian academic monetarists, holds that it should be M2 (roughly the British M3). The Swiss, as we have just heard, seek to control neither M1 nor M2 directly but target instead, in text-book fashion, on the monetary base.

I think it is safe to say that there is still disagreement and debate on this issue and that the papers and discussions in this conference have not clarified the issue. For every person I have encountered who holds that it does not matter, I have found someone else who holds that it does. I will conclude, therefore, with the suggestion that monetarists could do themselves, and their potential 'fellow travellers', a really great service if one of them would write a scholarly survey article on this question. What are the theoretical issues? In what models does it not matter much which aggregate is controlled and in what models does it matter? How do the views of various monetarist writers now stand on this issue? What, if any, relevant evidence is currently available to help us answer the twin questions so often raised at this conference: 'Does it matter which aggregate we seek to control?' and 'If so, which one should it be?'.

Comments on Dr Schiltknecht's Paper

Geoffrey E. Wood
The City University, London

Dr Schiltknecht's paper raises important issues in three areas. These are first, the appropriate choice of monetary aggregate for monetary control; second, the distinction between permanent and temporary fluctuations in variables, and how that distinction matters for the formation of expectations and the behaviour of the economy; and third, the interdependence of national monetary policies even in a world of floating exchange rates. I shall deal with these issues in that order—at one point distinguishing sharply between what is clearly generalisable and what is, perhaps, valid only for Switzerland.

However, before doing so I should emphasise just how unusual this paper is. It is unusual in that it is by a central banker who is willing to take responsibility for the maintenance of price level stability—rather than calling for incomes policies—and, not only that, it is by a central banker who has actually achieved his objective! Of course, the Swiss central bank was not under the kind of pressures imposed by deficit financing on some other central banks.[1] For that reason the task of attaining price stability may have been easier. But the fact remains that the task was carried out.

I. WHICH AGGREGATE TO CONTROL?

In his paper Michael Foot drew our attention to the wide range of monetary aggregates in existence, and pointed out that the monetary authorities of different countries, if they try to control the money supply at all, control different definitions of money in different countries.

Controlling the monetary base, as in Switzerland, does not entirely eliminate the problem of choice between aggregates, but it does nonetheless have some major advantages. The first advantage is that the base is something which is directly within the central bank's control; the amount of monetary base is not influenced by the portfolio decisions of the public. Secondly, unless the base multiplier is extraordinarily flexible, control of the base does ensure that there is no danger of a sudden explosion of money growth; this is in contrast to the situation in, for example, the USA, where the money supply is controlled by varying the Federal Funds rate and letting the supply of base then accommodate to demands for it, and where resistance to letting the funds rate change—especially upwards—can lead to large swings in money growth.[2] Third, if the base is controlled, then *all* definitions of money are controlled.

The problem of what rate of growth one should aim at is, of course, still unresolved, and one is still left with the difficulty that (in some countries) different monetary aggregates can behave differently for quite extended periods. These are the reasons why control of the base may not entirely eliminate the problem produced by the existence of a range of aggregates. But it certainly reduces these problems, and there is evidence which suggests that this reduction is very substantial.

II. PROJECTION ERROR AND CONTROL ERROR

In choosing a monetary aggregate, two questions are relevant. Which aggregate is most predictably linked to future economic activity? And which aggregate can the central bank control with smallest error? The central bank should choose an aggregate with the objective of minimising the *combined* effect of these two sources of error. Certain aggregates, such as the much touted wide definitions of money in the UK, may be closely linked to economic activity, but that certainly does not mean that they are desirable objectives of policy. Choosing them might minimise one source of error, but at the cost of maximising another.

The issue of how to minimise that total error has not often been explored. One very useful study was carried out by Andersen and Karnosky at the Federal Reserve Bank of St Louis.[3] Their study showed that targeting directly on the monetary base itself would in the United States do at least as good a job, in terms of stabilising nominal income, as would targeting on M1 or M2. In other words, the base could be not just a device for getting us to the monetary target, but could actually be the proximate objective of policy.

That is not how the base is used in Switzerland. Base growth was controlled, until the switch to pegging the exchange rate, with the objective of controlling M1. But the St Louis work, in conjunction with Switzerland's outstanding success at attaining price level stability, does make still more cogent the case for the adoption of a monetary base system of control in the UK. Now that the UK authorities are trying to control the money supply, it is time to move to a control system actually appropriate to that end, and to abandon the present system, the primary purpose of which was to facilitate the sale of government debt.

III. PERMANENT AND TEMPORARY CHANGES

A very striking feature of Dr Schiltknecht's paper is the distinction made between permanent and temporary changes in the monetary base. The distinction between permanent and temporary changes is not novel in economics. It was first highlighted by Milton Friedman, in his *Theory of the Consumption Function* in 1956. It is a distinction which has since proved fruitful in several areas—not just in consumption theory, but also in money demand estimation, and in the theory of investment.

With regard to its use in analysis of the money supply process, one should say first that the formulation is neat, and clearly shows that what is often described as evidence for the existence of unstable portfolio preferences is, when properly interpreted, in fact evidence for stability.

A question does, however, arise about the values of the multiplier. The errors in projections of the January 1977 forecast (page 215) are in part explained by the 'Chiasso fiasco'. But the convenient pattern of alternating positive and negative errors of the October 1976 forecast seems to be absent from the later forecast. Does that pattern resume on a longer run of undistorted data? And if not, has its absence been a sufficiently serious problem to warrant investigation and respecification of the multiplier? If it has not been, the stabilising consequences of the authorities carrying out policies which help the private sector distinguish between permanent and temporary fluctuations in economic variables are very dramatically emphasised indeed.

In any event, the specification in this paper is both elegant and, so far as the results are reported, useful. This distinction between permanent and temporary changes is also used very elegantly to explain why swings in money growth have not produced swings in the exchange rate—the swings were thought to be temporary. Long-lasting fluctuations are needed to produce exchange rate movements *in Switzerland*. This, it should be emphasised, is a fact which does not necessarily apply elsewhere, in countries where central banks have less of a tradition of financial rectitude. It may help explain, though, why sterling was strong throughout the first seven months of 1979 despite bursts of money growth that only a couple of years previously would have produced a sharp drop in the exchange rate.

IV. PEGGING THE EXCHANGE RATE

The most important part of the paper, and one which is linked to that last point, is the switch from a monetary target to an exchange rate target.

Before moving on to that, two minor issues should be noted in passing. First is the recognition that rational expectations do not rule out economic actors looking at a whole set of variables as well as the money stock when trying to predict the price level or the exchange rate. The behaviour of the money stock has often proved a good proxy for price expectations in wage equations, but in fast-moving financial markets where it is important for participants quickly to know whether a change is permanent or temporary, it is quite rational, as Dr Schiltknecht notes, for people to look at other variables also. This of course justifies the central bank's concern with money market conditions—for the central bank presumably knows whether they intend a change to be temporary or permanent, and so can have reason from time to time to smooth these financial markets. But a question does arise. Since these interventions have never led to deviations from medium-term targets for money growth, and since exchange intervention has generally reversed fairly quickly so as not to interfere with the targets, might not the markets by now be persuaded of the Swiss bank's commitment to price stability, thus rendering even their modest amount of 'fine tuning' unnecessary?

A second minor but noteworthy point is the discussion (on page 220) of how the bank controls the base. It can operate in either the foreign exchange market or the domestic money market to do so. The criterion for choice is whether the secondary objective (the principal objective always being money stock control) is to have a short-run effect on the exchange rate or on domestic money market conditions. Two matters arise here: first the 'assumption' (as Dr Schiltknecht terms it) which underlies the strategy—that domestic and foreign assets are not perfect substitutes in the short run. Quite a lot of work supports that assumption, and the paper by Hamburger and Wood (1979) tested it explicitly.[4] It can very reasonably be taken as a fact rather than as an assumption. Secondly, the similarity of the rule with the Mundellian policy assignment rule is notable. Although, as Dr Schiltknecht admits, the strategy was chosen without prior theoretical support there appears to be a very good chance that the strategy is the correct one.[5]

Finally, and most important, we come to the decision taken in the international monetary turmoil of autumn 1978, to move to pegging the Swiss frank against the Deutsche mark. That decision was taken to prevent a further rapid appreciation of the franc and, despite theory (and evidence from elsewhere) to the contrary, does not seem, at any rate yet, to have led to large-scale importation of inflation.

Dr Schiltknecht conjectures that the appreciation of the franc was due to some increase in demand for it; if so the appropriate response, given that the price level objective had been attained, was indeed to peg the rate and temporarily let the money stock rise as demanded. Resistance would have been severely deflationary. Econometric work on this conjecture is hard to produce, because of data gaps—particularly crucial here is that there are no quarterly GNP figures for Switzerland. But there is some evidence which suggests that he is right. This evidence arises from the behaviour of the US dollar.

That was the currency which was mainly under pressure, and the most satisfactory explanation for the pressure is portfolio diversification as a result of a weak and inconsistent anti-inflation policy in the USA.[6] Funds leaving the US dollar for such a reason would naturally flow to where anti-inflation policies were both strong and had been so for some years. Switzerland was a natural home for such funds.

This is why it is wrong to infer that a country can, without inflationary consequences, back off from its monetary targets whenever its exchange rate is under upward pressure. *The times when it can do so are a special case; the example of Switzerland does not provide a general rule.*

This policy change also highlights the interdependence of monetary policies in a world of floating exchange rates. With floating rates, countries are indeed insulated from flows across the exchanges. But they are still exposed to foreign monetary policy if that policy is such as to produce a change in portfolio preferences. Flexible exchange rates provide some insulation from monetary incompetence, but, as the Swiss bank recognised, there is a limit to the amount of folly from which they can protect one.

It is important to emphasise that the acceleration in Swiss money growth (from 0.4 per cent p.a. first to fourth quarters 1977, to 25.7 per cent p.a. from fourth quarter 1977 to second quarter 1978) cannot be ascribed to this decision to stabilise the franc. The expansion must have resulted from a decision to produce it by the Swiss national bank. The consequent modest acceleration of inflation in Switzerland, implying the presence of *excess* money, cannot therefore be taken as undermining the portfolio shift explanation for the behaviour of the Swiss franc relative to the US dollar on the foreign exchanges.

V. CONCLUSIONS

The conclusions of these comments must echo those of Dr Schiltknecht's paper. A monetary base approach to controlling the monetary aggregates is a very effective control instrument. That it had to be temporarily given up in Switzerland was a consequence of monetary disturbances abroad. Should every country simultaneously adopt such a sensible approach to policy, every country would find its economy running more smoothly, as they would no longer be imposing disturbances on each other.

NOTES

1. It is beginning to appear that R. J. Barro's finding that government expenditures rather than government deficits are the driving force behind money growth was due to a quirk in his data period. The issue is, however, clearly hard to resolve because of the generally intimate intertwining of deficits and expenditure. R. J. Barro, 'Are Government Bonds net wealth?', *Journal of Political Economy*, Dec. 1974.
2. There is considerable *short-term* flexibility in the Swiss multiplier. This dampens transitory interest rate fluctuations, while the long-run inflexibility maintains monetary and price level stability.
3. See Andersen, L. C.and Karnosky, Denis (1977), 'Some Considerations in the Use of Monetary Aggregates for the Implementation of Monetary Policy', Federal Reserve Bank of St Louis *Monthly Review* (September).
4. Hamburger, Michael. J. and Wood, Geoffrey E. (1979), 'Interest Rates and Monetary Policy in Regulated Open Economies', City University Centre for Banking and International Finance, Working Paper no. 10.
5. An important observation in allowing that strategy is that the composition of the base for money stock control does not seem to matter.
6. See Wood, G. E. (1979), 'The Dollar Rollercoaster', Vol. 1 of the Annual Monetary Review of the City University's Centre for Banking and International Finance.

Author Index

235

Subject Index

236

Gross National Product (GNP), 64,
65, 69
target, 86–8, 89–93

Income,
determination model, 70–2
nominal, 68, 74, 83, 84, 197, 199
Incomes policy, 48–9, 99, 100, 101
Inflation, 1–2, 28, 29, 32, 34, 47, 48,
50, 53, 57, 58, 76, 97, 123, 180,
187, 188, 224
cost-push, 87, 94
expected, 63, 97
and unemployment, 99–100, 124,
127, 130
Interest rate,
expectations, 103–4
policy, 22, 23
target, 7–8, 86, 89–91, 178, 181
Interest rates, 16, 24, 25, 32, 34, 47, 48,
50, 108, 115, 127, 132, 140
nominal, 32, 33, 49, 90, 91, 181
short-term, 63, 110, 147, 208
stabilisation of, 48, 91, 185–90
IS/LM analysis, 91, 178

Keynesian demand management, 87
Keynesians, 130

Labour market, 86–8, 123, 124, 142
Labour demand, 97
Local authority temporary debt, 144,
145

Minimum Lending Rate (MLR), 16,
22
Monetarism, 2, 18, 226
Monetarists, 50, 51, 52, 90, 100, 130,
181, 182
Monetary aggregate, 13, 42, 55, 57, 63,
70, 184–5
choice of, 52, 81, 91–3, 132, 227–8,
229–30
as target, 7–8, 90–93
Monetary aggregates,
control of, 227
income velocities of, 83

Monetary base, 19, 44, 45, 49, 53, 76,
83, 92, 118, 119–20, 212–15,
217–18, 234
control of, 219–21, 229–231, 232
Monetary control, 82, 115, 118, 132,
193
object of, 53
Monetary feedback rules, 3–8, 50
Monetary growth, 32, 50, 52, 84, 149,
188–9
rigid and discretionary rules of,
226–7
Monetary indicators, 2, 54, 96
Monetary instruments, 54, 58
Monetary policy, 1–2, 34, 50, 51, 52,
54, 58, 65, 87, 183, 184, 185–90,
217–18, 233
in Canada, 192–200
change in, 13, 75
instruments of, 55, 63
and rational expectations, 5
in the United States, 183–5, 188,
203–4, 205, 208–9
Monetary targets, 2, 15, 22, 23, 25, 28,
30, 31, 34, 35, 47, 50, 57, 86,
100–1, 105, 121, 128, 135, 177,
200–1
in Canada, 192–9, 203–5, 208–9
choice of, 3, 18–20, 131
control of, 21–2, 102–3, 194
and economic policy, 54
and expectations, 15, 58–9, 84
and fiscal policy, 159, 176
forward-rolling of, 21, 102
and inflation, 17, 99, 123, 124, 130,
192, 212, 221, 233
Keynesian view of, 17–18, 19, 97
monetarist view of, 17–18, 19, 97
problem of, 95, 120
rationale for, 47–9, 193–4
success of, 51, 202
in Switzerland, 211–12, 217–24,
232
Money,
measures of, 64
relation with income and credit,
72–5, 81, 85
Money multiplier, 213–15, 231
Money national expenditure, 55